CRASH LANDING

THE INSIDE STORY
OF HOW THE WORLD'S
BIGGEST COMPANIES
SURVIVED AN ECONOMY
ON THE BRINK

LIZ HOFFMAN

CROWN
NEW YORK

Published in the United States by Crown, an imprint of Random House,
a division of Penguin Random House LLC, New York.

CROWN and the Crown colophon are registered trademarks of
Penguin Random House LLC.

Library of Congress Cataloging-in-Publication Data
Names: Hoffman, Liz (Wall Street Journal reporter), author.
Title: Crash landing / Liz Hoffman.
Identifiers: LCCN 2022039607 (print) | LCCN 2022039608 (ebook) |
ISBN 9780593239018 (hardcover) | ISBN 9780593443538 | ISBN 9780593239025 (ebook)
Subjects: LCSH: United States—Economic conditions—21st century. |
COVID19 (Disease)—Economic aspects—United States.
Classification: LCC HC106.84 .H64 2023 (print) | LCC HC106.84 (ebook) |
DDC 330.973—dc23/eng/20221020
LC record available at https://lccn.loc.gov/2022039607
LC ebook record available at https://lccn.loc.gov/2022039608

Hardcover ISBN: 9780593239018
International edition ISBN: 9780593443538

Printed in the United States of America on acid-free paper

crownpublishing.com

2 4 6 8 9 7 5 3 1

First Edition

Book design by Victoria Wong

For my dad

"God shield our Empire from the might
Of war or famine, plague or blight
And all the power of hell,
And keep it ever in the hands
Of those who fought 'gainst other lands,
Who fought and conquered well."

—WINSTON CHURCHILL, 1890

"I don't think we're ever going to lose money again."
—DOUG PARKER, American Airlines CEO, 2017

CONTENTS

AUTHOR'S NOTE

On a cold, sunny Friday morning in late March 2020, I sat on my Brooklyn stoop, bathed in an eerie silence, and checked my email. It was the third week of the coronavirus pandemic and New York City was shut down. My then-employer, *The Wall Street Journal,* had closed down two weeks earlier along with the rest of the city, and I had taken to having my morning coffee outside, in what seemed both a thrilling change of pace and a quiet act of corporate rebellion. Atop my inbox was an email from one of my editors at the paper with the subject line "Ides of March."

My beat at the *Journal* was Wall Street—the flow of money among big banks, giant corporations, and the investors behind them. I had spent the previous few weeks writing about the virus's toll on financial markets, which after a decade of smooth sailing had now utterly freaked out. But the impact had spiraled well beyond trigger-happy traders. The virus that would come to be known simply as "Covid" had killed hundreds and sickened thousands. Nobody was buying anything. Massive layoffs were being announced every day. It was a seismic event for the global economy, with impacts spiraling out in every direction. The task from my editor that morning was to try to capture the moment and its complexity. The resulting story, published on the first Saturday of April, was an eight-thousand-word chronicle of March 2020, the month the world shut down. It told the stories of two dozen corporate executives and investors as they faced the biggest challenge of their careers.

What became clear, in one interview after another, was that the economic elite was just as stunned as the rest of us. For most of them, the past decade had been a glide path—and for me, too. I became a financial reporter at the beginning of that decade, in 2011, at the start of what turned out to be a remarkably dull and benign stretch for the economy. Stocks went up. Debt was cheap. Corporate profits climbed to new records. Nobody on Wall Street trading floors lost an embarrassing amount of money, or at least not in a fashion that lent itself to rollicking stories in the newspaper. I wrote about a merger boom and chronicled the banking industry's return to profitability after the 2008 meltdown. It was fun enough, and I learned a lot. But I sometimes found myself a little jealous of predecessors who had established themselves in the thick of reporting on past crises.

And now suddenly one had arrived.

It didn't feel like it at first, of course. The onset of the coronavirus pandemic in the early months of 2020 had no parallel in recent history. And then, suddenly, it was the only thing that mattered. In writing this book I aimed to capture that slowly-then-all-at-once feeling, exploring the decisions that the chief executives of some of the world's biggest companies were making through a lens that was changing by the hour.

Most of us don't run giant companies, but almost everyone can remember the uneasiness of March 2020, when things were fine until they weren't, until the springs that held our daily lives together suddenly sprang loose. I vividly remember sitting, maskless, on a flight from Tampa to New York on March 8, returning from a family vacation to a Gulf island that we had joked a week earlier about canceling, and wiping down the airplane armrests with hand wipes pilfered from Chick-fil-A. Three days later, I left the *Journal*'s office in midtown Manhattan. I would not be back for almost two years.

In the days that followed, we would all make monumental decisions, quickly and with information that was imperfect at best, about how to live in this new world. Some of these decisions proved silly in retrospect—I bought a pulse oximeter, though not a Peloton—but some would profoundly affect the course of our lives. We moved; we quit our jobs; we decided to write a book. Three years on, we are now living with those decisions and the unexpected consequences.

This book grew out of my early reporting on the immediate economic carnage of the pandemic. It began as an attempt to chronicle the extraordinary economic events that occurred as the pandemic froze the nation's economy. I wanted to understand what it was like to be in the driver's seat of the world's biggest and most influential companies, firms where leaders were used to talking about strategy in quarters, if not years, and be forced to make decisions on the fly—decisions on which a company's very survival might hinge. Who were the losers—and were there some surprising winners?

To answer these questions, I set out to find the most compelling corporate stories I could, ones that captured different kinds of companies and their leaders—Wall Street financiers, Midwest manufacturers, a Silicon Valley travel upstart and a legacy company it was trying to disrupt, and an airline industry brought to the brink of collapse, begging the government to save it.

I began this project not knowing whether these companies and the economy they stood astride would survive, or how their businesses might be reshaped. Like so many things during the pandemic, my project in time began to take on new dimensions. As the months went by, I realized that I wanted this book to be more than just an account of the greatest black swan event in contemporary economic history. I wanted to use the backdrop of this moment to explore the job of a modern CEO—and how it would be changed by this crisis and the grief, social unrest, and general anxiety it fomented. On paper, the corporate hierarchy in 2023 might resemble that of 2019, but the job has taken on new dimensions. CEOs stepped into the leadership void left by the Trump administration, whose dithering and optics-obsessed response to the crisis cost thousands of lives. That, coupled with the perceived politicization and flip-flopping of public health agencies, eroded millions of Americans' faith in institutions; many looked to their employers for steady leadership. The furor over masks and vaccines put CEOs in the political hot seat, forced to choose between adopting federal guidelines and alienating a portion of their employees and customers.

Each chapter of the postindustrial economy has brought its own archetype of corporate leader. The robber barons of the nineteenth century gave way to the first class of bosses skilled in the science of corporate and financial management. The postwar age churned out plodding, paternalistic stewards. Faced with one or two critical decisions in the course of their long tenures, they built the lazy, sprawling conglomerates that gave rise to the empire-smashing corporate raiders of the 1980s. The raiders didn't last, but the financial discipline and pursuit of profit they brought with them to corporate boardrooms did. The CEOs who followed merged, outsourced, and engineered their balance sheets on a scale never seen before during a period that saw a burst of innovation but also two crashes in the course of a decade. The biggest and most charismatic of them— Amazon's Jeff Bezos, JPMorgan's Jamie Dimon, Disney's Bob Iger— seemed to escape the corporate world altogether, as bona fide celebrities who had governments on speed dial and could make news simply by opening their mouths.

That changed in 2020. Their worlds became virtual, small, tactical. The globe-trotting stopped, replaced by endless Zoom calls and painfully awkward Zoom happy hours. Employees panicked. Hundreds of decisions had to be made in an instant. As the pandemic dragged on, the toxic politics around it seeped into seemingly every boardroom decision.

There are signs that we are in a new chapter of corporate meaning and management, one underway before the pandemic but fueled by it, as well as the social, political, and racial unrest that coursed alongside it. The pandemic will end one day. But I suspect that, just as the legacy of the corporate raiders of the 1980s bred new traits in the CEOs who came after them, the forces that shaped companies and their leaders during the crisis are, to some degree, here to stay: navigating fractured politics, building financial cushions, chucking out procedure and making decisions on the fly, and genuinely—not just in the jargon of glossy annual reports, but in a lived, everyday way—balancing profits and people.

This book is the result of interviews with more than a hundred people, and I've tried to write it in a way that captures the narrative tension of the moment—a moment that was continuously made obsolete and even foolish as the pandemic built into a global trauma whose human and economic fallout we'll be dealing with for years to come. Dialogue is rendered to the best recollection of people who were there or who were briefed on the discussions, and is supported by contemporaneous notes, emails, and text messages where possible. Readers should not assume that anyone in a particular scene was the source of the reporting it contains.

A note about accuracy: Where possible, I corroborated facts that were told to me with calendar entries, personal communications, public documents, and media reports. When individual recollections conflicted with primary-source documents, I deferred to the documents. But, as most of us can attest, the pandemic did something strange to our memories, warping them, stretching and compressing time in ways that have invariably introduced some errors—inadvertent and immaterial, I believe—to this book.

PROLOGUE

February 11, 2020

Bill Ackman winced as he watched the line of selfie-seekers form. It was a few minutes after 9 P.M., and Ackman, in a crisp white shirt and a pale blue tie, had just finished giving a talk at the London School of Economics. As he reached for his suit jacket, draped over the back of his chair, a horde of young finance students hurried down the auditorium aisle, smartphones in hand.

This kind of thing happened with surprising frequency to the fifty-four-year-old hedge fund manager. Following his graduation from Harvard Business School in 1992, Ackman later launched an investment firm, Pershing Square Capital Management, and over the course of nearly three decades on Wall Street had become a bona fide celebrity for the wannabe billionaire crowd. His name had become synonymous with bold market bets—a reputation enhanced by refined looks tailor-made for New York's tabloids, where he was reliable clickbait, and cable television, where he appeared to tout his investments and occasionally trash-talk rivals. With deep-set hazel eyes under dark eyebrows and a shock of white hair that he'd had since his twenties, Ackman could have passed for a Hollywood leading man of a certain vintage, or at least a handsome commentator on the Golf Channel.

He made more than $3 billion rescuing a mall owner, General Growth Properties, out of bankruptcy in 2010, then lost $1 billion on a crusade to prove that Herbalife, the maker of protein shakes and vitamin supplements, was a fraud. He had won big betting against the housing market in the run-up to the 2008 collapse, and lost even bigger investing in the drug company that owned Botox, a disaster that had prompted a public mea culpa. He sniffed out executives who were some combination of fat, happy, and lazy as the new century dawned. No blue-chip boardroom was out of range of his idea gun: JCPenney and Borders (misses), Wendy's and Canadian Pacific Railway (hits).

At its peak in the mid-2010s, Pershing Square managed more than $20 billion for investors ranging from billionaires to Arkansas teachers' retirement funds, and though its assets had dwindled after a string of losing investments, he remained in 2020 the model of a Wall Street high roller: charming and loquacious, wrong almost as often as he was right, but never in doubt, and with billions of dollars to put behind his ideas. It was a reputation that inspired fear in corporate CEOs, whose shares he bought and whose strategy he was prone to publicly skewer. It also won him a legion of fans, especially among fawning young financiers back in New York, where he was easy to spot on the streets of midtown Manhattan. He usually indulged them.

Not tonight.

It had been six weeks since the first reports about a mystery virus circulating in China. In early January, health authorities in Wuhan, an inland industrial city of eleven million people about four hours by train from Beijing, had flagged a few dozen cases of a new respiratory illness that caused pneumonia, in some patients severe. The cases all appeared linked to a "wet market" on the city's outskirts—a term denoting markets common in Asia that sell live seafood and animals, including exotic ones, for slaughter. The first confirmed death came on January 11, a sixty-one-year-old man who was said to be a market regular.

By the time Ackman took the stage at the London School of Economics in February, there were more than 40,000 reported cases in China and a few thousand in neighboring countries. More than 1,000 people had died. As he spoke, some 350 Americans were on their way home, courtesy of U.S. government charter planes, from the hot zone in central China, to spend two weeks in quarantine at American military bases in California. On the day of Ackman's talk, the virus had been given a name by the World Health Organization. "I'll spell it," the group's director-general told reporters. "C-O-V-I-D hyphen one nine."

The name was a mash-up of what little was known at the time. COVI: It belonged to the coronavirus family of viruses. D: It caused disease, distinguishing it from the myriad viruses that fulfilled their genetic destiny without sickening their hosts. And it was first discovered in the final days of 2019. Scientists had quickly sequenced the virus's genetic code and identified it as a type of coronavirus, a family of pathogens known to virologists as a neighborhood nuisance: mostly mild but prone to obnoxious variants. They are so named because the spiky proteins that cover their surface, which pierce human host cells and allow the virus to replicate, resemble what a child might produce if asked to draw a crown.

Ackman had been voraciously consuming news reports out of China that confirmed that the virus could pass between people, even among those who weren't showing symptoms and didn't know they were sick—a crucial indicator of how quickly a virus might spread. When the mayor of Wuhan admitted in late January that as many as five million people had left the city in the days following the Chinese New Year on January 25, before a regional lockdown was imposed, it confirmed the hedge fund manager's fears. "This isn't going to stay a Chinese problem," Ackman had told his wife.

He worried about his father, a lung cancer survivor, and moved his parents into a guest room in his estate in the Hamptons. He sold Pershing Square's stake in Starbucks, which had more than three thousand stores in China.

And he had nearly canceled this trip to London. He had ultimately kept the commitment because the main event was Pershing Square's annual shareholder meeting in Guernsey, the tiny English Channel island known for sweeping coastlines and lenient tax laws that made it a popular domicile for investment funds. The island was lax about many things, but annual meetings were a must. Canceling would have invited a regulatory headache.

Toward the end of his lecture at the London School of Economics, Ackman opened up the floor for questions. One audience member raised the specter of the new coronavirus, and as Ackman started to respond, a student in the front row coughed. Ackman leaned back sharply, half in jest, to laughter from the crowd. Then he struck a more serious note: "It is one of the black swans out there right now," he said.

"Black swan" is a ubiquitous term in economics. It comes from a historical belief that all swans were white, which held for centuries until colonizing Europeans stumbled onto Australia and found black swans among the continent's menagerie of strange creatures. Adopted more recently by economists, the term is now a warning: The most dangerous and costly crises come when something that has never happened before—something that everyone has assumed could never happen—happens.

The economist who coined it, Nassim Taleb, assigned three characteristics to "black swan" events: They are rare, they are extreme, and once they have passed, hindsight tends to rationalize them. Of course a web of ill-conceived European alliances could drag the world into war in 1914. Of course determined terrorists could bring down a New York skyscraper with a plane. Of course home prices could go down just as surely as up, a lesson learned in 2008 at huge cost.

In February 2020, as Ackman spoke to the next generation of financiers and corporate executives in London, the idea that the coronavirus would spread unchecked, crippling and reshaping the global economy, sounded far-fetched. Supervirus scares, including bird flu and swine flu, had long been fodder for cable news programming but had fizzled out in the end. The idea that the coronavirus would be uniquely disruptive or deadly seemed like a crank theory.

But on paper it checked the first two of Taleb's boxes. First, true pandemics are rare. The last big one, the 1918 influenza outbreak, was more than a century ago. You'd have to go back another hundred years to find the global cholera scourge that began in 1817, and more than four hundred more until hitting the Black Death of the 1300s. More recently, the 2004 outbreak in China of Severe Acute Respiratory Syndrome, or SARS, and the Ebola outbreak in east Africa defied doomsayers and stayed mostly contained.

But when pandemics do happen, they are extreme, satisfying the next of Taleb's criteria. The 1918 flu killed an estimated one in thirty people on the planet and sickened as many as one in three. Today's world was far more interconnected, Ackman told the students gathered in the London lecture hall. The costs, both in lives lost and economic fallout, would almost certainly be worse this time around.

With a wife and a nine-month-old at home back in New York, Ackman had no interest in being an early patient. The norm, at lectures like this, was to stick around for a while and hold court. Instead, Ackman ran out the clock, taking a few extra questions from the crowd to skate past the scheduled 8:30 P.M. end time. As the finance fanboys drifted down the aisles—many of them, Ackman assumed, international students who had just returned from holiday breaks in Asia—he waved apologetically over his shoulder and made a quick exit into a car waiting in the London chill.

Months later, he would apply to the lecture a word that had by then seeped into the public lexicon. He had worried, without having the vocabulary for it at the time, that his evening with the university students would be a superspreader event.

CRASH
LANDING

CHAPTER 1

BORROWED TIME

Steven Mnuchin was sick of talking about global warming.

Half an hour into a private dinner at the World Economic Forum in Davos, Switzerland, the conversation had been of little else. Executives from the biggest companies in the world had gathered in the ritzy ski town's famed Grand Hotel Belvédère. A shrine to a nineteenth-century European version of wellness, nestled into the side of Davos's steep hill, in recent times the hotel served as the power center of the annual summit. For one week a year in late January, snipers patrolled its rooftops as the world's corporate elite gathered. It was a long and annoying trip, even by private jet, but the chance to rub elbows with their peers and senior government officials—and to be seen as masters of the universe, thought leaders for the century to come—was irresistible. Among the attendees at that evening's dinner were Uber CEO Dara Khosrowshahi, Facebook's Sheryl Sandberg, Chevron's Mike Wirth, IBM's Ginni Rometty, Volkswagen chairman Herbert Diess, and Wall Street dealmaker Ken Moelis, along with Mnuchin and his colleague in Trump's cabinet, Wilbur Ross, the octogenarian commerce secretary.

This kind of dinner was exactly what these corporate executives had come to the Alps for. Squeezed around a long table covered in white linen and dotted with fresh-cut flowers and elegant candle tapers, the group had somberly—if not soberly—discussed the need for more radical action on climate change.

It was the kind of tin-eared talk that was as much a part of Davos as alpaca-lined parkas and galosh-covered Armani loafers. The organization behind it all, the World Economic Forum, had been founded in 1971 by a Swiss university professor as a humble academic venue for resolving international conflicts and promoting shared prosperity.

But in recent years it had become a capitalist cheerfest, where the highest-tier tickets cost more than $500,000 and even a spartan hotel room fetched more than $600 a night. Corporate executives, hedge fund titans, and government officials disembarked from helicopters and black cars to spend five days doling out management advice to the developing world and patting themselves on the back for it. In 2020, more than a hundred billionaires were in attendance, and even for Mnuchin—a wealthy man himself, a former Goldman Sachs executive turned Hollywood producer who had been one of Trump's first cabinet picks—the hypocrisy was a bit thick. He also thought their attention was misplaced.

"Global warming is an issue, but it's not the only issue," he told the room, as tuxedo-clad waiters circled to refill wineglasses. Iran's nuclear program was growing more sophisticated by the day and should be higher than it was on everyone's worry list, he said. "Also, you know, there's a city of eleven million people in China that's on lockdown."

It was January 25, 2020, more than three weeks since the virus had been reported by Chinese authorities. It had already sickened some five hundred people in the country and killed seventeen, by the country's official tally.

But how bad was it? Reports of the virus struck many of the evening's attendees as the kind of thing that cropped up from time to time in the developing world—and China in particular. Decades after the communist revolutionary leader Mao Zedong had penned a poem bidding "farewell to the god of plagues," promising to eradicate a deadly parasitic fever, spread by the use of human waste as fertilizer, and bring China into the modern age, the country remained fertile ground for pathogens. Rapidly expanding cities butted up against stubborn old-world customs, creating the ideal conditions for what epidemiologists call "spillover," in which diseases that might otherwise have circulated harmlessly through animal populations jump to humans, with unpredictable consequences. By 2004, a respiratory disease, SARS, had killed hundreds in China. It was later genetically traced to a colony of cave-dwelling bats, from which, experts theorized, it had jumped to civets, small catlike mammals commonly sold for slaughter as a delicacy in village markets. Before that, in 1997, it was a virulent strain of flu that traveled from poultry to humans, stamped out only by the slaughter of millions of chickens. Another flu variant had originated in Hong Kong in 1968 and was ultimately blamed for as many as a million deaths globally.

Now, in late January 2020, a new virus had appeared. It didn't yet have a name, much less a forensic footprint or a treatment protocol. But to those global observers who knew what to look out for, it had all the markings of a killer. While much remained unknown as Mnuchin admonished his fellow elites for their misplaced attention, it was clear the virus could spread between people. Early studies suggested it could live on surfaces, possibly for days. Chinese authorities had moved to seal off Wuhan ahead of the Lunar New Year, a major travel holiday that would send millions of people out from cities that were breeding grounds for a highly contagious disease back to their homes in suburbs and rural villages. Officials canceled planes and trains out of the city, and suspended subway and ferry service within it.

They were too late. Cases had already spread to neighboring countries, including Taiwan and Japan. And a few days before the conference in Davos, the virus had been confirmed in the United States, in a thirty-five-year-old Washington State man who had recently returned from China. An official at the U.S. Department of Health and Human Services warned that "the virus may already be here. We just don't have a test to know."

But none of that had pricked the bubble of optimism at Davos. When the virus was raised at all, it was largely dismissed, notably by U.S. president Donald Trump, who, unlike his predecessors Barack Obama and George W. Bush, had opted to attend the elite conclave. He had boasted in recent months about "the greatest economy ever," which he believed would carry him to reelection for a second term in the fall. "We have it totally under control," Trump told an interviewer in Davos—the first of what would prove to be a string of overly optimistic and often deliberately misleading comments from the president about a deadly virus.

Trump, for all his political blinders, wasn't alone in shrugging off reports from halfway around the world. Nobody at Davos seemed particularly worried about the virus, not the hundreds of corporate executives in attendance nor the reporters who chased them down icy sidewalks and into exclusive parties in hopes of gleaning a morsel or two. "All the right things are happening," the CEO of pharmaceutical giant Novartis told an anchor at CNBC, the financial-news channel. Attendees crammed into coat-check lines and swiped toothpicked olives and cubed Gruyère off communal trays. They packed a chalet piano bar to hear pop star Jason Derulo perform and stayed for the aftershow, a turntable set by David Solomon, the Goldman Sachs CEO, who, in addition to running the country's sixth-biggest bank, was a house-music deejay hobbyist.

Even as Mnuchin voiced his misgivings at dinner, he wasn't exactly ringing the alarm bell publicly. In an interview that morning with CNBC, he hadn't been asked about the coronavirus and hadn't brought it up. He'd spent most of the interview talking up the Trump administration's plans for further tax cuts. Jamie Dimon, the CEO of America's biggest bank, skated past the topic, too. JPMorgan had just reported its most profitable year on record, and he summed up the mood in Switzerland with a rousing endorsement of the economic system that had made Davos's attendees rich: "Capitalism is the greatest thing that ever happened to mankind."

Nobody makes friends at Davos by being a bummer.

—

THE EXECUTIVES GATHERED at that dinner in Switzerland could hardly be faulted for their optimism. The global economy in early 2020 was, by plenty of measures, the strongest since the end of World War II. Stock markets around the world were setting new records almost daily. In America, the previous July had marked ten straight years of economic growth—the longest expansion on record, eclipsing the Clinton-era boom of the 1990s. With unemployment at a fifty-year low, the biggest problem for many corporate executives was finding enough workers.

But on closer look, the story of the post-2008 economy was playing out on a split screen. On one screen, the companies that made up its economic backbone were thriving. Corporate profits hit a record high of nearly $2 trillion in 2019, padded by the Trump administration's tax cuts, passed two years earlier. Silicon Valley campuses and urban office towers pulsed with white-collar employees whose income was on the rise. Flush with cash, they splurged on new homes, cars, and streaming services and plowed their savings into the stock market, which hit one record high after another.

The other screen showed an economy uniquely vulnerable to crisis. The stable, high-paying union jobs that had powered previous economic expansions and built the middle class were vanishing at an alarming pace. Wages were flat, adjusting for light inflation, leaving many workers struggling to afford essentials. Benefits like pensions and health insurance became less generous or vanished altogether. In a little over a decade, the share of corporate earnings paid out to private-sector workers shrank by 5.4 percentage points.

As the virus began its international spread in February of 2020, U.S. government data showed that the vast majority of working adults enrolled in Medicaid or food stamp programs weren't unemployed and on the dole but were in fact working full-time, their below-sustenance corporate wages subsidized by taxpayers. A day's work no longer guaranteed a stable existence.

In the mid-twentieth century, the growing fortunes of America's corporations were shared with workers. Now it increasingly went to shareholders, a one-way rejiggering of a social contract that had underpinned capitalist growth for a half century. What's more, millions of people were no longer corporate employees at all, but rather "gig workers." They drove cars for ride-hailing apps, scanned documents for law firms, and rented out their homes on Airbnb, often without the job-based benefits like pensions and 401(k) funds that previous generations of workers had counted on to build wealth. "We built an economy with no shock absorbers," the Nobel-winning economist Joseph Stiglitz would later say. And debt had grown at every level—household, corporate, government. "Such conditions," the Federal Reserve Bank of Boston had warned in September of 2019, in the bone-dry language of central bankers, "have the potential to amplify a downturn should it occur."

Corporate debt, after easing in the wake of the 2008 blowup, had come roaring back as companies borrowed heavily to finance acquisitions and buy back their own stock. Between the end of 2010 and the end of 2019, this debt had risen from $6.1 trillion to $10.1 trillion. Banks and bond investors found themselves in a race to the bottom, willing to overlook high levels of existing debt and unproven business models to keep lending. Speaking to a House of Commons committee in early 2019, Mark Carney, the governor of the Bank of England, warned that the situation looked a lot like the pre-2008 subprime housing boom, when banks eager to feed a Wall Street mortgage-securities machine wrote loans with their eyes closed.

Even the soaring stock market, on closer examination, held worrying signs. Corporate profit growth, though still robust, had slowed in 2019, and a simmering trade war flared up between the United States and China, the world's two largest economies. Yet the stock market barely flinched, hitting one record high after another. Between 2013 and 2020, the S&P 500 rose twice as quickly as the profits its component companies produced. The price-to-earnings ratio of the S&P 500 index cracked 25:1 in January of 2020, the largest gap between stock prices and actual corporate earnings since 2009. Decades of investing fundamentals were being tossed aside in a frenzy.

And it wasn't just stocks that were rising. The decade-long rally benefited nearly every kind of investment. The benchmark U.S. bond index rose by 6 percent in 2019. Gold gained, too. This is unusual. Stock market rallies are usually accompanied by declines for safer assets like bonds and gold, and vice versa. Investors run to safety in times of crisis, and then back again when the fear recedes. But in 2019 everything went up.

Conventional wisdom says no economic trend has a single cause, but the decade-long bull market that grew out of the wreckage of the 2008 meltdown may come as close as anything to proving that wrong. The Federal Reserve, the U.S. central bank, had kept interest rates historically low in the years after the global financial crisis, which started as a market crash but quickly became a credit crunch. Available credit is essential for companies to launch, expand, and hire. By keeping interest rates low, the government tried to force banks to lend, thereby supporting the economy.

Ten-year U.S. Treasury bonds yielded about 5 percent annually in 2007; by 2019, investors were getting half that. When the safest financial investment on the planet—the U.S. government has never defaulted on its debt, and Treasury bonds are among the easiest assets to convert into cash—is returning fractions of a penny, investors look for alternatives. They pile into stocks, corporate bonds, real estate, and anything else that promises a return. So everything goes up.

The ten-year economic expansion had made investors blind to risk, forgetful that markets can go down just as easily as up. With their stock prices continuing to rise, corporate executives began to feel invincible. They embraced the financial engineering that Wall Street craved—cheap debt, billions spent wooing shareholders, and a wave of corporate consolidation unseen in twenty years. Companies riding a post-2008 wave of economic growth grew increasingly sure that the good times would never end. Executives spent billions of dollars buying back their own stock, a move that served to boost the share price, enriching investors and themselves. They borrowed heavily and socked little away. The biggest U.S. airlines, for example, spent 96 percent of their free cash flow between 2009 and 2019 on stock buybacks. It was all underpinned by a false sense of security brought on by a decade-long bull market.

The global economy was teetering on a precipice, but everyone was simply admiring the view.

WITHIN WEEKS, IN a world transformed overnight by the pandemic, everything about the Davos meeting would come to seem ridiculous: the gathering of people, the private jets many of them took to get there, the wine tastings and private dinners. It was the sort of backroom cavorting that had gone away under the glare of populist anger after the 2008 crisis but had crept back as America had prospered. And, billionaires or not, it was the kind of gathering of people in close quarters that would soon come to seem like a relic of the "before times," when proximity in the business world was an asset—a deal sealed, a sale advanced—and not a potential infection.

As the coronavirus spread across the world in the early months of 2020, the moments of reckoning came quickly for America's corporate chiefs, who faced an economic shutdown swifter and more total than any in modern history. By the end of March, leaders of the world's biggest companies were on their heels. Macy's department stores and Ford's factories went dark. So did Disney World and professional sports. Hollywood studios called "cut." Flights were grounded, airports deserted. On Wall Street, trading grew so panicked that there was talk of closing the markets, which hadn't happened since the terrorist attacks on 9/11.

As the virus gained steam, CEOs had global operations and supply chains that should have provided sight lines into its spread. They had access to government officials across the world, and global workforces that should have tripped health alarms. But few saw the crisis coming. And when it did, they bumped along in the dark like everyone else, never feeling they had enough information to run companies that they had steered, in some cases, for almost a decade through a benevolent, easy-money world. Many sought out government officials or health experts, tapping trustee boards, country-club memberships, and other informal networks unavailable to regular Americans to find their way.

The decisions they made, they hoped, would save their companies and preserve the engine of the U.S. economy for when the virus eventually subsided. Just as they didn't foresee the screeching halt of the global economy, they couldn't have predicted the unprecedented flood of money from the federal government, filtered through the private markets, that would keep them afloat.

And they would spark a rethinking of the corporate-management orthodoxy that had dried in the post-2008 cement. The pursuit of growth at any cost, an underpinning of American capitalism, would be questioned.

The tinder was already there. The economy that they dominated had changed over the past four decades in ways that made it more vulnerable to a shock like the coronavirus. Corporate debt skyrocketed. Wages stagnated. Millions of workers were pushed out of stable corporate jobs into the gig economy, renting their homes on Airbnb, their cars on Uber, and their time on TaskRabbit. Manufacturing, an industry likely to bounce back more quickly after the shutdown as companies backfill orders for sprockets and widgets, is no longer the economic driver. Instead, America has become a service economy, fueled by consumption of soft goods—haircuts and cocktails and hotel stays—whose demand has been slower to return.

A relentless march toward efficiency gave rise to just-in-time management strategies that prized small inventories and relied on a humming supply chain, finely tuned to deliver a screw to an industrial factory at just the moment it was needed, lest precious shareholder money be wasted financing that screw before the door it was supposed to secure to a chassis skimmed off the assembly line. Hospitals stockpiled fewer masks, ventilators, and drugs, and converted excess bed space into outpatient clinics that could rack up billings. Companies packed their offices tightly. Airlines did the same with their planes. And Wall Street cheered them on. Analysts slapped "buy" ratings on companies that focused on cost cuts. Hedge funds and buyout firms marked those that didn't for shake-ups, buying up big positions in their stocks and pushing their CEOs out.

For the country's corporate leaders, Covid-19 would be trial by fire. They scrapped their business plans and adjusted to life in quarantine. In the pandemic's early days, they struggled to reassure employees who were as scared of joblessness as of the virus itself. As it wore on, they grappled with their workers' newfound sense of work-from-anywhere autonomy, needling them to get back to the office with little success. They thought themselves masters of the corporate universe, products of three decades of management fine-tuning, but were tossed into the tidal pool of central-bank policy, beneficiaries of an unprecedented opening of a monetary spigot as Washington raced to keep the economy from imploding.

CHAPTER 2

CHAMPAGNE DECADE

Chris Nassetta closed his eyes and pressed his head into the seat-back for the five-hour flight to Cabo San Lucas, the Mexican beachside town where a handful of other couples, all longtime friends, were awaiting him and his wife for an annual holiday tradition. It was a few days before Christmas, and the chief executive of Hilton was ready to close the books on 2019.

He had logged more than 250 days on the road during the year, crisscrossing the globe to open new hotels, meet with investors, and partake in various celebrations to mark the company's centennial. It had been one hundred years since Conrad Hilton, born to a Norwegian immigrant father and German American mother in what was then the New Mexico territories, had bought his first property, a squat brick inn in Cisco, Texas, that rented rooms in eight-hour blocks to workers in the nearby oil fields. The company that Conrad had built was now the second-largest hotelier in the world, with 970,000 rooms in 119 countries, an annual revenue of $9.45 billion, and a market valuation of $31 billion. Though it was still nipping at the heels of Marriott, the industry king, it was closing the gap, and 2019, Nassetta's twelfth year in the job, had been a good one.

He had rung the bell at the New York Stock Exchange and sipped piña coladas on the set of *Good Morning America,* toasting a decade-long economic boom that had been very good to corporate America and to Hilton. The company had opened more than one new hotel a day in 2019, riding a continued rise in global travel and an appetite from Wall Street investors who were all too eager to put their dollars into new properties, spurred by easy-money policies in Washington that pushed them to invest in anything, everything. Hilton was preparing to launch its eighteenth brand in mid-January, about two weeks away. Dubbed Tempo, it was aimed at younger travelers who had increasingly come to shift their dollars away from hotels, with their stuffy concierges and nosebleed minibar prices, in favor of sites like Airbnb and Vrbo, which offered a sense of adventure and authenticity. Nassetta had toured mock-ups of its Bluetooth-wired rooms and communal workspaces, confident they would attract the millennial travelers—what the company called "modern achievers"—his shareholders craved. Hilton's stock had started the year at $71 and closed at $112, an all-time high. Investors were pleased. So was the company's board of directors, who would soon approve a $21.4 million pay package that would make Nassetta one of the highest-paid CEOs in the world.

But now, taxiing on the runway toward his first vacation in a year, the fifty-five-year-old wasn't feeling in the mood for a victory lap. Nassetta was tired—and he was worried. The eleven-year economic boom that had followed the 2008 crash was too good, and had gone on too long, to last. Hilton may have been opening new hotels at its fastest rate in its history, but its older properties were struggling. Revenues at existing hotels, which had typically grown comfortably by 5 or 6 percent per year, were now stuck in neutral. Demand from Hilton's business travelers was waning, a sign that big companies weren't optimistically chasing new business around the world. That wasn't just bad news for Hilton's hotels in convention hubs like Washington, Las Vegas, and Atlanta. It was also a sign of bigger problems on the horizon. When global companies stopped hitting the gas, Nassetta knew, the economy tended to stall. It was a replay of a tape Nassetta had seen before, one that had made him a realist about the inevitability of recessions and the euphoria that precedes them.

Silver-haired with a wide smile, Nassetta was industrious and warm, a born hustler. He grew up in the Washington, D.C., suburbs, shoveling driveways in the winters and working summers in the engineering department at a local Holiday Inn, where his parting gift was a toilet plunger, spray-painted gold. He had launched his career in the early 1990s sorting through the wreckage of the savings-and-loan crisis, restructuring commercial real estate mortgages after banks' slipshod standards had caught up with them. He had been a young first-time CEO when the dot-com bubble burst in 2001, sparking another recession. And he had taken the job at Hilton in October 2007, just a few months before the start of an economic crash from which the company would barely emerge.

Now deep into a career defined by crises, Nassetta was determined to see around the next corner more keenly. For months, even as stocks hit new highs and the economy continued to grow at a fast clip, he had quietly been preparing Hilton for a downturn he was sure was coming, even if he didn't know from where. He had slashed marketing spending, mothballed nonessential technology projects, and told his chief financial officer, Kevin Jacobs, to refinance Hilton's debt so it didn't have any big bond repayments looming in the near term, which would give it some financial breathing room if things turned south. "Cycles are cycles," he told Jacobs before packing up for the Christmas holiday. "This one won't last forever."

In Mexico he toured the Waldorf Astoria resort that Hilton had just opened and spent Christmas Eve in a suite at the company's Los Cabos resort with his wife and six daughters, clad, in family tradition, in matching onesies and elf hats. He swapped pleasantries with Treasury Secretary Steven Mnuchin and Steve Schwarzman, chairman of the private-equity giant Blackstone, who both happened to be spending the holidays in the Mexican beach town. He probed them for confirmation of the gloomy knot in his stomach but detected little.

He finally unburdened himself to David Solomon, the chief of Wall Street powerhouse Goldman Sachs. The two were close friends.

They had met in the early 1990s, when Nassetta was making a name for himself as a real estate investor and Solomon, then a junior executive at the investment bank Bear Stearns, had helped to raise money for Nassetta's deals. In the two decades since, they had risen to the pinnacle of their industries, now both CEOs of Fortune 500 companies. They counted each other as confidants, members of a small club of leaders who sat atop their respective industries. After a round of golf at the El Dorado, the polo-clad friends sipped a rosé that Solomon, a wine aficionado, had picked out.

"I've got a bad feeling," Nassetta told his friend and former banker. The U.S. economy, he said, was "like a car running out of gas. And I don't see a gas station anywhere."

A few days later, he hosted a New Year's Eve dinner for his family and friends in a private dining room at the Cabos Waldorf, which bore the Hilton name. The group toasted the new year, and Nassetta tried to put his angst behind him. Everyone seemed jubilant. And why not? America's business class was closing a decade that had been almost too good to be true.

Seven thousand miles away, health officials in Hong Kong had just issued a report that went little noticed in the foreign press. They were monitoring twenty-seven cases of pneumonia, seven of them severe. "Causative pathogen" still unknown.

A FEW WEEKS later, hundreds of guests poured into an eight-story Greek Revival building in lower Manhattan, pausing for photographs on a red carpet covered by a makeshift tent shielding them from a frigid winter night. It was late February and there wasn't a mask in sight.

New York's financiers were there to toast, naturally, themselves. It was the Museum of American Finance's annual gala and was taking place in a venue that was itself a monument to American capitalism's global expansion. The chandeliers overhead glimmered above a six-story ballroom that was the former home of National City

Bank, which evolved into the modern Citigroup as Wall Street continued its consolidation and global domination in the waning part of the twentieth century.

The guest of honor was easy to spot as he floated through the cavernous space. James Gorman was six-foot-one with slicked-back hair and a thin frame, draped this evening in a navy suit and a purple tie, carrying a glass of scotch that was mostly a prop. A bit of a control freak, Gorman drank sparingly in public settings, and anyway, tonight he had a speech to give.

The well-wishers who stopped to glad-hand him weren't just offering congratulations on the evening's leadership award. They were saluting Wall Street's latest merger mogul. A few days earlier, Gorman had sent eyebrows shooting up by spending $13 billion to buy E*Trade, the giant retail trading brokerage. It was the biggest deal in more than a decade on Wall Street and a huge bet on the bull market that was now entering its second decade. Project Eagle, as the E*Trade takeover was known inside Morgan Stanley, had been negotiated in secret for months and finally announced on the morning of February 20. U.S. stocks had closed the night before at a record high.

The deal said much about Wall Street's past and future. High finance had emerged from the 2008 crisis rightly hobbled and, equally rightly, brought to heel by new rules and contempt from a bruised public. In the years that followed, the securities-trading businesses that had gotten it into trouble in the first place had fallen out of favor, replaced by the business of helping ordinary individuals manage their money and plan for retirement. Three of the biggest retail brokerages—Scottrade, TD Ameritrade, and Charles Schwab—had all merged in quick succession. E*Trade was the last one standing, probably too small to survive on its own, but with more than five million clients that big banks, hungrily eyeing the space, would love to have.

Unlike trading or investment banking—the business of helping companies merge, go public, and issue new securities to raise money—wealth management is relatively stable. When markets turn, mergers wither and corporate bosses retreat. But people still need someone to manage their money, and in his decade on the job, Gorman had staked Morgan Stanley's future on helping them do it. By the end of 2019, the firm managed $2.7 trillion for more than three million Americans. But it wasn't enough. Money management is what is known on Wall Street as a "scale business." With fixed overhead costs, profits grow with every incremental account. Buying E*Trade would bring another $360 billion in client money into the firm, squeezing more profit out of each dollar. It would also put an exclamation point on Gorman's tenure—a headline-grabbing takeover that was by far the largest on Wall Street since the pre-2008 halcyon days.

Morgan Stanley was a somewhat unlikely suitor. The firm had nearly failed in 2008 and for years afterward bumbled along as the weakling of Wall Street, lurching from one crisis to another. The E*Trade takeover—a deal that landed them on the front page of the *Journal*—was a coup. It was the biggest takeover by a major bank since the 2008 crisis. That it came from Morgan Stanley, not so long ago the industry's resident basket case, was a testament to the firm's turnaround under Gorman, and on this snowy night a week later, the mercurial CEO was in an unusually good mood.

Wall Street bosses tend to come in two flavors: brash trader and smooth-talking banker. The sixty-one-year-old Gorman was neither. Born into a family of ten in a suburb of Melbourne, he had disappointed both his father, who'd hoped he'd be an engineer, and his mother, who'd hoped he'd be a priest, by becoming a lawyer. After stints at McKinsey, the consulting firm, and Merrill Lynch, the investment bank, he had joined Morgan Stanley in 2006 with a mandate to transform its "thundering herd" of stockbrokers, who earned commissions peddling shares to Middle America, into a profit-generating force that offered concierge financial advice to wealthier clients.

Clinical and aloof, Gorman was a tough nut to crack, even to longtime Morgan Stanley insiders. Even as he fired the two thousand lowest-performing advisers, colleagues would catch him in more human moments, delighting in standing at the window of his suburban New York office with binoculars, watching the Australian shepherds kept there to chase away deer.

Morgan Stanley had largely hung back as new types of exotic, risky trading swept Wall Street in the early 2000s. Under Gorman's predecessor as CEO, John Mack, the firm charged in at the worst possible moment, just as credit and real estate prices were peaking. In 2007, it lost $9 billion on a single mortgage trade, beginning a spiral that brought it to the brink of bankruptcy a year later. A major cash infusion from Mitsubishi, the Japanese bank, bought it time. Had regulators not intervened, it would almost certainly have failed.

The crisis ushered Mack out and Gorman in. It was quite the contrast. Mack was a backslapping Southern bond trader, a former college football player who liked to mingle in the Morgan Stanley cafeteria. Gorman preferred the quiet of his office, where he tallied in longhand the daily revenue figures from each of the firm's major divisions each night, sticking the loose-leaf sheets into a folder on his desk. He axed Morgan Stanley's proprietary trading desks and shrank its bond-trading operations, the source of repeat blunders. He sold off a fleet of oil tankers and a half-finished eyesore of a casino in Atlantic City, remnants of the freewheeling culture that once ruled Wall Street. Instead, he doubled down on the steadier business of money management and household financial advice, adding retail brokerage Smith Barney in his early years.

And now he had bagged a giant fish in E*Trade. The dot-com darling, once known for its Super Bowl ads featuring a talking baby, had long dominated the world of retail investing, catering to small-time traders chasing riches in the market. It was a coup by any standards, a chest-beating one by Wall Street's.

As a light snow dusted the streets of lower Manhattan outside, Gorman took the microphone. He offered the requisite appreciation, then opined on the duty of capitalists—as he saw it, "to help issuers and investors meet, and to help savers and borrowers meet," and to do so without getting out over their skis. He reminded the audience what happens when risks are overlooked, when ebullience gets the better of reason. "As we saw twelve years ago," he said, "it can be catastrophic."

A SHARP BREEZE hissed through the desert palms outside as the two men sat in the great room, framed by the lengthening shadow of the San Jacinto Mountains. Jim Hackett, the chief executive of Ford Motor Company, and Bill Ford, the company's executive chairman and scion of its founding family, were at the tail ends of their Christmas breaks, dressed casually and sipping cold mineral water.

Hackett had driven in from Newport Beach, where he had been spending the holidays in a rented bungalow a short drive from where his kids and a baby granddaughter were staying. He was meeting Ford at the storied Smoke Tree Ranch outside of Palm Springs, California. It was a rustic, moneyed community so deliberately off the grid that Hackett had gotten lost using Google Maps to get there and needed Ford to guide him over the phone. Bill had wintered there as a child at the family cottage, where he had waved at Walt Disney, who had a place down the street, and waited for his father, William Clay Ford, Sr., the last surviving grandchild of Henry Ford, to return from a round of golf with Frank Sinatra, whom a young Bill called "Uncle Frank." He later bought a home on the ranch himself, and today he had invited Hackett down for a chat.

Hackett had only been in the job two years. He had been appointed as an outsider after a long career running Steelcase, the biggest maker of office furniture in the world, and then a year and a half as the athletic director at the University of Michigan, where he had been a backup center on the football team in the 1970s. (He may have been a rare outsider at Ford, but his deep roots in the state and an abiding love for the U of M Wolverines helped win over the Michigan employee base and union members.)

On the drive down, Hackett's thoughts kept returning to an article he had read on a battered iPad back in the bungalow, about the growing case count of the coronavirus in China. Ford, like most U.S. industrial powerhouses, relied heavily on Chinese suppliers to provide the raw parts that went into its pickup trucks and sedans. Ford had embraced the "just-in-time" model pioneered by its Japanese rival, Toyota, a decade earlier, which frowned on big inventory holdings in favor of the right rivet or seatback arriving just before it needed to be installed. It was part of the broader push in corporate America toward efficiency and had helped juice profits. But it left little wiggle room. Ford's warehouses didn't hold the supply of components and parts they once did, and any delay in shipments from China could be costly. It had been two weeks since the Chinese authorities had announced they were tracking the virus, and Chinese ports were already starting to report delays.

But that wasn't the topic of today's desert sit-down. The two men were there to discuss the future of Ford—specifically, how long Hackett would remain its CEO. The sixty-four-year-old had always been something of a temporary boss, brought in after his predecessor, Mark Fields, was ousted after losing support of shareholders and the Ford family, which owned 5 percent of the company's stock but controlled 40 percent of its voting power.

The two had been a click-and-clack duo. The patrician Ford was born into industrial royalty, the son of a Ford scion and an heiress to the Firestone tire fortune. He had gone to Hotchkiss, the elite Connecticut boarding school, then off to Princeton with the keys to a rare green Mustang. Hackett was the youngest of four sons whose Irish Catholic parents had stopped having kids because they couldn't afford any more. Cerebral and dough-faced, he had hustled his way to his first CEO job at the age of thirty-nine.

But the two men had grown extraordinarily close. Ford had taken a chance on Hackett. He had never worked in the auto industry before joining Ford in 2016 to run its skunkworks unit, which was exploring self-driving and car-sharing technologies in a desperate attempt to catch up with Silicon Valley. When Fields left, Ford offered the job to Hackett. He had accepted the job coolly, warning his patron that "Wall Street's not going to like me." He was right. Wall Street didn't like him, or more charitably, they didn't understand him—and neither did a large swath of his own employees.

Hackett had tried to push Ford, which was conservative to the point of being stodgy, to move faster and think bigger. But his vision was hard to follow at times and didn't resonate with the go-left-go-right engineers who struggled to follow his road map. He became known for his late-night emails, which tended to land long after the family-oriented Midwesterners who worked for him had gone to bed. The emails sometimes included links to TED Talks—meccas for big thinkers and influencers but derided by others as self-indulgent displays of intellectualism—and articles from science magazines. He once answered a question about why Ford should be in the smart-car business by saying that "the nature of what makes a business win over time is not unlike any other kinds of system—the way our bodies win in battle, or the way a football team wins, or the way a market moves. I'm a student of this, complexity theory." It was the kind of head-scratching answer that had failed to win the loyalty of the rank and file. When he mandated that all the companies' new models be Wi-Fi-connected by 2019, engineers complained that technology could be glitchy, that Ford's reputation for quality might suffer, and who needed their car to be a computer anyway?

He was prone to quoting behavioral economists to confounded Wall Street analysts. Ford fell short of its own profits projections repeatedly in Hackett's early tenure. When asked by a Morgan Stanley analyst in the summer of 2018, after Ford had postponed an investor event set for September, whether he'd still be in the job by then, he said "Hell, yes." And yet the stock had fallen 20 percent on his watch. Had America's founding carmaker lost its way?

As 2020 dawned and the two men met in Palm Springs, there was promising news on the horizon for Ford. The electric-powered Mustang had just been launched in Los Angeles, a new-age take on the classic muscle car—its three driving modes were "whisper," "engage," and "unbridled." (It would later beat out models from Tesla, Audi, Volvo, and Porsche for *Car and Driver*'s coveted Car of the Year prize.) Development of the company's first electric F-150 truck was chugging along in secret. Hackett had just wrapped up discussions with Bob Iger, chief executive of Disney, to run a series of promotional videos of the coming new Bronco across Disney's TV and streaming properties. However dim its past few years, however far the company had drifted from the entrepreneurial spirit of Henry Ford, it now seemed to have found its way back.

"Don't you want to see those things through?" Ford asked Hackett.

But Hackett was sixty-four, and now, he thought, was the time to go. He told Ford that he believed Jim Farley, the company's head of strategy and technology, was the right successor. Farley had little direct experience with the financial workings of the company—not an insignificant blind spot, given that Ford was heavily indebted and relied on an intricate web of financing subsidiaries to move its cars from factory floors to dealerships to garages across America. But he was a car nut—he owned a half dozen collective sports cars and raced a red 1966 Ford GT40 in amateur contests in Europe—and that counted for a lot at Ford.

"It's your decision, Jim," Ford said tactfully as the sun's rays bounced off the yucca trees outside.

"Well, it's your company, Bill," Hackett responded. They agreed to start laying the groundwork, including promoting Farley to chief operating officer, and see what 2020 brought. Maybe it would be an easy on-ramp for the new guy.

BRIAN CHESKY SPENT the holidays preparing for the most consequential moment in the life of any startup: an initial public offering. The company he ran, Airbnb, had grown from a hastily conceived idea he'd shared in an email with his San Francisco roommate, to make a little extra money by renting out an air mattress on their living room floor, into a behemoth in Silicon Valley. It had been valued by venture capitalists in its most recent fundraising round at $31 billion, and thirty-eight-year-old Chesky had decided the time was right to go public.

Airbnb had all the requisites of a Silicon Valley darling: fast growth, a lofty valuation, and a brand that had busted out of grammatical prison to become a verb in its own right—and none of the investor drama or toxic-workplace complaints that had plagued other high-flying startups like Uber. It was branching out beyond its traditional business of connecting homeowners and vacationers. It had hired a former CEO of Virgin America, the airline, to spearhead a push into transportation; Chesky figured that Airbnb could own not just the vacation but how people got there and how they moved around once they did. There was talk of partnering with tour bus operators, taxi fleets, even riverboat guides. And as befitted any tech company worth its salt in 2019, it was establishing itself in media. It had put out a glossy magazine with Hearst, the media giant, and had aims of being a player in Hollywood, producing a television show for Apple's streaming service that featured quirky homes all over the world. As one headline put it: "Airbnb wants to get into streaming media . . . because why not?"

All that remained was a splashy initial public offering, the moment when a private company lists its shares for public trading and joins the ranks of the corporate elite. Airbnb was aiming for an IPO as soon as that summer, one that Chesky's Wall Street advisers had told him could value the company at $50 billion or more. That would cement Airbnb's status as a Silicon Valley elite and mint Chesky a billionaire many times over before his fortieth birthday. His staff had sent him off for the Christmas break with a heavy stack of offering documents, known as "prospectuses," that other Silicon Valley startups had used to launch their IPOs.

Hopping from New York City to Orlando to the Caribbean, he

scribbled notes in the margin about what he liked, what he didn't. The document would announce Airbnb to the world, and Chesky, who had attended art school and was obsessive about design and branding, wanted Airbnb's launch to be different. Ringing in his head was an article he had read in the *Times* of London, published in the final days of 2019, that called the 2010s "the decade of disconnection." Mobile technology and social media were supposed to bring people closer together but instead sowed division and isolation. The public square had moved online, leaving the physical gathering places of old empty. He was committed to using Airbnb to bridge that gap and bring people together. It was a goal shared by many in Chesky's generation of techno-evangelists—Facebook's mission had long been to make the world more "open and connected"—but Chesky thought Airbnb had a chance to achieve it without the damage other companies had wrought.

This year, 2020, he typed out in a missive to himself on his iPhone's Notes app, would be about *connection*.

ED BASTIAN HURRIED into the vast hangar at Atlanta's Hartsfield-Jackson Airport and tried to shake off his annoyance.

The CEO of Delta Air Lines had just finished a television interview in which he got sucked into a discussion on live air about the etiquette of reclining seats on airplanes. A video had gone viral online a few weeks earlier of a passenger on an American Airlines flight repeatedly punching the back of the fully reclined seat in front of him. It hadn't happened on a Delta flight—thank God for small favors, the deeply religious Bastian had thought—but it was a no-win question for an airline CEO after a decade in which passengers had been crammed into increasingly smaller seats and charged fees for extra legroom. Bastian, a polished interviewee, had turned the moment into an opportunity. When he flew in coach—which was often, the six-foot-three Bastian told the television interviewer—he did not recline. If you must, he said, the polite thing to do was to ask. *Manners.* Now, as he hustled into bay 12, he was eager to turn his attention to happier matters. It was, after all, Valentine's Day.

Bastian was there at Delta's largest hub to deliver a love letter of sorts to his employees. The company had recently announced financial results for 2019 that made it the world's most profitable airline, with $4.1 billion in profits on $44.9 billion in revenue. In a black-on-black pinstriped suit and a forest-green tie, he announced that Delta would be paying its employees their share of those profits—$1.6 billion in total, the equivalent of about two full months of pay for the average employee. The crowd cheered and pumped their arms. "Valentine's Day to us now is not red, it's green," he told the crowd. "It's profit-sharing day." The 115-acre hangar thundered.

It was an unusual arrangement at a modern corporation, a legacy of Delta's bankruptcy filing more than a decade earlier. In 2005 the company had begged employees to accept cuts to their pay and pensions, promising them that when the company rebounded, they would share in the bounty. The arrangement was key to Delta's efforts to stave off several union organizing drives over the years; only Delta's pilots and dispatchers were unionized, while its twenty-five thousand flight attendants, plus its mechanics and customer-service agents were not. (The president of the national flight attendants' union, Sara Nelson, was in the crowd at the Atlanta airport, casting a wary eye on the proceedings. Her union had tried three times to unionize Delta's flight attendants and was preparing for a fourth.)

True to its word, Delta had paid out about 15 percent of annual profits to its workers each year since then. At first it was a meager sum as the company staggered out of Chapter 11. Now, for the sixth straight year, it was more than $1 billion—the biggest such payout by any company in history, Bastian told the crowd.

He gestured to a maintenance worker, who pushed a button. A huge white curtain fell to reveal an Airbus A321, a 199-seat, $116 million jet that had rolled off an assembly line in Hamburg, Germany, two months earlier, inscribed with the names of each of the company's employees and emblazoned with "Thank You" in Delta-red block letters. Ninety thousand names, many belonging to people who had stood by Delta in what Bastian had called its "darkest hour" and were now being rewarded for it.

The employees didn't know it then, and neither did Bastian, but another, even darker hour was coming. By the end of the year, eighteen thousand of them would no longer be collecting a paycheck from the company.

JUST A FEW weeks earlier, Bastian had taken the stage at the Las Vegas Convention Center, where thousands of journalists, analysts, and tastemakers had gathered for the Consumer Electronics Show, the largest annual conference for tech gadgets. Bastian was giving the keynote address, the first airline executive to do so at an event that usually hosted executives from companies such as Netflix, Mercedes, and the National Football League. For years, Bastian had been repositioning Delta not as an airline—a commoditized, capital-intensive, and competitive industry that was given low marks by both customers and Wall Street investors—but as an innovator. Delta didn't sell a product, he believed. It sold an experience.

To be sure, Delta the airline had plenty to brag about: the best on-time rate of any major U.S. airline, the healthiest finances, and a perceived premium status that allowed it to command ticket prices 10 percent above industry average per available-seat mile. And back at headquarters in Atlanta, Bastian's team was almost finished crunching the company's 2019 financial results that would make Delta the world's largest airline by revenue. The previous summer had been the best on record for Delta, whose planes were flying on average 90 percent full, ferrying six hundred thousand passengers a day to more than three hundred airports around the world. The company was predicting 6 percent sales growth in 2020.

But Las Vegas wasn't the place to talk about all that. Instead, Bastian laid out a futuristic vision of air travel that was seamless, even pleasant—a new jet age that would restore the magic of air travel. Biometric kiosks would usher travelers into airport lounges. Real-time bag tracking would assure them that their luggage was making the trip, too. He demoed a robotic exoskeleton that would let baggage handlers lift heavy suitcases with ease. Bastian spent seven minutes interviewing the director of *The Farewell*, a film available on the in-flight seatback entertainment systems that Delta had been pitching to Hollywood as a new way to reach movie audiences, a complement to streaming platforms like Netflix and Hulu. (He cited data showing that people are more likely to cry on airplanes, which he said could be a selling point for tearjerkers.)

Don't think of Delta as an airline, the chief executive told the crowd in Las Vegas, branding it instead a digital travel concierge that would organize travelers' ride-shares to the airport and mine real-time data from the Transportation Security Administration to steer them to shorter security lines. "Parallel reality screens," co-developed by Delta's in-house venture capital arm, would recognize travelers who stopped at airport flight-information screens and show them, in their own language, only their itinerary and no one else's. It was the next iteration of what Delta had for years been calling the "travel ribbon," packaging the entire experience, from the moment a passenger booked a ticket to the moment they collected their baggage, in a neat bow.

Rather than rely on the vagaries of the oil supply chain for its jet fuel, Delta had bought its own refinery in Philadelphia. It manufactured its own seatback entertainment screens. Its mechanics weren't only fixing Delta planes; they had more than 150 other airline and airport customers paying for those same services. In a few weeks, Delta would announce $1 billion of investments to help it go carbon-neutral over the next decade.

Under Bastian, it had climbed to the top of the industry—so much so that it seemed to escape it. It was the master of its own destiny.

It wasn't just Delta. The airline industry had enjoyed a champagne decade. The bankruptcies that swept through the big U.S. carriers in the mid-2000s were a distant memory. A wave of mergers, rubber-stamped by hands-off regulators under a series of administrations, both Republican and Democratic, had consolidated dozens of U.S. airlines into three majors—Delta, American, and United—whose dominance allowed them to ruthlessly cut costs, drive tougher bargains with their labor unions, and charge passengers for perks that used to be free, like checked baggage and on-board food. Passengers had gotten over their grumbling about it—or if they hadn't, it wasn't stopping them from traveling. Spending on air travel doubled between 2006 and 2019, to more than $800 billion. The industry was increasingly an engine of the U.S. economy, driving 5 percent of the country's gross domestic product and supporting, directly or indirectly, one in every fourteen jobs in the country.

Executives had paid down debt and replaced tired aircraft with spiffier new planes. And they had spent tens of billions of dollars buying back their stock, using 96 percent of their free cash flow between 2010 and 2019 on buybacks, such was their confidence that the boom-and-bust days of the 2000s, and the 1990s, and the 1980s, were behind them. Industry profits nearly quintupled between 2011 and 2017, to $38 billion. Their biggest concern was a looming pilot shortage. During the first few days of March 2020, the head of the industry's lobbying group, Airlines for America, had sounded out the CEOs of the country's nine carriers ahead of the group's annual strategy meeting, set for March 5, where environmental and sustainability efforts were set to top the agenda. Six had told him to make sure they didn't get thrown off-topic by the coronavirus.

The irony was that the industry was about to be felled by a disease that it had itself helped to spread. The world in 2020 was connected as never before, by increased global commerce and airfare within reach of more and more of its citizens, to a degree that allowed the virus to spread not slowly over land crossings but instantaneously. The number of global city pairings connected by a direct flight doubled in less than two decades, to twenty-two thousand by the end of 2019. From the first reported cases in China in late December, the virus conquered countries and hopped oceans, first to Thailand, Taiwan, South Korea, and Japan, and then to Iran and Italy, which by late February was the global epicenter.

The first reported U.S. case, a thirty-five-year-old man who lived in Washington State, had strolled through the Seattle-Tacoma Airport on January 15 on a returning flight from China. He had felt fine on the plane.

CHAPTER 3

THE BIG ONE

James Gorman nervously eyed the gold-plated tissue box.

He was in the royal palace in Riyadh, Saudi Arabia, seated to the right of the country's crown prince, Mohammed bin Salman. It was early March, a week after the awards gala at Cipriani's, and the Morgan Stanley CEO was on the second leg of a three-day trip through the Middle East to visit with clients and dignitaries. The United States had just reported its first death from Covid-19 a few days earlier—a man in his fifties in Washington State. There appeared to be an outbreak of cases at a long-term care facility near Seattle, and there were pockets of cases in California, Illinois, and Massachusetts, too. Life was continuing mostly as normal, though, in America. It hadn't occurred to him to cancel the trip.

Globe-hopping was central to the role of any modern CEO, especially on Wall Street, where bankers lined up to advise governments on modernizing their economies and investing their money. These trips also provided a window into global trends that was hard to get even from New York, the crossroads of global capital, and in early March, such windows were hard to come by.

Gorman's first stop had been Kuwait, where a security officer had put a temperature scanner to his forehead before clearing him to enter the building for a meeting with executives from the emirate's sovereign wealth fund. The check had rattled Gorman. The emirate had been through Middle East respiratory syndrome (MERS), another type of coronavirus that had struck the Saudi peninsula in 2012. (MERS was extraordinarily lethal, killing four in ten people who caught it—deadlier than smallpox—but turned out not to be particularly contagious and petered out on its own.) Given their recent experience with a deadly virus, Gorman took the caution of his Kuwaiti hosts as a sign that the West was underestimating the dangers of this one. By the time he landed in Saudi Arabia two days later, Gorman was spooked enough to let the protocol officers at the royal palace know he wouldn't be shaking hands. They asked whether he was sick. "No," he said, "just concerned."

He had mostly managed to stick to his plan of limited physical contact, though the Saudi energy minister insisted during a brief meeting on draping his arm around the lanky CEO and leaving it there. And now, as Gorman chatted with the controversial thirty-four-year-old crown prince about ways Saudi Arabia could diversify its economy and reduce its reliance on oil, the young royal kept sneezing. Each time he did, he grabbed a tissue from an ornate gold-clad box that sat on a marble table next to a vase of freshly cut white tulips, then dropped the wadded tissues into a wastebasket that sat on the floor between the two men's knees. Gorman had already been iffy about taking the meeting; Saudi Arabia was a fast-growing economy and was using its oil riches to become a key player in global finance and investments, but the murder of a *Washington Post* journalist in 2018—pinned by U.S. intelligence squarely on the young crown prince—had tarnished its reputation in the West. Now, as the pile of tissues grew, so did Gorman's angst. As he left the palace, he shared his concerns with Franck Petitgas, head of Morgan Stanley's international business, who had accompanied him on the trip. "This could be the big one," Gorman mused.

The Big One. Pharmaceutical executives and public health experts had been warning for years of a deadly pathogen, a superbug perfectly evolved in ways big and small, conniving and accidental, to do maximum damage. That trope was a popular vein of inspiration for Hollywood, which tapped pandemic storylines in hits like the 1990s classic *Outbreak*, inspired by the bestselling book *The Hot Zone*, in which a deadly tropical fever sweeps the globe, carried by a monkey captured in an African jungle and sold to an exotic pet store. Ebola, the closest thing in real life to that fictional virus, had flared up in the mid-2010s in Africa, killing more than eleven thousand people and sowing panic as photos of bloodstained hospital floors and funeral pyres were distributed across global news services.

But tropical diseases like Ebola simply kill their victims too quickly to go global. Those who don't die are rendered too sick to venture out to restaurants or movie theaters or other communal gathering places where they might infect others. And these diseases are mostly blood-borne, which means that only close contact with bodily fluids can spread them.

The real threat, public health experts warned, was far more mundane: a virus that spread through the air or casual touch, something resembling the seasonal flu. It would look more like the SARS virus that had emerged in China in the mid-2000s than anything cooked up in a Hollywood studio. It wouldn't go to the trouble of liquefying organs or shredding blood vessels. It would instead set down roots right where it entered the body—in the lungs—and wreak a slower, quieter havoc there. Early symptoms would resemble any of the thousands of viruses that are typically dismissed as a bad cold. And rather than the near-certain death that fictional bogeyman pathogens promised, The Big One would live in the mortality sweet spot that terrifies virologists. It would kill enough of its victims to cause alarm in the halls of public health departments but would leave most of them alive and even ambulatory, with a high enough viral load to be infectious but well enough to go about their daily lives.

Such a middle ground might well be a biological quirk, a mutation in a strand of genetic code. But it would be an evolutionary triumph. Viruses have a single-minded purpose: to spread. Killing a host too quickly is counterproductive.

As March 2020 arrived, Covid-19 seemed to tick each of those boxes. While signs pointed to an origin at the Wuhan market, the early cases in China included several family members, and it was unlikely that each person had been infected by the same caged marmot, Malayan porcupine, or other exotic animal for sale there. That suggested the virus was spread by close contact, possibly by airborne droplets that all humans swap when they speak. And one early scientific study, from February, had pegged the mortality rate at 5.25 percent, about half as deadly as SARS and fifty times more lethal than the typical winter flu. That was squarely in the virological sweet spot. Early reports suggested, and later ones would soon confirm, that people with Covid-19 were infectious before they showed symptoms, which would make it drastically tougher to contain. As any workplace or school can attest, it is hard enough to get people to stay home when they know they're sick. Getting a healthy person to quarantine would prove to be nearly impossible.

The virus had hopped international borders with ease and eluded a lockdown by the Chinese government—admittedly belated, but far more drastic and strictly enforced than anything that would likely be achievable in less authoritarian countries. And while it shared its genetic roots with a family of viruses well known to modern medicine, viruses are notoriously unpredictable. Some respond well to treatments, some do not. Some can be tackled by vaccines, others can't. (There is still no cure for the common cold, and decades of research have failed to produce an HIV vaccine.) Viruses are wily, complex, and single-minded. And this one had a head start.

A few days later, Gorman landed back in New York, where life seemed to be continuing as usual. He dined at Elio's, a white-linen Italian joint on the city's Upper East Side, with three other couples, including the Australian consul general in New York and his wife, who were in town for an event the next day at the consulate, where Gorman would be receiving the Order of Australia, the country's highest civilian honor. When asked months later about the last normal thing he had done—his last untroubled outing in what would, in the grim tongue-in-cheek-speak of the pandemic, become known across America as "the before times"—he would mention this dinner.

ED BASTIAN SIPPED his drink as the sun set over the desert. It was the end of January and the Delta CEO was in the Atacama Desert, in northern Chile, with a half dozen lieutenants to celebrate their recent $2 billion investment into LatAm, South America's biggest airline. The deal, which had been completed a few weeks earlier, was a coup: Delta had snaked LatAm away from its longtime U.S. partner, American Airlines, negotiating the deal for months in secret meetings in New York and Miami. The four-day trip to the Atacama was the first time the two broader management groups were meeting. The LatAm team was eager to show off their country, and the Delta team was eager to see what their $2 billion had bought. Group hikes, mud baths in local hot springs, and a tour of the world's largest underground mine had given way to cocktails and Chilean barbecue on a hotel terrace overlooking a martian landscape, red and jagged.

Bastian had heavier matters on his mind. He quietly slipped away from the crowd, motioning to Delta's president, Glen Hauenstein, and the head of the airline's international business, Steve Sear, to follow. They huddled in a corner of the terrace. "We have to figure out what to do about China," Bastian told them.

China's reported death toll from the coronavirus stood at around 170, with about 7,700 cases, surpassing a grim milestone for infections set by the SARS outbreak in 2003. In Beijing alone, fifty million people were effectively in quarantine, a population equal to that of the entire west coast of the United States. And those were just the official numbers. There were widespread reports of Chinese officials suppressing information on social media apps and silencing those, including some medical professionals, who tried to speak out about the threat. The global business community had seen this before, during the SARS outbreak, and many had quickly come around to the view that the coronavirus was almost certainly worse than the government was letting on—or, at the very least, that the official numbers couldn't be trusted.

They were now beginning to back away. A week earlier, Disney had shut down its parks in Shanghai. McDonald's had closed its restaurants in Wuhan, the city at the center of China's outbreak. Starbucks had closed its cafés in the entire Hubei province and was distributing masks to baristas elsewhere in China, its second-biggest global market. Delta itself had halved its daily flight schedule between the United States and China after demand for new bookings began to fall, while United Airlines had canceled key routes from Los Angeles to Shanghai and Beijing.

Bastian thought it was only a matter of time before the U.S. government forced them to stop flying to China altogether. Tom Cotton, a conservative senator from Arkansas, had been publicly pressuring the Trump White House to do so, and senior administration officials had told executives at several airlines that a move was being considered.

Bastian wanted to move first, especially given Donald Trump's penchant for simply tweeting out policy decisions. The company had already allowed thousands of ticket-holding customers traveling the last week of January to change their flights without paying a fee, but Bastian told his lieutenants that was a half measure. They should scrap the entire China schedule, which meant canceling dozens of daily flights that were some of the company's most lucrative on a per-mile basis.

"That's a pretty dramatic step," Hauenstein said. "Are you sure?" Hauenstein knew such a pronouncement would throw the industry into turmoil and panic passengers who were already abroad. Plus, Asia accounted for about 7 percent of Delta's business, less than some rivals but big enough to hurt. And looking past the immediate financial hit, Delta had worked hard to establish a foothold in China, which was increasingly important to Western business travelers. It hadn't been easy. China isn't an "open skies" country, meaning air travel is controlled by the government. Foreign carriers have to run a gauntlet of agencies to add airport gates and secure the most sought-after routes. In 2015, Delta had invested $450 million to buy a small stake in China Eastern, one of the three major airlines in the country, in an effort to deepen its inroads and prove its intentions to the country's government. A knee-jerk reaction might hamper Delta's ambitions there, Hauenstein now warned, particularly if the virus turned out to be milder than feared. It was one thing if the White House ordered it, he said, but voluntarily canceling all service to China wouldn't go over well with officials whose blessing Delta would need as it eyed further expansion in the country. He gently urged his boss to consider all the arguments.

Bastian's eyes narrowed. "Knowing what we know, would you want to crew those flights?" Passengers, after all, had a choice about whether the risk of getting on an international flight was worth it. Delta's pilots and flight attendants, on the other hand, had to go where they were sent. Plus, he added, if the White House was going to make them do it anyway, there was value in getting ahead.

Sear's deputy, Perry Cantarutti, wandered over, drink in hand. "I think we just made the call to pull our China schedule," Sear told his dumbfounded colleague.

The decision would be announced a few days later, alongside similar plans from United Airlines and American. That the three largest U.S. carriers, fierce competitors, all made the same call showed that the fear was acute. This was no time to try to steal market share, to push ahead while a rival backed away.

But while they were united in their concern and simultaneously reached for the bluntest possible instrument, there was no consensus on how long a China flight suspension might last. American's plan was to stop flying to the country immediately through March 27. Delta and United would keep flights as scheduled for another week before wiping their schedules—United until March 28, Delta through April 30. Nobody had any idea how long the virus would remain a threat. Airlines, which plan their schedules out for months in advance and feed huge amounts of data into their software to decide whether to, for example, add an extra route from Chicago to Orlando or seize on a *Game of Thrones*–inspired surge of tourism to Iceland, had nothing to go on.

As executives and analysts tried to size up the potential impact to the airline industry, the only real precedent they had to draw on was SARS. That outbreak, in 2003, had wiped out about $10 billion in global airline revenue after trans-Pacific flights were grounded and fearful travelers stayed home. But China's importance to the industry had exploded over the intervening years. By 2020, international travel in and out of the country was ten times what it was in 2003, representing an additional 450 million passengers a year. Business travelers, the most lucrative passengers for major carriers, were flocking to the country to open factories, clinch deals, and gain insight into China's burgeoning technology scene and prosperous consumer class. It would be far worse this time. How much worse was anybody's guess.

So began a stumbling effort by corporate CEOs to rework their existing plans with no idea what would happen next. As case counts rose day by day, and the blurry biological science began to be filled in, directives changed on a daily basis. Executives who were used to three-year plans were making decisions on the fly, only to have to amend them days later, time and again.

MARY FLEURY WAS sitting in a nondescript hallway of a nondescript hotel near the Detroit airport when she heard her name. The longtime head of security for Ford, Fleury was tasked with keeping watch over dozens of plants and executives around the world and protecting politicians and other dignitaries who came for a factory-floor photo op. Her current assignment was comparatively low-rent. She was standing watch outside a hotel suite where her boss, Jim Hackett, and Bill Ford, the company's chairman, were working on a top-secret project. It had been a few weeks since the two men had met in Palm Springs to lay out a timeline for Hackett's retirement, and they were now planning step one: a management shake-up that would see the long-serving head of the company's automotive division passed over and Jim Farley, Ford's head of strategy, anointed as Hackett's heir apparent.

It was the next piece of Hackett's $11 billion restructuring of Ford, which for years had plodded along, outpaced by competitors in China and Silicon Valley and under fire from Wall Street. The discussions were too sensitive to be held at Ford's headquarters, just outside of downtown Detroit, where Hackett, who maintained an open-door policy, worried about prying eyes. So Hackett had booked the suite in the airport hotel, and its walls were now covered with organizational charts mocking up the management changes. He had posted Fleury outside to stand guard.

During a break in the discussions, Hackett's mind had returned to the virus. A week earlier he had been in Las Vegas at a conference of Ford dealers, shaking hands with many of the three thousand attendees who had flown in from around the country. "What if the virus is already here?" he had mused to his chief of staff. That concern had only intensified in the days that followed as the virus hopped to Iran and then Italy, which was now the focus of apocalyptic news coverage of full hospitals running out of ventilators, patients suffocating to death as nurses held plastic-covered iPads to their ears to say goodbye. Hackett was no weekend epidemiologist. But his father had been a large-animal veterinarian, and Hackett remembered how his face would change at the dinner table when he talked about outbreaks he was treating in cattle herds. The diseases moved fast, with little regard for anything else.

He popped his head out into the hallway and locked eyes with his security chief. "Mary, do we have a crisis management team? Like, some kind of emergency-response task force?" Hackett asked his security chief. She said Ford did indeed have a crisis task force, made up of executives from across the company. "I need you to call them," Hackett said.

The fast-moving virus and its potential to wreak havoc was

threatening to upstage Hackett's carefully laid succession planning. The next Monday, an early February morning that was cold even by Michigan standards, Hackett was at his office at 6 A.M. for the first of what would be weekly, then twice-weekly, then daily calls with that task force, which was made up of executives in key regions across the world. The focus was on China, the disease's epicenter. Like other industrial manufacturers, Ford relied on a finely tuned supply chain, bringing in raw parts and materials, largely from Asia, and assembling them into finished products at plants in North and Central America. The lockdowns inside of China, as well as diminished commercial and cargo flights out of the country, were stranding millions of components earmarked for assembly in Ford autos. Any delays would be costly, and shipping containers were starting to pile up at Chinese ports, held up by a shortage of workers and government restrictions on commerce and transportation. So the company chartered several commercial airliners, Boeing 747s that were sitting idle on the tarmacs in Chinese airports as trans-Pacific travel ground to a halt. They landed in Detroit in mid-February, the seats stripped out and the cabins crammed with boxes of wire clips, gas caps, window buttons, and other components.

Now Hackett told his team their focus needed to change. It was no longer just a question of Ford's supply chain in China. The company needed to consider the likelihood that the virus would hit in the United States and might sweep through its factory floors. If it did, he warned, there might not be enough workers to man the assembly line. Even if Ford could keep up production, shoppers might be wary of going into showrooms. At worst, he said, laying out a doomsday scenario that sounded far-fetched even as he said it—weeks of complete lockdown in the United States, followed by a sustained economic pullback—spelled bad news for car companies. Who would drop tens of thousands of dollars on a new car, especially when there wasn't anywhere to go?

BRIAN CHESKY FLICKED through Airbnb's numbers on his iPad, swiping through colorful charts that relayed a worrisome trend. Bookings in China, a small but fast-growing market for Airbnb, had fallen 80 percent in the three weeks between early February and now, the last day of the month. As cases of the coronavirus continued to rise across the country—there were now more than 80,000 reported cases, with 2,900 deaths—new bookings had virtually disappeared and requests for refunds for trips already booked were pouring in. The panic was starting to spill over into South Korea, and then Japan, and even thousands of miles away to Italy, where by early March there were 1,700 confirmed cases and more than 30 deaths. The daily dashboard of Airbnb's business that Chesky received looked like a mirror image of the data that were being released by global health authorities and dotting the homepages of news organizations: one set of charts climbing sharply up and the other dropping off a cliff.

Chesky fired off a note to his board of directors: "For the first time, Airbnb is a smaller company than it was a year ago. We are now shrinking."

Shrinking. It was a dirty word in Silicon Valley, where ravenous growth was not only applauded but expected. While mature public companies are expected by their shareholders to turn a profit, a strange ethos had taken root in startup land over the preceding decade: a single-minded focus on growing revenue, adding customers, and squeezing out competitors, profits be damned. Hot technology startups burned hundreds of millions of dollars each year, but, as long as their revenue kept growing and new users kept coming to their apps and websites, those losses were forgiven and even encouraged by venture capitalists, who gave them more and more money. The thinking was that with enough money, companies could buy their way to success, subsidizing new users until they cornered the market.

Airbnb had been happy to oblige. Its revenue had grown from $919 million in 2015 to $4.8 billion in 2019. And its costs had risen just as fast, with losses ballooning fivefold over that period, to half a billion dollars. In 2019, one out of every three dollars the company brought in went to marketing expenses. Another dollar went to pay for servers, engineers, and fees to the companies that processed its online payments. In 2019, the last full year before Chesky sketched out an IPO, the company lost $674 million. And yet its valuation kept marching higher. The last time it had raised money from private investors, in 2017, it was worth $31 billion, making it the second-most-valuable startup in the country, behind only Uber, which hadn't yet gone public.

Now all that was at risk. Gross bookings at Airbnb for February 2020 had been $3.5 billion, not quite an all-time high but close to it. Within a month, it would be negative—that is, the company was refunding more money to panicked customers who were canceling trips they hadn't yet taken than it was bringing in from new bookings. Chesky, one of the brightest stars of Silicon Valley, was about to find out what happens when an already unprofitable company, bringing in plenty of revenue but spending it just as quickly, suddenly sees business drop to zero.

A SIMILAR WAVE had hit the industry Airbnb was trying to disrupt.

By mid-January, Chris Nassetta, the CEO of Hilton, was taking daily calls with his head of Asia, Alan Watts. The company had four hotels in Wuhan and hundreds across China, part of a major international push that had been a centerpiece of Nassetta's tenure.

Hilton was once the paragon of glamour for the jet-set crowd of the mid-twentieth century, opening opulent hotels in exotic places like Bogotá and Istanbul. By the early years of the next century, it had retreated from international expansion, becoming a sleepy company whose California headquarters closed at noon on Fridays. When Nassetta took over in 2007, with a mandate to restore the faded brand to its former glory, he pushed the company hard into international markets. At the time, about 15 percent of Hilton's hotel rooms under construction were abroad; by 2014, that figure was 70 percent, including a major push into China, where the company would soon build a new corporate headquarters in Shenzhen to keep a closer eye on the burgeoning market in the country. One in every three hotels that was built in the country in 2019 carried a Hilton brand. The same year, Hilton had announced plans for a thousand-room hotel in Singapore, which would be one of its largest hotels anywhere in the world. And now in early 2020, it was in talks with a Chinese developer, Country Garden, to sign an agreement for a thousand new hotels, which would make it by far the largest foreign hotel chain in the country.

Now that headlong expansion looked like a liability. By the end of January, with 10,000 cases confirmed in mainland China and at least 250 people dead from the disease, two of Hilton's hotels in Wuhan had been fully booked by the local authorities to house quarantine patients. The other two were shut down. Watts organized an Asia-wide crisis task force of Hilton managers for the first time since the Fukushima earthquake in Japan in 2011. Unable to trust the case counts coming out of Chinese state-owned media, they pored over more reliable data like international flight cancellations to model how quickly business would evaporate, and shuttered dozens of hotels alongside those ordered closed by local governments.

As March dawned, 60 percent of Hilton's hotels in China had been at least temporarily closed since the start of the pandemic. The market on which it had pinned its future, where Nassetta had reembraced Conrad Hilton's corporate creed—to "fill the earth with the light and warmth of hospitality"—the rooms were dark.

CHAPTER 4

BUBBLES

Bill Ackman woke up in a cold sweat with a single thought: The stock market is going to crash.

It was the early hours of February 23, a Sunday. The investor's anxiety had only intensified after he returned from London to New York, where life seemed to be marching on as usual. He had watched that week as the S&P 500 index hit a new record high, wondering why nobody else seemed worried.

One person with whom he shared his concerns was his wife, Neri Oxman. The two had married a year before, and Ackman credited their relationship with a comeback of sorts for Pershing Square, which had just weathered its worst five-year stretch on record, in the middle of which his twenty-two-year marriage had ended. He had met Oxman in 2017, a year in which his firm lost money for the fourth straight year. In 2018, it finished flat, and in 2019 it had its best year ever, with gains of nearly 60 percent, and he attributed some of the turnaround to their romance. "It's very helpful when you're going through a difficult period to be in a great relationship," he had told a room of conference-goers that spring. The couple's fortunes had risen together. They welcomed a baby girl, Raika, in the spring of 2019.

Ackman and Oxman seemed to be good for each other. Not only was Pershing Square making money again, but Oxman had landed an exhibit at the Museum of Modern Art that brought a besuited Ackman out into an unseasonably balmy February evening. The centerpiece of the exhibit was a thirty-foot-high pavilion spun by silkworms, an example of the kind of organic, functional art that Oxman called "material ecology." The seventeen thousand insects had been imported from Padua in northern Italy, near the epicenter of that country's spiraling coronavirus outbreak—now the second-worst in the world, behind China. Ackman wondered whether the silkworms or their handlers could have brought the virus with them, then felt silly for the thought. Still, he shooed well-wishers away from Oxman, body-blocking at least one fan who came in for a con-gratulatory hug, and the couple made an early exit. In the Uber to a restaurant for a celebratory meal, Ackman took a call from Nicholas Christakis, a renowned biostatistician, peppering the scientist on the virus's course. The couple ate at Le Bernardin, a restaurant with three Michelin stars and Manhattan's power set on its VIP list, and he relayed what he'd heard to Oxman, musing that it might be their last meal out for months.

By late February, as life in New York and in the financial markets it anchored seemed to be carrying on like normal, Ackman's agita had congealed into a sharp panic, one that woke him before dawn that Sunday. He assembled a conference call for 8:30 P.M. that night with his investment team, rousing a few from leisurely weekend activities. Such meetings were unusual. Pershing Square tweaked its portfolio infrequently, and built positions after months of deep analysis, which tended not to change all that much on the prevailing market winds. Plenty of investors like to call themselves "long-term"—putting dis-tance between themselves and twitchy-fingered opportunists—but Ackman could comfortably wear the label. He kept many of his posi-tions for years, often holding on long past the point of economic ra-tionality. That he had convened his lieutenants now spoke to the uncertainty that had settled over the economy.

Dialing in from the sitting room of his Manhattan penthouse— a 13,544-square-foot duplex that, when he bought it in 2015 for

$91.5 million with a group of investor friends, clocked in as the second-most-expensive residential purchase in New York City's history—Ackman laid out the ultimate bear thesis: Coronavirus cases in China were still rising. Fashion week had just wrapped up in Italy, sending an exodus of designers, retailers, and media from Milan back to New York, Paris, London, Tokyo, and Los Angeles. "They've just distributed this virus to every important city around the globe," he argued into the phone. The United States wasn't a nation of rule-followers, which would make the virus hard to contain and make the kind of strict lockdowns that the Chinese government was pursuing all but impossible, he observed. The market, lulled into complacency and trading near all-time high prices, would tank. Unemployment would be massive. Ultimately, he warned them, it could end in civil unrest.

"Guys, this is just math. It's compounding. We need to either sell everything," he said, "or put on a massive hedge."

Hedges are the financial equivalent of insurance. At their simplest, they involve taking a position contrary to an existing investment that will pay off in case the original thesis turns out to be wrong. An investor who buys Apple Inc. shares might "sell short," or bet against, a broad bucket of technology stocks on the theory that if she is wrong about Apple, she'll at least make some money if the index falls. ("Selling short" involves borrowing shares, usually from an investment bank, with the promise to redeliver them to the bank at a later date. Investors who believe their price will fall can sell the borrowed shares now, buy them back later at a lower price to satisfy the contract with the bank, and pocket the difference.)

There were two options, Ackman told his team. Pershing Square could sell billions of dollars of stock holdings that he worried were about to crater in value, the equivalent of taking money out of the bank and putting it under the mattress. Or the firm could hold on to them and instead buy an insurance policy that would pay out if stocks cratered as he suspected. The team went through each position in Pershing Square's portfolio, which included household names like fast-food chain Chipotle, Starbucks, Hilton, and Lowe's, the home-improvement store. Ackman suggested dumping its stakes in Hilton and Berkshire Hathaway, the conglomerate run by legendary investor Warren Buffett. Together, the two companies accounted for about one-third of Pershing Square's stock portfolio.

His argument for selling Hilton was straightforward. Hospitality would be the first industry hit by any lockdowns, whether ordered by the government or self-imposed by panicked travelers, Ackman said. Hilton may not own many of the hotels that carried its banner, but it made its money by skimming a take of their revenue. If that dried up, it could be "game over," he told his deputies.

The argument for selling Berkshire Hathaway was twofold. Pershing Square's investment in the conglomerate was only six months old and hadn't significantly gained in value, so selling it would bring in cash without triggering a big tax bill. Berkshire, which owned companies ranging from Dairy Queen to GEICO to Burlington Northern Railroad, was also something of an odd fit in Pershing Square's portfolio. Ackman had long admired Buffett and was a regular attendee at the company's annual meeting in Omaha. (At the 1994 affair, as a twenty-eight-year-old rookie hedge fund manager, he rose to ask the billionaire about Berkshire's investment in Wall Street's Salomon Brothers. "My name is Bill Ackman, and I'm from New York," he began.) Twenty-five years later, in the spring of 2019, he had plowed 11 percent of Pershing Square's money into Berkshire stock, which he thought was wildly undervalued at the time.

But Ackman was what is known as an "activist" investor. His typical strategy involved taking stakes in public companies and pushing them—sometimes with private charm, sometimes with public pressure—to change tack, whether by spinning off a weak division, replacing their management, or putting themselves up for sale. Berkshire was immune to that kind of pressure. Buffett controlled about one-third of Berkshire's voting stock, which meant that he didn't particularly have to listen to his shareholders; and anyway, he was so revered in the investment community that he was essentially untouchable. If Ackman's investment style was predicated on unstoppable force—making enough noise to pressure corporate managers into adopting his ideas—Berkshire Hathaway was an immovable object. With turbulent times ahead, he said, he wanted Pershing Square's money to be invested in companies where he could make a difference.

His lieutenants pushed back on both ideas. For starters, Ackman had long tried to shed his reputation as a corporate raider for a softer image as a long-term investor. Abandoning Hilton, one of Pershing Square's longest-term holdings, would only reinforce that reputation. Plus, he knew the company well and admired Nassetta, its chief executive. As for Berkshire Hathaway, Buffett had a knack for making money during times of stress. It had booked huge profits after the 2008 crash as desperate companies turned to Buffett for a lifeline. He had turned one of his oft-quoted investment aphorisms— "Be fearful when others are greedy, and be greedy when others are fearful"—into billions of dollars. "This is when Buffett shines," Anthony Massaro, a Pershing Square lieutenant, told his boss. No selling. A massive hedge it was, then.

Ackman landed on an idea that was simple in design but bold in its size. In a twist of irony, it involved a strategy that was widely blamed for the 2008 financial crisis: credit-default swaps. These instruments are essentially insurance policies, but instead of protecting a homeowner from the risk of fire or a car owner from the risk of an accident, they protect lenders from financial losses. Bond investors live with the risk that whoever owes them money, whether it's a Fortune 500 company or a municipal government or thousands of individual homeowners, won't pay it back. This is where financial engineering takes over: Somewhere out in the world is another investor willing to take on that risk for a fee. The credit-default swap connects them. The buyer of the swap makes periodic payments, akin to insurance premiums, to the seller of the swap. If the borrower defaults, the seller pays the lost interest and principal, making the buyer financially whole. In the middle, of course, are investment banks, who collect a fee from both sides for making the match.

Cooked up inside JPMorgan in the 1990s, the financial instrument became very popular, very fast. The market for credit-default swaps was worth $6.4 trillion by 2005 and $61.2 trillion three years later—more than three times all the money invested at the time in global stocks. In theory, they were a social good: Lenders that could protect themselves from the risk of losses were more likely to keep lending, allowing lower-rated companies access to needed capital.

But by the mid-2000s, credit-default swaps had outgrown their roots as staid insurance products and become a new casino game, allowing any investors to speculate on debt. Ackman had been one of them. In 2007, he had bought credit-default swaps on the bonds of two municipal-bond insurers, MBIA and Ambac, and had made more than $1 billion. The popularity of swaps had waned after the global financial crisis, in part because new regulations made them harder and less profitable to trade. They still hummed along in the background of financial markets, but by the end of 2019, about $7.6 trillion was invested in outstanding contracts, down 87 percent from their precrisis peak. In the words of one commentator, swaps were no longer "evil, or feared, but boring."

Ackman didn't think they were boring. To him, they were a classic lopsided bet. For relatively small sums of money, the potential rewards were vast. In his talk at the London School of Economics, Ackman had laid out the case for using credit-default swaps, calling them "amazing instruments. If you're right you make a fortune, and if you're wrong you just pay this little premium."

Like all kinds of insurance, credit-default swaps only work if they're priced correctly. After all, a car insurance company will go broke offering cheap policies to a reckless driver. Similarly, an investor will have to pay more for credit-default swaps covering the bonds of a company on the brink of bankruptcy, while bonds issued by an ultrasafe company like Microsoft, which carries a pristine triple-A credit rating, can be insured for a pittance.

But by late February, something strange had happened. Sellers of this financial insurance didn't seem especially concerned about Covid-19. Credit-default swaps could be bought for fractions of a penny, even on companies that didn't carry the highest credit ratings from Moody's and Standard & Poor's. The sellers of these financial insurance policies weren't charging much more to insure the bonds of low-rated companies than those of more creditworthy companies. In other words, they didn't seem to be discriminating between riskier borrowers and safer ones. "The market is completely mispricing this," Ackman told his team on that Sunday conference call. What's more, if the coronavirus required the kind of nationwide lockdowns that he thought probable, those triple-A credit ratings would be meaningless. No company would be spared if their revenue went to zero, no matter how creditworthy some analyst at Moody's had decided they were.

So, while the value of Pershing Square's stock positions might fall, it could recoup that money by betting against corporate bonds. And he could do it at historically cheap rates, thanks to the general lack of alarm among other investors, who were happy to pocket small insurance premiums against what was widely seen as a remote risk.

"Start buying," he told his traders, who the next morning began putting on one of the biggest trades of Ackman's life.

THOUGH HE DIDN'T use the word, Ackman was calling the financial market what it had clearly become: a bubble, and one that was at risk of popping.

Financial bubbles are as human as anything. In the 1600s, merchants in Amsterdam went crazy over tulip bulbs. Market investors did the same with U.S. stocks in the 1920s, Japanese real estate in the 1990s, dot-com companies in the late 1990s, and U.S. homes less than a decade later. Some bubbles are obviously ludicrous even in the moment (see: Beanie Babies) and some only in retrospect, but the pattern is reliably the same. Evangelists, driven by a belief that their chosen asset will change the world, pile in. Investors, seized by a fear of missing out on big gains, follow on. Frenzied buying pushes an asset's price well beyond what a sober economic analysis of profits and prospects can support. Skeptics grumble while others get rich.

In the decade between 2009 and 2019, the same thing happened. Except instead of being concentrated in one place—residential property, Dutch tulips, tech stocks—it came for nearly the whole of the global financial system.

The S&P 500 shot up 400 percent between March 2009 and March 2020, a decade-long bull market that rose from the ashes of the 2008 meltdown and seemed to defy logic. It survived a trade war between the world's two biggest economies, the United States and China, that threatened the hum of global commerce. It shrugged off hurricanes, political upheaval, the first-ever downgrade of the United States' credit rating, and a debt crisis in Europe. To be sure, corporate profits had risen, too, but stock prices had climbed far faster. In 2011, an investor could buy a slice of the S&P 500 for about thirteen times the per-share annual earnings of the companies that made up the index; by early 2020, that ratio was twenty-five. Doubters warned repeatedly that it couldn't last, and over and over they were proved wrong.

And while stocks got expensive, debt got cheap and plentiful. The oddity that Ackman had noticed—a lack of discernment among bond investors who charged barely more interest to riskier borrowers than safer ones—grew more pronounced. In 2016, lenders were charging U.S. companies an interest rate that was 2 percentage points above Treasuries. By early 2020, they were charging only 1 percentage point more. In other words, they were assuming that corporate America was almost as safe a bet as the federal government, which has never missed a debt payment in its history.

Even those who didn't believe were sucked in by the rise of new computer-driven strategies that used algorithms to sniff out trends in microscopic price moves and then ride the wave. At its simplest, this strategy means buying when others are buying and selling when others are selling. It is essentially the opposite of fundamental investing, which holds that stocks or bonds become overvalued when they rise too far (and thus should be sold) and are cheap when they fall too far (and thus should be bought). This strategy went by an official-sounding name: momentum investing. But it would be better characterized by borrowing a term that by the late 2010s had been popularized in the world of social media—FOMO, or the "fear of missing out," which captured the blend of anxiety and exclusion seeded by scrolling through posts on Facebook and Instagram that display the glamorous lives of others. By the decade's final years, FOMO had replaced fundamentals as the dominant force in financial markets. It was a bubble—not as patently absurd as the rush for Beanie Babies or Dutch tulips, but a bubble nonetheless—and the only question was what would burst it.

Bill Ackman was waiting, holding out a bucket.

HE DIDN'T HAVE to wait long.

On February 25, the day after Pershing Square started executing its trade, Nancy Messonnier, director of the CDC's National Center for Immunization and Respiratory Diseases, held a teleconference with reporters, where she said in the starkest terms the American public had heard to date that the virus was coming. "It's not so much a question of if this will happen anymore but rather more a question of exactly when this will happen and how many people in this country will have severe illness," she said. Worldwide, 2,800 people were dead from Covid-19 and 82,000 had fallen sick. The coronavirus would soon be spreading in communities across America, she said, if it wasn't already. There was no widespread testing available, so any reported numbers would likely be underestimating its spread. She urged parents to ask their children's schools how they planned to deal with an emergency closure, and urged employers to think about how their workers might do their jobs from home. It was the first time many Americans had heard terms that would soon be commonplace—telework, teleschool, telehealth.

The next day, February 26, American authorities would identify a patient in California who didn't appear to have traveled abroad or come into contact with anyone who had, making it seemingly the first U.S. case of community spread. This would later be proved false, after epidemiologists tracked cases in the United States far earlier than was thought, but in the moment, it represented a sea change in how Americans viewed the virus. It was no longer an "over there" problem. It had hit home.

For Wall Street, the coronavirus represented something they hadn't seen in more than a decade: an exogenous shock whose impact on the global economy was potentially huge and essentially unknowable. Would offices and factories and schools in America and Europe close up like those in China had? Would streets and stores empty out? How long would it take for scientists to develop medicines that could slow the virus down, or a vaccine that would stop its spread? Was that even possible? With no clear answers, traders struggled to see the bottom and sold everything they could.

On February 27, the stock market posted its biggest one-day point drop in history. The S&P 500, a collection of the largest publicly traded companies in America, was worth 12 percent less than it had been at its peak, just a few weeks earlier. Even shares of electric utilities and consumer-staples companies, which investors typically turn to during times of volatility because of their steady dividend payments, were hit. Stock indexes in Europe and Asia plummeted, too. Federal Reserve Chairman Jerome Powell attempted to reassure investors that the central bank was in control: The coronavirus "poses evolving risks to economic activity," he said that Friday, which ended the worst week for U.S. stocks since the 2008 crash. The central bank would "act as appropriate to support the economy," he said.

The drop pushed the market into what economists call a "correction," which means a drop of at least 10 percent from a recent peak.

It's a vague, even helpful-sounding term. A fitness instructor might correct sloppy technique. A first-grade teacher might correct a backwards letter. On Wall Street, it means a swift decline—exactly what qualifies as a "recent peak" is subjective—that tends to spark panic.

Even though many analysts had been predicting that stocks were overdue for a pullback, given how quickly their prices had risen over the preceding years, the speed of this decline was rattling. Of the twenty-six previous market slides of similar size in history, the average had taken four months. This one took just six days. The longest-ever U.S. stock rally was in danger of falling into "bear market" territory, a term that marks a 20 percent decline from a recent high.

Apple and Microsoft, two profit machines whose shares are bell-wethers for broader market moves, began warning investors that they would make less money because of the virus. Analysts at Goldman Sachs predicted that if the virus wasn't quickly brought under control, corporate earnings in 2020 wouldn't grow at all from 2019 levels. Hopes of a quick bounce-back, a "V-shaped" recovery in which a short, sharp recession was quickly neutralized by an equally acute rebound, were evaporating.

Investors sold stocks and high-yield bonds. They fled to the safety of government debt, dropping the yield on the ten-year U.S. Treasury to a record low of 1.127 percent. (Bond yields, or the annual return an investor will realize, fall when the price of the bond rises. So when investor demand for a particular bond surges, its price rises, and its yield goes down.) In Europe, where coronavirus caseloads were higher and the virus was beginning to dramatically upend commerce and travel, interest rates on government debt fell even further, diving deep into negative territory, meaning that investors were actually paying for the privilege of lending their governments money.

"It's a brand-new thing," Chris Stanton, chief investment officer at Sunrise Capital Partners, a California-based quantitative fund, told *The Wall Street Journal*. "If the next headline says Disney is shutting its theme parks, we will start seeing moves like 2008."

It would take less than two weeks.

CHAPTER 5

DO YOU GUYS NEED HELP?

J im Hackett had an idea. In late February 2020, the Ford CEO called his old friend and corporate sounding board Arne Sorenson, the chief executive of Marriott, who was heading a committee at the Business Roundtable—a group of corporate executives who occasionally get together and try to solve the world's problems and their own. Founded in 1972, it was nakedly self-serving in its early days, helping to beat back a major piece of antitrust legislation in 1975 and thwarting a push to stiffen punishments for corporate crimes in 1990. In recent years it had softened its edges, becoming more overtly involved in global affairs and seeking to improve the business community's image in the eyes of an increasingly hostile public. That shift was cemented in 2019, when it dumped long-held corporate orthodoxy and embraced what it called "stakeholder capitalism," arguing that companies should no longer serve only the interests of their shareholders, but also of their employees, customers, and communities.

Its more than 200 member companies, including Apple, Bank of America, supermarket chain Albertson's, and Pfizer, employed one in six American workers and had $9 trillion of combined annual revenue. The virus was spreading and would soon hit the United States in force. With little clear guidance out of the federal government, Hackett thought the Business Roundtable was in a position to lead.

"Leadership," he had told an interviewer just a year before, "is having a point of view."

He reached Sorenson at his home in Chevy Chase, Maryland. The Marriott boss was a notoriously hard worker, but he had cut back his hours in the office as he underwent treatment for pancreatic cancer, which had been diagnosed a year earlier. Those who had seen Sorenson in recent months had been shocked by the toll it had taken; his thick brown hair, styled for years in a classic CEO left part, had thinned considerably, and his shirt gaped at the collar. After asking how Sorenson was feeling, Hackett pitched him on an idea he thought might save the economy.

"We should close the country for four weeks," he told Sorenson. "I mean, completely close it."

The plan he laid out was a series of concessions from corporations, from workers, and from the government, with each side giving just enough that he thought it might be palatable to all. Business Roundtable member companies, and any others that wanted to sign on, wouldn't be allowed to lay off any workers. Any employee who could stay home would do so and receive 60 percent of their pre-virus wages. In exchange, they would surrender their vacation days for the remainder of the year, save for one holiday of their choosing, which would allow companies to get some of the lost productivity back. The government wouldn't tax those wages but would avoid a spike in unemployment that seemed inevitable to Hackett.

It was the opposite of the "tragedy of the commons" problem that often derails good ideas, he told Sorenson. Everyone would have some skin in the game. If enough big companies agreed to shut down, there would be no concerns about competitive advantages. "In four weeks we can kill this thing," he said.

Sorenson thought it sounded like a good idea, but there was a problem—one that Josh Bolten, CEO of the Business Roundtable, had quickly identified when Hackett presented the idea to him a few days earlier.

"Who's going to convince the president?" Bolten had asked.

Donald Trump had been downplaying the virus for weeks, since his comments at Davos that the situation was "totally under control." The president had come to see the booming stock market and low unemployment rate as his tickets to reelection in November. Sorenson knew that the president was unlikely to respond well to a wholesale shutdown of the economy, even if it was just temporary.

Hackett tried. In February he called a senior White House adviser, but the administration was in chaos, trying to get its arms around the virus and wrangle a president with little interest in lockdowns. And so, the idea went nowhere, and an opportunity for corporate America to help lead the country out of crisis was squandered. But the dance between the nation's CEOs and the federal government about what it would take to forestall economic carnage was only just beginning.

DOUG PARKER, THE CEO of American Airlines, pushed open the door to the Roosevelt Room in the White House and took a seat at the polished wood table. It was March 4. Across from Parker sat President Trump, and around him, the CEOs of Parker's biggest rivals: Southwest's Gary Kelly, Alaska Airlines' Brad Tilden, Peter Ingram of Hawaiian Airlines, Robin Hayes of JetBlue, and Oscar Munoz of United Airlines, who, as the president pointed out, was at a greater risk of getting seriously ill from the coronavirus after having a heart transplant in 2016. ("I don't recommend it," he told Trump.) Only Bastian was missing; the Delta chief was in upstate New York burying his mother, who had died a few days earlier at age eighty-four of a sudden respiratory infection. Doctors had been unable to explain her quick decline, and in the months to come, as cases mounted and evidence later suggested the virus had been circulating in the United States longer than previously thought, Bastian would wonder whether she had contracted it. Now, though, he was giving a eulogy in Poughkeepsie as his rival CEOs gathered in Washington.

The White House wanted the airlines' help in tracing travelers who might have come in contact with infected passengers. For their part, the airline CEOs wanted a clear message from the president that it was safe to fly. Passenger volume through U.S. airports was holding steady—about fifteen million people passed a TSA checkpoint the final week of February, similar to the amount a year prior—but there were signs that travelers were getting nervous. Bookings for future flights were falling sharply. It had been a busy week for the biggest U.S. airlines, which had scrambled to rework schedules and accommodate customers who were increasingly wary of flying. Three days earlier, United had become the first major airline to trim its domestic routes, announcing a 10 percent reduction that would take effect in April, and had postponed a training program set to begin March 1 for a new class of pilot recruits. American had waived change fees for customers who booked a new flight before March 20.

The CEOs had been invited to a meeting with Vice President Mike Pence, who was heading the White House's coronavirus task force, and his public health advisers. But when the door swung open to the Roosevelt Room, where the White House press corps had lined up with cameras running and notebooks open, Trump was the first one through, flanked by Pence and Deborah Birx, a longtime public health official serving as the coronavirus response coordinator for the White House.

Trump started out in rare muted form, turning the meeting over to Pence for prepared remarks, but his restraint in front of a bank of pool cameras only lasted so long. He soon interjected, blaming the Obama administration for a shortage of testing kits, noting—falsely—that he had reversed a Food and Drug Administration policy that had limited the ability of private laboratories to develop their own tests. (In fact, the policy had been put in place by Trump's own FDA and did little to shackle private labs.) He introduced the CEOs to the press pool as "the biggest and the best." When his secretary of homeland security, Chad Wolf, provided an update on screening efforts at U.S. airports, Trump asked instead about screening efforts at the United States' southern border, "where we're doing so well."

The executives discussed actions they were taking to disinfect their planes and keep passengers and crew members safe. Munoz, the United CEO, said he had been promoting fist bumps instead of handshakes at his ninety-six-thousand-person airline, calling himself the "poster child" of a high-risk Covid patient. "Fantastic story," the president said, nodding approvingly.

As the meeting wrapped up, a reporter asked Trump whether he was weighing financial support for the industry. "Don't ask that question, please," he said, to nervous laughter from the CEOs. "I don't want you to give them any ideas." The executives got what they came for, though: When asked on live camera whether it was safe to fly, the president said it was.

The CEOs then walked the two blocks west to the headquarters of Airlines for America, the lobbying arm known as A4A. Unknown to the besuited honchos as they ambled down Pennsylvania Avenue was the fact that Parker had another iron in the fire. The Roosevelt Room meeting was just for show; any real progress was going to be made behind closed doors, away from the cameras, and the ambitious Parker wanted to be there. Nate Gatten, American's head of government affairs, grabbed the CEO's elbow and pulled him aside. Gatten had confirmed a one-on-one meeting for his boss with Mnuchin that afternoon. A few minutes before the 3:30 meeting, Parker rose to leave and let his fellow CEOs know where he was going.

"What are you meeting with Mnuchin for?" Gary Kelly, the Southwest CEO, asked. It was a fair question. Parker had been an airline CEO for twenty years and had never met with a Treasury secretary—not even in the days after September 11, 2001, when the industry required billions of dollars in aid. Airline bosses stayed in close touch with federal aviation regulators and key congressional members, but if they were talking to a Treasury secretary, something had gone terribly wrong. And mistrust was running high among the bosses of America's airlines, who hadn't yet quite come around to the idea that they were all in the same load of trouble.

Mnuchin, who, back in January at Davos, had been among the first Trump officials to begin raising the alarm bells about Covid's potential toll on the economy, was a member of the White House's coronavirus task force. The task force's meetings had been increasingly chronicled on cable news, with Mnuchin taking a prominent role. "Gary, at every meeting of the task force, Mnuchin is sitting right there front and center," Parker told Kelly. "Before this is all over, I think he's going to be negotiating for the government." Implicit in his words was something the CEOs hadn't openly discussed: that despite their assurances to the contrary just a few hours earlier in the Roosevelt Room, the airlines might need money after all. If the guy holding the purse strings wanted to talk to Parker, he'd go. He headed across the street to a meeting room in the Treasury building.

Outside the glare of the White House press pool and the television cameras, Mnuchin dispensed with the theatrics. "No bullshit, Doug. Do you guys need help?"

"Honestly, I don't think we do right now, but if we do, you'll be the first to know," Parker said.

A week later, the world would change again, and Parker would find himself the spokesman for an industry seeking a $50 billion bailout. And as he predicted, it would be Mnuchin sitting across the table.

As THE AIRLINE executives met in the Roosevelt Room, below them in the White House Situation Room, a group of top government economists were meeting to discuss the growing financial fallout from the virus. While Larry Kudlow, who was best known as a television personality with a financial-commentary show on CNBC before he was tapped as Trump's top economic adviser in 2018, worked with the White House's official coronavirus task force, a shadow group of economic whizzes had begun gathering regularly to assess the on-the-ground reality.

Andrew Olmem, Kudlow's deputy, was there, along with Mike

Faulkender, a top Treasury Department economist; Tyler Goodspeed, a member of the Council of Economic Advisers, a sort of mini think tank inside the White House that has been around since the 1940s; as well as staffers of Ivanka Trump and Peter Navarro, the president's protectionist trade adviser. Olmem had organized the group a few days earlier, with marching orders to identify data that the government should be tracking that might produce better intelligence and flag warning signs about the virus's effect. Treasury had been put in charge of the domestic economy, the Council of Economic Advisers had been tasked with international issues, and Olmem's team at the NEC were tracking disruptions to the nation's supply chain.

Now the mandate had changed. Yesterday, it was "What are we monitoring?" Today, Olmem told the group, it was "What are we going to do?"

Faulkender's team of less than two dozen, mostly economists, at the Treasury Department had been working on some ideas. They had hewed to the advice Larry Summers, the preeminent economist, had publicly given in early 2008, just as cracks in the credit markets were appearing that would later shake the nation's entire financial system. He had then urged policymakers to step in, but to do so in a way that was "timely, targeted, and temporary." Treasury staffers felt that advice applied now, too. (Within a few months, the government's response would pivot to Summers's advice in late 2008, as Wall Street was melting down, when he urged government action that was "swift, substantial, and sustained.")

A top priority was executing an idea that would come together quickly, a government guarantee of paid sick leave for workers sick with the virus. Congress would pass that in an initial, small coronavirus relief bill a week later. But the group was focused on things that could be done without congressional action. Promising ideas included delaying the upcoming April 15 tax filing deadline, which Mnuchin could do unilaterally; pausing collection of interest payments on debts owed to the government, like student loans; and using a pot of money controlled by the Treasury Department to support financial markets.

That pot, the Exchange Stabilization Fund, held just under $100 billion, and Mnuchin had substantial leeway to deploy it as he saw fit. It was a relic of the 1930s when Congress gave the Treasury Department funds to stabilize the dollar after U.S. currency was unpegged from the value of gold, which lawmakers feared might send the greenback's value crashing. Since then, Treasury secretaries have used the ESF to step in when Congress won't. In 1995 it was used after Congress voted down a bailout of the Mexican government, and in 2008 it was briefly tapped to stabilize plunging money-market funds to stem panic on Wall Street.

The group now discussed whether it might be used again. The wheels were starting to turn in Congress for a major stimulus bill, but that would likely take weeks to pass into law, they figured, correctly. The Treasury could use the ESF to backstop financial markets that were in turmoil and possibly to send direct aid to small businesses affected by the virus's spread. The latter idea would, within a few weeks, morph into one of the biggest single federal aid programs in history—the Paycheck Protection Program, an initiative that ultimately spent more than $500 billion covering the payrolls of millions of small businesses.

Details of the discussion quickly appeared on CNN.com. Olmem sent around an email to everybody, with a link to the article and a comment saying, "Not helpful." Rumors were swirling about if and how the government might step into what was fast becoming an economic crisis, and the financial markets were swinging daily as information—some of it true, some of it not—surfaced. Keeping control of the narrative was a priority for Olmem's boss, National Economic Council director Larry Kudlow, and so far, it was off to a rocky start.

Congress passed the first of what would be several Covid-19 relief packages. The $8.3 billion bill sailed through Congress and was signed by Trump on March 6, the same day the number of Covid-19 cases surpassed one hundred thousand. Its speedy passage through an otherwise bitterly divided Congress showed just how seriously the government was taking the threat. Less than two weeks later, the Families First Coronavirus Response Act was signed into law. It covered paid sick leave for workers struck ill with the virus, allowing companies to use the money they withhold from payroll checks for social security taxes. It also allocated money for Covid testing and expanded food assistance and unemployment benefits.

These bills would prove to be warm-up acts for the mother of all government stimulus efforts—more than $4 trillion approved over the next year in an effort to buoy an economy in crisis. It would, mostly, work. Despite its critics, who argued rightly that the policies pursued by the government helped large corporations and the wealthy individuals who own the biggest chunk of stocks, the efforts undertaken by Mnuchin and others in the government—like the actions taken by their predecessors in 2008, many of them equally unpopular—would keep the largest economy in the world from imploding. By the early twentieth century, economists had largely internalized the lessons of the Great Depression. Then, the government had responded to an economic crisis, mass unemployment, and the lack of credit available from banks by tightening the purse strings. That playbook had, in the intervening decades, come to be seen as a catastrophic mistake. Governments needed to spend their way out of crises, and that was what the United States would do in 2020.

But those drastic steps were still a few weeks away. The intervening days would be as harrowing a time as the modern global economy had ever seen and reverberate for years to come.

AMERICA GOT ITS last good jobs report on Friday, March 6. The economy had added 273,000 jobs the previous month, nearly 100,000 more than economists had expected, and the unemployment rate held steady at 3.5 percent. The total number of Americans with jobs held steady, near December's record of 158.8 million.

But the news did little to stop markets that had moved beyond jittery and into panic. The S&P 500 dropped as much as 4 percent before closing down 2 percent. The yield on the ten-year Treasury bond dipped as low as 0.68 percent as investors flocked to the security of U.S. government debt. Britain's blue-chip stock index, the FTSE 100, closed at its lowest level since the Brexit vote in 2016, putting the coronavirus's spread on par, at least in the minds of investors, with one of the most consequential financial and geopolitical events of the past half century. "We should prepare for a short-term but severe global recession," Nigel Green, chief executive of deVere Group, an investment firm, told *The New York Times*.

A few days earlier, the Federal Reserve had sought to calm the markets by cutting its benchmark interest rate by half a percentage point. But investors weren't buying it. The world was nearing 100,000 confirmed cases, and deaths had topped 3,300. True to the warnings that Nancy Messonnier, the CDC official, had given ten days earlier, the virus was very much here. Maryland, Indiana, Nebraska, Kentucky, and Pennsylvania reported their first infections. Massachusetts had traced a cluster of cases to a conference hosted the previous week by Biogen, a biotech company. A cruise ship, the *Grand Princess,* was being held off the coast of California with at least twenty-one confirmed cases on board. Two deaths in Florida brought the U.S. fatality count to sixteen.

On March 6, the University of Washington became the first major college to cancel in-person classes. The same day, city officials in Austin, Texas, canceled South by Southwest, the buzzy film, technology, and media festival that was set to host, among others, Twitter's CEO, the Beastie Boys, and Ozzy Osbourne, promoting a new documentary. Google and Facebook called off their annual developer conferences, cultlike events that the tech giants typically used to roll out new products and features.

America was beginning to shut down.

CHAPTER 6

THE GREAT UNWIND

By late February, as his traders were busy executing a giant bet against the credit markets, Bill Ackman was reaching out to anyone he could think of, testing his own gut against the reactions of others who had been through crises before. He called Jon Gray, the head of Blackstone, the private-equity giant. Dispensing with the normal pleasantries, he asked simply: "What do you think?"

"I don't think you have much to worry about," Gray replied. "If Bernie is the nominee, Trump is going to win in a landslide." Ackman realized Gray thought his concern was about the chaotic Democratic primaries, in which the far-left Bernie Sanders appeared to be running away with the nomination over centrist candidates like former vice president Joe Biden, who was seen as friendlier to big business. But politics wasn't anywhere near the top of Ackman's list of concerns. "I'm calling about the virus," he told Gray.

He emailed Warren Buffett at Berkshire Hathaway, whose stock Ackman had flirted with selling just a few days earlier before being talked out of it by his investment team. Berkshire's annual shareholder meeting, known in the press as "Woodstock for capitalists," drew tens of thousands of people each spring to Nebraska to hear the oracle of Omaha and his longtime sidekick, Charlie Munger, talk about financial markets with their signature folksy charm. Ackman had missed the 2019 event to attend the birth of his daughter but had watched the live video stream from the hospital room while his new baby slept. "A beautiful memory," he wrote to Buffett over the last weekend in February, before switching gears.

"On a more cautious note, I was just thinking about coronavirus," he wrote. "Query whether it is advisable for 40,000 to gather from around the world at the meeting." It was a tactful effort to peek inside the famed investor's head; Buffett had been through crises before and had shown his ability to make money off them.

The billionaire was as folksy as ever in his reply. In an email dictated to his longtime secretary—the octogenarian doesn't use email—he said that he hoped to see Ackman at this year's meeting, set for May 2, and invited the investor and Oxman to a private brunch. "Unfortunately we can't include Raika," he said of Ackman's infant daughter, "though if she owns Berkshire, I hope she continues to vote for me and Charlie" as members of the board of directors. He added: "I have no idea if the coronavirus will affect attendance, but Charlie and I plan on having a great time."

Starting to feel somewhat foolish, Ackman tried another of the world's richest men. "I believe I have an accurate and differentiated view of the economic impact of coronavirus, if you're interested in comparing notes," read the email that he typed out to Bill Gates on the afternoon of February 28. The Microsoft founder and philanthropist, who had donated hundreds of millions of dollars to fight malaria in Africa, had authored an op-ed piece the day before in which he said the coronavirus was starting to look "like the once-in-a-century pathogen we've been worried about." Finally Ackman had found someone who shared his concerns. "I thought your editorial was spot on both with respect to the current situation and what is required going forward," he wrote. "Bottom line, I am gravely concerned."

He never heard back.

—

THE SUN WAS barely peeking over the buildings as Jay Clayton made the mile-long walk from his rented apartment in Washington, D.C., to the headquarters of the Securities and Exchange Commission, the country's top regulator of financial markets. It was Monday, March 9. Clayton had left a charmed life as a Wall Street lawyer three years ago to run the SEC. Appointed to the post by Trump in 2017, he had been an odd pick to those who knew him as a mostly apolitical centrist, and had pursued a middle-of-the-road regulatory agenda, filing lawsuits against fraudsters and cracking down on cryptocurrency scams but largely keeping a light touch on corporate America. His tenure had gone smoothly until a few weeks earlier, when the coronavirus had jolted the U.S. stock market from its steady upward march.

Clayton had gotten just three hours of sleep the night before, having been on the phone with his top markets deputy, Brett Red-fearn, until nearly 4 A.M. Clayton took a swig of coffee as he walked, pressing his phone to his ear. On the other end of the line was Stacey Cunningham, the president of the New York Stock Exchange. She had also slept fitfully and had arrived early to pace the exchange's iconic trading floor in downtown Manhattan. As the head of the biggest stock exchange in the country and the regulator overseeing it, the two spoke often, particularly in times of market unease. But today's call was different.

Both Cunningham and Clayton knew what was coming when the opening bell rang in two hours. Unlike the stock market itself, which is active from 9:30 A.M. to 4 P.M. Monday to Friday, stock futures trade continuously, and their moves during the market's off-hours tend to predict the action when it reopens. Stock futures had fallen nearly 7 percent on Sunday. With more than 100,000 people infected and 3,600 dead worldwide, investors were starting to lose their cool.

A week earlier, on February 28, signs had appeared at the security desks of the New York Stock Exchange: Any employees who had traveled to countries with significant case levels—though exactly what that meant, outside of China, was anyone's guess—should stay home for two weeks. Two days later, it extended that policy to guests. The news anchors who hosted all-day coverage from its trading floor packed up and left. The same day, Cunningham met with top lieutenants to begin planning for what, even then in late February, seemed an unthinkable possibility: that the iconic trading floor, perhaps the foremost symbol of American capitalism, would close.

As Clayton turned left onto E Street, his main concern was whether the measures put in place years ago to handle a market decline that sharp would stave off a panic. In the decades since 1987's "Black Monday," when the stock market had plunged more than 20 percent in a matter of minutes, the exchange has implemented a series of safeguards, known as "circuit breakers." The circuit breakers were designed to automatically halt trading for fifteen minutes if shares fell more than 7 percent, and were a high-tech, high-stakes version of a switch designed to shut down an overloaded home electrical system in the event of a surge. The idea is that a forced halt will allow investors to calm down and clear the backlog of panicked sell orders. The system hadn't been triggered since 1997 and had been reformed significantly in 2014. The circuit breakers were tested every three months, always on a Saturday, when a digital feed of simulated trades was fed through the systems of the New York Stock Exchange and its biggest rival, Nasdaq. But those were the equivalent of testing the battery in your smoke detector every few months and hoping your house won't burn down. Nobody was quite sure that the main event would go as well as the dress rehearsals.

The NYSE had also spent tens of millions of dollars upgrading its technology systems the previous summer. The new system, dubbed Pillar, was intended to give the system more headroom on days when trading volumes surged. Cunningham was confident in the pricey redesign, which had required a major overhaul of arcane systems, but it hadn't been through a real-world test. Any glitch wouldn't just be embarrassing. It could actually spark a panic. A system that failed to respond in the right order and in the right manner to trading tickets would be the digital equivalent of crashes in the days before Wall Street was computerized, when frazzled brokers would take their phones off the hook rather than receive a flood of "sell" orders from clients. An unresponsive market quickly becomes a broken market, where sellers outnumber buyers and prices plummet.

The previous Friday had given Cunningham a bit of comfort. The NYSE's systems had handled 330 billion "messages"—electronic pings sent across the exchanges systems that signaled orders to buy and sell, and changes in order prices and ticket sizes. That was by far a record, and the system had held up with no outages or major hiccups. Cunningham was cautiously optimistic it would hold again today.

"Good luck," Clayton told her. She knew she'd need it.

MICHAEL BLAUGRUND WAS also up before dawn, groggy and in a strange bed.

The forty-one-year-old head of operations for the New York Stock Exchange, one of Cunningham's top deputies, had arrived back in the city on a red-eye flight from Henderson, Nevada, where he had been visiting his grandmother, who was ill. His mother had sent him back with a small bottle of hand sanitizer. It seemed to him a bit dramatic. *Mothers,* he thought on the flight home as he thumbed his phone, monitoring the futures market.

However, with 550 confirmed cases of Covid-19, there were starting to be signs that the virus was disrupting daily life. But it had been business as usual when Blaugrund had left New York a few days earlier, and he expected the same when he landed. Blaugrund glanced around the packed cabin at the unmasked passengers, sipping sodas and chomping on airline pretzels, and wondered what the market sensed that they didn't.

Investors were starting to lose their cool. By the time he was on the ground at Kennedy Airport, stock futures were down 5 percent and still falling. If the sentiment was unchanged by the next morning, the market was heading for "limit down"—Wall Street jargon for a situation in which stocks hit the maximum 7 percent decline that triggers an automatic halt. He knew it was likely to be an early morning, so rather than schlep to his home in the suburbs, he booked a room at the Beekman Hotel in downtown Manhattan. Now that he was up, he took a minute to orient himself. He grabbed a coffee at a Starbucks around 6 A.M. and headed out.

The financial district, on the tip of lower Manhattan, was always quiet and dark, its narrow streets perpetually covered in scaffolding that promised sparkly renovations for the city's oldest quarter but never quite delivered. But now in the first week of March, it was a ghost town. The tourists who usually gathered for selfies in front of the stock exchange were gone. Empty cabs passed at a crawl. He checked his phone again. Sellers were outnumbering buyers. An automatic halt looked almost certain.

As the NYSE's head of operations, tasked with overseeing the plumbing that millions of global stockholders rely on, Blaugrund's chief concern was a technical snafu. Unlike its entirely computerized cousin, the Nasdaq, the New York Stock Exchange still used brokers to find the opening price for stock. The human touch was in many ways an anachronism, a nostalgic touch meant to keep the allure of the country's oldest exchange alive for the companies whose listings it sought and the media outlets that crowded its trading floor—though Cunningham was always quick to defend their utility, arguing that experience trumps algorithms in times of market stress.

These brokers call investors each morning to find an opening price that balances orders from buyers and sellers, and it can take a few minutes after the opening bell at 9:30 for every stock to notch a first trade. If enough stocks that were part of the S&P 500 index opened down far enough, it would trigger a halt, even if other stocks hadn't officially opened yet. The result would be an unwarranted trading freeze that would sow panic across the market.

He walked the floor reminding operations staff and brokers how the circuit breaker would work. They would need to be ready to re-open stocks fifteen minutes later, which meant canvassing investors by phone and electronic inquiries to find a price that would balance demand from buyers and sellers. Everyone was watching screens. Blaugrund's boss, Cunningham, was bouncing between a contingent from Citigroup—the designated bell ringer that morning—and staffers briefing her on the premarket moves. The bank's president, Jane Fraser, rang the bell, then elbow-bumped executives on either side.

It took less than five minutes. At 9:35 A.M., after stocks fell 7 percent, a deafening single bell rang out on the floor of the New York Stock Exchange, signifying a halt to trading for the first time in eighteen years. Cunningham hopped in front of a waiting CNBC camera and assured investors that the system was working the way it was supposed to.

Back at SEC headquarters, Jay Clayton, Brett Redfearn, and a half dozen deputies had gathered in Redfearn's office to await the halt. Redfearn was a veteran of the Wall Street trading floors, having spent years at JPMorgan Chase before joining the agency in 2017. He, too, was confident that the trading halt would be initiated as intended but worried what would happen when the fifteen minutes were up. A circuit breaker, after all, is just a time-out, meant to give investors a chance to gather their thoughts. But would investors who had been panic-selling their shares feel any differently about the state of the world in fifteen minutes? The virus would be just as scary.

"What if there are no buyers?" he asked the room. Without a two-way market—that is, enough buyers of stocks who could be paired with sellers to find a clearing price for thousands of securities— "we could be in free fall." He took a deep breath, and as he did, he looked around the room, which was suddenly a bit too crowded for comfort. Lower-level aides, sensing a historic moment, had moseyed in as the market had plummeted. "Six feet apart," Redfearn barked, and kicked the backbenchers out into the hallway.

Trading resumed at 9:49 A.M. Major indexes managed to come

off their lows and hold above them for the rest of the morning, but it was a bloody day for stocks. The S&P 500 fell 7.6 percent, its worst day since 2008. The Dow Jones Industrial Average, a less representative but more iconic index that includes industrial heavyweights like Boeing and IBM, lost 2,000 points in a single day for the first time in its history. The Nasdaq Composite Index, heavier on technology stocks, slid 7.3 percent. Peter Cecchini, a strategist at brokerage firm Cantor Fitzgerald, had given *The Wall Street Journal* a succinct eulogy for the longest winning stretch for financial markets in modern history: "The eleven-year bull market is over."

Into one of the most stressful moments of Blaugrund's professional life careened a personal bomb. A few minutes before 4 P.M., with stocks heading for their worst decline in a dozen years, his phone rang. It was his wife. Their three-year-old son was having trouble breathing, she told him, and they were on their way to the hospital. Blaugrund grabbed his laptop and his coat and bolted off the trading floor as the closing bell rang out behind him, marking an end to the stock market's worst day in thirty years. He wouldn't be back for two months.

Before the day was out, more bad news would come in. The SEC had its first suspected case of Covid-19, an employee who worked on the ninth floor of its D.C. headquarters. Clayton had spent the day fixated on tumult in the stock market. But he wasn't just the country's chief securities regulator. He was a boss, too, with more than four thousand employees who were increasingly worried about their own safety. He found himself issuing the same words of comfort that other bosses would reach for in the weeks to come, well-intentioned but light on reassurances.

"Our thoughts are with them and their families," he wrote in an email to staff that evening, of the staffers who had tested positive. "You are our greatest asset," Clayton wrote, the kind of hand-holding email that went out at thousands of workplaces as executives with few answers faced employees with endless questions.

IT WASN'T JUST the stock market. Financial markets were unraveling quickly.

The market declines of late February and early March had been unnerving but had at least had the ring of sanity. Investors sold stocks and risky bonds and fled for the safety of government debt and money-market funds—a product that was considered as safe as cash and offered tiny yields. The market might have been spooked, but it acted in line with the well-established Wall Street playbook. In times of crisis, investors sold riskier things and bought safer things.

By the second week of March, that had broken down. Publicly traded money-market funds, which make short-term loans to companies, would see 30 percent of their assets, some $100 billion, withdrawn by investors no longer comfortable lending overnight on any terms. Borrowing costs in the money markets hit their highest levels since 2008. Another type of short-term funding known as "repurchase agreements," or repos, saw similar spikes in borrowing costs, as did the $1 trillion market for commercial paper, short-term notes that big companies issue.

These three financial markets—commercial paper, money markets, and repurchase agreements—are canaries in the financial coal mine. Because they are the shortest-term kinds of borrowing, with terms as short as overnight and as long as a few months, they reflect the real-time moods of investors and often foreshadow more momentous moves.

The Federal Reserve moved quickly to try to stem the panic. The economic effects of the virus hadn't yet shown up in data the central bank monitors closely to gauge the health of the U.S. economy, such as the cost of bank loans, unemployment figures, and manufacturing data. Just 211,000 people had filed initial unemployment claims in the week ending March 7, about average for this time of year. And just a week earlier, the governors of the regional reserve banks that make up the Federal Reserve system had said it was too soon to make any drastic moves in response to the virus's spread.

But now the markets were in complete turmoil. And history has shown that what starts as a financial panic, confined to corners of Wall Street that most people have never heard of, can quickly become a broader economic crisis. Banks stop lending, cash-strapped businesses shut down, and layoffs ensue.

On March 3, the Fed cut its benchmark interest rates by half a percentage point, to a target range of between 1 percent and 1.25 percent. (For most of its history, the Fed, like most central banks around the world, set a single benchmark rate, which is used as the baseline for all sorts of borrowing—from consumer mortgages to corporate loans. That changed in 2008 when, in an effort to avoid the sticker shock of rates dropping all the way to zero for the first time in history, it set a range of 0 to 0.25 percentage points. When the economy began to recover after the crisis and the Fed started to increase that benchmark rate, it stuck with the range.)

It was the Fed's largest ever one-time cut to interest rates, and the first time since 2008 that it had made any change to rates between regularly scheduled meetings that happen roughly every six weeks. The central bank also lowered the interest on a special type of emergency loan available to big banks, known as the "discount window." "We do recognize that a rate cut will not reduce the rate of infection. It won't fix a broken supply chain," Fed Chair Jerome Powell said. "But we do believe that our action will provide a meaningful boost to the economy." With the Fed's support, Powell hoped, banks would continue to lend, investors would continue to purchase corporate bonds, and consumers could continue to buy homes.

Answering questions from reporters sitting shoulder to shoulder and passing a microphone between them, Powell, dressed in a soft blue suit, lavender tie, and square tortoiseshell glasses, said, "So, what changed? We've been carefully monitoring the situation since it first became known and waiting to see how it would evolve. And I think we've come to the view now that this is the time for us to act in support of the economy." Asked whether further interest-rate cuts were to be expected, he was vague but sought to reassure: "We are going to use all of our tools, in a strong way, to try to support the economy. . . . Financial markets are functioning in an orderly manner."

They were not. Stocks rallied for all of fifteen minutes after Powell's announcement, and by the end of the day, major stock indexes lost 3 percent. The yield on ten-year U.S. Treasury bonds had dipped below 1 percent for the first time ever, though it closed slightly higher.

That Friday, March 13, Trump held a press conference outside the White House where he said he had instructed the Energy Department to purchase—"at a very good price," the self-titled dealmaker in chief added—large quantities of crude oil for storage in the country's strategic petroleum reserve. "We're going to fill it right up to the top," he said of the reserves, located in salt caverns near the Gulf of Mexico. The administration's move to purchase oil came after the worst week for crude-oil prices since 2008, as investors worried that lockdowns would sap demand for oil. Exxon stock had fallen 20 percent over the week. Chevron had fallen 12 percent.

He started speaking at 3:52 P.M., just a few minutes before the closing auction of U.S. stock markets, a time of heavy buying and selling, and his comments sent shockwaves through the market. Oil stocks rose sharply, dragging other listings along with them. The moves were so wild that brokers on the New York Stock Exchange had trouble finding a closing price for some stocks and decided to delay the closing auction, which is important because the closing prices of stocks set the prices of thousands of indexes and mutual funds across the world.

It was yet another example of how Trump was prone to saying—or, often throughout his presidency, tweeting—things with little regard to how they might be received. Had he waited just ten minutes to make his announcement about the strategic oil reserves, investors would have had the evening to digest the news, and the exchange's market makers would have been prepared for oil stocks to open higher in the morning. Instead, it was bedlam. Energy stocks, including Exxon, rallied sharply in the final five minutes of trading, leading to a chaotic closing auction.

Cunningham, the NYSE president, reached out to Mnuchin Monday morning and tactfully asked for some help. Market-moving announcements from the Rose Garden that close to the end of the trading day were not helpful, but her text message was tactful: "Press briefings earlier in the afternoon would put less strain on the market at a critical time." He promised he would talk to the president and circled back a few hours later, assuring Cunningham that the administration wouldn't hold press conferences during the final hour of the trading day.

Around the same time, investors and other financial professionals had begun whispering about the prospect that the markets might be closed entirely. The idea was quietly being pushed by some hedge fund investors—several well-connected people on Wall Street and Washington would later mention Tom Barrack, a property magnate and close friend of Donald Trump who was heavily invested in the tanking market for real estate securities.

The chatter was also filling up Stacey Cunningham's inbox, as investors watching their savings evaporate from all over the country wrote and called, begging her to make it stop, writing, in some cases, in remarkably personal terms. "Will you please consider closing the market for a while?" read one such note on March 15. "The markets aren't 'correcting' . . . they're being driven by manufactured panic and work stoppages. My dad was born in a steel town and clawed his way out. He put money in the market and was on the verge of retiring. If the market stays open, we could see an entire generation's retirement wiped out and create another massive crisis on the back end of this. Thank you for reading if you've made it this far."

Each message cut deeply, and Cunningham understood the instinct but knew the idea was a bad one. If investors were anxious now, finding a closed sign on the busiest and richest financial market in the world would unleash full-fledged panic. Unable to sell stocks, they would rush to offload anything they could to raise cash, which would likely lead to a collapse of corporate and government debt at the worst possible moment. And billions of dollars of financial instruments that sat on the books of banks, money managers, and corporations were linked to stock prices. If the market closed, they would become a black box. That might sound like a small problem in the scheme of things, but the 2008 financial crisis was sparked by an inability to slap a price on a single financial asset—in that case, real estate bonds. Nobody knew what they were worth, and so began a cascade of collateral seizures, forced liquidations, and a self-feeding downward spiral. Mortgage securities in 2008 was a $3 trillion market. U.S. stocks were worth $40 trillion.

Mnuchin had floated the idea of a shortened trading day, perhaps closing the markets at 1 P.M. to allow Wall Street's back offices to work through the mountain of trade tickets that were piling up. The usually mundane business of "trade allocation"—ensuring that a specific order was routed to the correct legal entity within larger trading firms—was turning into a mess as trading volume surged. But that, too, Cunningham told him, was problematic. The financial exchanges of the twenty-first century run on millions of lines of computer code that assume a 9:30 A.M. opening bell and a 4 P.M. closing one.

The markets stayed open, and all anyone could do was watch them fall.

CHAPTER 7

DASH FOR CASH

It was a picture-perfect evening in Bridgetown, Barbados. Vacationers strolled the white sand beaches under clear skies while a
live band played reggae by the tiki bar at the resort below. Kevin
Jacobs, though, was eight stories up in a hotel room, phone pressed
to his ear, having heated conversations with bankers. Hilton's
forty-six-year-old chief financial officer had weeks ago promised a
vacation to his wife and twin teenaged daughters and was now
regretting it.

It was March 7, and the hotel industry, like the financial markets,
was in free fall. Customers were canceling reservations at a rapid
clip and booking few new ones. Just a few days earlier, Jacobs and
his boss, Chris Nassetta, had made a presentation to Hilton's board
of directors, warning that revenue per available room, the most important financial metric in the hotel industry, might fall 20 or 30 percent. That would roughly match what had happened to the company
during the 2008 meltdown, and it was a dire comparison. Hilton
had barely survived that crisis.

Now, just seventy-two hours later, those estimates were looking
wildly optimistic. Corporate travelers, who tend to spend more than
leisure guests, had disappeared overnight. Big conferences, the lifeblood of Hilton hotels in cities like Las Vegas, Washington, and Atlanta, were being canceled. Spring leisure bookings were dropping

by half. At those levels, Jacobs had warned his boss, Hilton might not make it.

Hilton might be one of the world's biggest hotel companies, but it doesn't actually own many hotels. Shortly after taking over as CEO in 2007, Nassetta embraced a strategy, one pioneered by Marriott a decade earlier, that emphasized branding and services over ownership. The idea, simply, was to shift the burdens of owning physical buildings to someone else while collecting steady fees for designing, franchising, and in some cases managing them. Marriott had spun off a chunk of its hotel properties in 1996 into Host Hotels & Resorts—the company Nassetta had once run—and then done the same with its time-share business in 2011. Wall Street had cheered the move, because it freed up the company's capital to be reinvested in new brands and initiatives. In 2017, Hilton spun off half of its hotels into a new company, Park Hotels & Resorts. Its vacation-booking and time-share business morphed into another new entity, Hilton Grand Vacations, with forty-six resorts and a points-based club reward system. The new Hilton was, to a large degree, not a real estate company anymore. It was, in Nassetta's telling, a purveyor of consumer experiences, relegating the risks of property ownership—heavy borrowing, interference from local government officials, leaky faucets—to others while collecting steady fees by charging property owners to use its brand, its room-booking software, even its key-card technology.

In Wall Street parlance, Hilton had become "asset light." The company made money by skimming a percentage of revenue, anywhere from 8 to 20 percent, from the property-investment firms that actually owned the hotels operating under its eighteen brands, which included Waldorf Astoria and DoubleTree. On an average day, the company brought in about $25 million and spent $20 million of it on overhead, payroll, and other operating costs. But now that revenue was disappearing quickly, and it still had bills to pay: taxes, utilities, salaries for its few thousand corporate employees, plus upkeep and staff at the roughly sixty hotels it owned or managed itself.

While his wife and kids relaxed by the pool, Jacobs picked up his cellphone and steeled himself for some tough conversations.

JACOB'S BOSS, CEO Chris Nassetta, had been warily eyeing Hilton's coffers, too. Hilton had about $500 million in cash, but he knew that wouldn't last long if the booking numbers kept tanking. A casual comment from Hilton's head of human resources, Matthew Schuyler, who was also chairman of the board of trustees at Penn State, told him: "Every college in America is going to be shutting down." That was all Nassetta needed to hear. He quickly called Hilton's general counsel to ask whether he needed board permission to draw on the $1.75 billion line of credit that the company held with Wall Street banks. He had only done that one other time in his career—on September 12, 2001. She said he didn't.

Nassetta told Jacobs to tap the company's existing $1.75 billion lines of credit at banks and start working up new financial projections in case the company needed to float a bond offering to raise more cash. "I want every dollar I can get," Nassetta said. "I mean it." If it turned out Hilton didn't need the money, the company could always repay it. The few million dollars it would have to pay in interest in the meantime would be cheap insurance against a worst-case scenario that was getting worse by the day.

But making the call was one thing. Getting the bankers to send the money was another, and that's how Jacobs found himself holed up in the Hilton resort in Bridgetown, phone pressed to his ear while his teenaged daughters frolicked by the pool. Before he had left Washington, he had sent official notice to Deutsche Bank, the lead bank on Hilton's loan, and told them the company was drawing the entire thing.

This was unusual. Corporations maintain emergency bank lines of credit that they can draw on if money gets tight. These loans are almost engineered to be problematic. Banks are happy to offer them for next-to-zero interest rates in good times to curry favor with corporate executives who might hire them for more lucrative work on acquisitions or securities offerings. But when economic stress sets in, they start to look, in the classic Wall Street parlance, "mispriced"—money guaranteed at below-market rates, at the exact moment companies are in distress. And sure enough, by the time Jacobs had landed, his inbox had filled up with anxious bankers who wanted to know why Hilton needed so much cash.

"We're looking at forward bookings that are falling off a cliff," he told bankers on a hastily assembled conference call. He said it matter-of-factly. He didn't think he needed to explain himself. The banks had signed a contract promising to send the money if Hilton asked, and Hilton was asking.

In truth, though, there was another reason the company was pulling its credit lines, a concern that had been festering in Jacobs's mind all week. What if the banks themselves ran into trouble? What if they didn't want to wire the money? If Hilton's business continued to deteriorate, the banks might invoke a little-used clause in corporate contracts, allowing them to declare that Hilton had suffered a "material adverse change" in its business—essentially, to say that Hilton was no longer the same company they had agreed to lend the $1.75 billion to in the first place, and thus they weren't obligated to do so. If hundreds of companies pulled their credit lines at once, bankers might get squirrely. Jacobs wanted Hilton to be at the front of the line.

"I'm not smart enough to know if this is going to be a banking crisis or not," he told his bankers. "But I've studied the past. I've read *Too Big to Fail*"—the definitive telling of the near-collapse of the banking system in 2008. "You don't know that your bank is about to fail overnight until it's about to fail overnight," Jacobs said.

His message was clear: Send us the money now.

No COMPANY COULD have been financially prepared for an economy that turned off virtually overnight. Still, the coronavirus's spread—slow at first and then seemingly all at once in March of 2020—exposed the dangers of a financial playbook that had become the default in corporate boardrooms over the previous two decades. Companies doled out nearly all of their profits to shareholders in a bid to keep their stock prices climbing. Those that kept large cash reserves were ridiculed as fat and lazy, relics of a sleepier age of American business when rainy-day funds were common. Hedge fund investors went off in search of companies with excess cash on their balance sheets, then waged public campaigns to get them to part with it, ideally by buying back stock or paying dividends—both of which tend to increase stock prices. It was all part of the broader push toward efficiency that was a hallmark of twenty-first-century corporate management. Bloat was out. Thin was in.

Senior managers, who are largely paid in stock themselves, were happy to oblige. Stock buybacks by companies in the S&P 500 index rose from $299 billion in 2010 to $800 billion in 2018. The total amount of cash returned to shareholders, in buybacks and dividends, doubled over that period, rising faster than both the profits they reported and the amount they put toward investments, like new factories or research facilities. As a result, companies had little financial cushion when the pandemic hit and their revenues evaporated.

Hilton had spent $4.7 billion on buybacks and dividends since 2017, trying to close the gap with Marriott, whose shares traded at a higher value. It used virtually all its cash profits, and borrowed the extra, to keep shareholders happy—and they were. By the time the virus started shutting down its hotels in China, Hilton's stock had outperformed both that of its archrival and the broader market over the past three years. But the company was holding 25 percent less cash than when it had gone public in 2013. And now it was asking Wall Street banks to pony up.

A few days later, reporters caught wind of the move. "Hilton Draws Down $1.75 Billion Credit Line to Ease Virus Hit," read the headline of a March 11 Bloomberg article that cast Hilton as the first blue-chip company to max out its available bank borrowings. The move, the article suggested, meant that fear was taking hold in corporate America: Here was a blue-chip company, a household name that appeared on the itinerary of many American families planning their vacation, scrambling for dollars.

An aide forwarded the story to Nassetta, who was working late in his office in suburban Washington, D.C. As he read it, the lights of the nation's capital spooled out under him. His mouth curled in a grim smile. *Just wait,* he thought. *In a week, this won't even be worth writing about.*

He was right. In the days that followed, companies around the world would do exactly what Hilton had done, borrowing every dollar they were contractually entitled to from their bankers and begging for more. Reporters stopped taking notice.

A SIMILAR DRAMA was playing out in the corner of an airport lounge at Atlanta's Hartsfield-Jackson Airport.

Ken Morge, Delta's corporate treasurer, pressed his forehead into the window overlooking the runway and his cellphone to his ear. There were some very nervous lawyers on the other end of the line. Morge was at the finish line of what in normal times is a box-checking exercise for someone in his job. Delta had a $1 billion loan that was coming due in a few weeks, and Morge had been tasked a few weeks earlier with talking to the banks and renewing the debt on similar terms. It was a routine process for most companies, and especially for airlines, which are heavy borrowers and maintain relationships with a large number of banks. Delta had launched the new loan a few days ago—that is, its bankers had sent out detailed documents to their investor clients who might want to buy a slice of the debt detailing the terms of the loan, the protections they would have, and some information about Delta's financial health. This was the final call with lawyers at white-shoe New York firm Simpson, Thacher & Bartlett, which was representing the banks.

Typically, these calls go something like this: The lawyers ask if anything major has changed since the documents were sent out, and the person in Morge's seat says no.

Morge gave it his best. "So, uh, I've got the due diligence list in front of me, and I'll just go down it really quickly," he said.

"Hold up," one of the lawyers said. "I want to go through these very distinctly." Morge swallowed hard. He wasn't trying to pull one over on Delta's bankers; nothing will get a company blacklisted on Wall Street faster. But he knew any detailed discussion as to what exactly had changed about Delta's circumstances in the preceding few days—about the world in general, as he sat in a noticeably quieter, emptier airport—was unlikely to leave anyone feeling better about the loan.

Morge and his boss, Delta CFO Paul Jacobson, had spent years building back their relationships with big banks after the airline's 2005 bankruptcy filing. They had paid Wall Street hundreds of millions of dollars in fees. They had rebuilt their balance sheet and restored their investment-grade rating—a point of pride for their boss, CEO Ed Bastian. Now he could tell from the tone of the lawyers that it wouldn't be enough. Banks were getting nervous.

And it wasn't just this loan that was at risk. Morge and Jacobson had, at Bastian's direction, been feeling out another group of banks about a new, far larger loan of about $4 billion that would help shore up Delta's finances for whatever was to come.

The conference call was the first sign to Morge—a Delta lifer who had joined the airline's finance department as an analyst in 1997, had been through its bankruptcy, and was named its treasurer in 2012—that things were getting bad. He texted Delta's head of investor relations, Jill Greer: "Need you on this call now. It's not going well."

A week earlier, a group of senior Delta executives had gathered in a conference room at the airline's Atlanta headquarters. The question on the table was whether to seek aid from the federal government. None of them found the idea especially palatable. For starters, Delta had publicly complained for years about Middle Eastern governments that subsidized their national airlines, which allowed them to undercut Western rivals on lucrative long-haul routes. Secondly, the executives knew that any government aid would come with strings attached, likely in the form of an equity stake that would make the Treasury Department a significant shareholder for years to come. A similar playbook had been used to rescue big banks in 2008 and had included stock warrants for the U.S. government, caps on bonuses paid to top executives, and a freeze on buybacks and dividend payments. Wall Street had found it such an unpleasant experience that most of the firms rushed to repay their emergency aid as quickly as possible.

But Delta's cash was running low. For one thing, it had just paid out $1.6 billion in profits to its employees in February and had also paid off some maturing debt. Nobody was booking flights. In mid-February, the company was selling about $140 million in tickets every day. By early March, it was down to $80 million. And thousands of customers were canceling flights they had already booked.

Cancellations create a giant financial problem for airlines. Passengers pay for trips before they take them, which means airlines collect money from a customer before they have to spend it on that same customer. Known as an "air traffic liability," it is essentially a loan from passengers, and by the time the coronavirus spread started accelerating, Delta's was about $6 billion. Now its customers, by canceling their flights, were essentially calling in the loan. It may have been masquerading as refund requests, like a retail customer returning an unwanted sweater, but on closer look, it was more dire than that. It was a run on the bank.

Delta tried to nudge passengers to convert their tickets into vouchers for future travel and, for those still optimistic about travel, waived its standard $200 fee to make changes to a ticket. But by the middle of March, the company's daily net sales were negative, meaning the company was paying out more in refunds every day than it was selling in new tickets. By the end of the month, it was losing $100 million a day. Every morning at 8:30 A.M., top executives including Bastian, his lieutenant Glen Hauenstein, Jacobson, Morge, and Jill Greer gathered to answer a single question: How much cash do we have? Every dollar that went out the door had to be justified. The new loans and drawdowns of existing loans had given Delta about $6 billion in cash. At the pace it was burning money by late March, that would last just two months.

Two days later, on March 18, Delta announced a slew of cost-cutting measures. Senior executives would take pay cuts of 50 percent, and Bastian gave up his salary for six months. It closed its airport lounges, consolidated facilities at its hub in Atlanta, and said it would ground more than six hundred planes—half its fleet. Some would not return; the company was accelerating the retirement of older planes, including its Boeing 767s. Bastian said talks with the government had been productive and he was confident that aid would come through. "That said," he added, "we have to continue to take all necessary self-help measures. Cash preservation remains our top financial priority."

Meanwhile, Bastian asked his general counsel, Peter Carter, to work with the top lawyers at other airlines to come up with an initial proposal that they could take to the government. It had been about a week since the airline executives—save for Bastian, who had been attending his mother's funeral—had met at the White House and reassured the president they weren't asking for money. In a document swapped back and forth over email in the following weeks, Carter, Steve Johnson at American, and Brett Hart at United hammered out a two-page document with three main points.

First, the industry was looking for grants, not loans. This was partly informed by the emergency loans that had been extended to some airlines in the wake of the 9/11 attacks, which had left them in weak financial shape and contributed to several bankruptcy filings, including Delta's in 2005. Second, the airlines wanted a suspension of the 7.5 percent tax that the federal government collects on all flights. Third, with enough financial support from the government, they would promise not to lay off employees.

It was designed to be simple and address the cash crunch facing the industry. It was also designed to keep the federal government as far away as possible from the companies' actual operations. The executives might have needed Washington's money but they weren't keen for its input. Notably, the proposal didn't include an offer to give the government a financial stake in the companies. The airlines also weren't agreeing to limits on executive pay, or federal control over their routes and schedules. And they weren't offering to suspend stock buybacks or dividends. Such programs are a key underpinning of stock prices, and any limits on their ability to distribute their profits to shareholders going forward was a one-way ticket to a tanking stock price.

That they were even thinking about profits and how they might spend them reflected a miscalculation that titans of industry across the economy would make in the early days of March: that the crisis would be over in a few weeks, maybe a few months at most.

THE TREASURERS OF the eight biggest U.S. banks dialed in to a series of calls with officials at the Federal Reserve, the Treasury Department, the FDIC, and the Office of the Comptroller of the Currency. Together, those four agencies oversee the nation's financial system, each with their own jurisdiction and priorities. The banks represented on the calls were: four commercial giants—JPMorgan Chase, Bank of America, Citigroup, and Wells Fargo—which collectively held 40 percent of Americans' savings and trillions of dollars in business and home loans; investment-banking heavyweights Goldman Sachs and Morgan Stanley, better known for securities trading and dealmaking; and two custody banks, State Street and Bank of New York Mellon, which are essentially storehouses for stocks and bonds and handle much of the back-office paperwork that makes the financial system function.

In the wake of the 2008 crisis, these eight firms had been designated as "global systemically important banks." It was regulator-speak for the fact that they were so large, so wired into the global economy, that their survival and strength were not simply a matter of private profits but of public necessity. Translated into the vernacular, they were simply "too big to fail." The label had brought with it new government scrutiny, and regulations that required them to hold more capital in reserve and submit to annual "stress tests" to ensure they were strong enough to withstand a deep economic shock.

But the 2008 crisis had also made the eight banks bigger and more powerful. They had survived efforts to break them up and had beaten back a populist, anti–Wall Street movement. They had learned to live with the onslaught of new regulations, which were onerous enough to discourage smaller banks from getting too big and competing with them. They were a financial "gang of eight" that rivaled the congressional leadership group of the same name in their sway over the economy.

Their treasurers met quarterly with regulators, and that Wednesday's meeting was supposed to be in Washington. But the market tumult had the bankers glued to their office screens, and so a series of conference calls was hastily arranged.

Beth Hammack dialed in from her office high in Goldman Sachs's downtown headquarters. Before becoming the firm's treasurer in 2018, Hammack had spent years on the trading floor, where she traded government bonds and learned the Wall Street art of sensing weakness—a quiver here, a hedged statement there. She quickly recognized the unease she heard from the other bank treasurers on the line. Cash was leaving each of their firms, and quickly.

Banks, in their simplest form, pay depositors interest for their savings and lend out that money at a slightly higher rate, pocketing the difference. But the global behemoths that dominate finance today bear almost no resemblance to that model. Keeping enough money moving to the right places around a giant firm like Goldman and the seven other banks dialed in to the conference call involves an intricate dance. Customers make deposits and withdrawals. Hedge funds put up cash as collateral for trades, then ask for it back when the value of the trade changes. Short-term borrowings come due and are re-upped, their maturities extended for a day or week or month.

Layered on top of this constantly moving ledger is a maze of regulations put in place after the 2008 crisis, which give favorable treatment to some sources of funding deemed stickier, like long-term bonds or consumer deposits, over others, like repurchase agreements—overnight loans underpinned by collateral. Put simply, banks must keep enough cash on hand to replace funding that is expected to be lost in the next thirty days.

They didn't have enough.

THE WORLD HAD changed while Ken Morge was skiing—or trying to.

When Delta's treasurer had flown to Colorado a week earlier, hoping to catch the peak of the season in Aspen with his wife and kids, he had been negotiating the outlines of a $4 billion loan from a group of Wall Street banks that would shore up the airline's finances. As far as corporate loans go, this was a pretty easygoing one. Its bankers weren't demanding collateral, a sign that its lenders were comfortable lending to Delta's good name alone. And why shouldn't they be? The company carried an investment-grade credit rating. It had plenty of assets—planes, airport slots, coveted flight routes—that it could borrow against if needed. And its bonds traded at far higher prices than those of rivals United and American, which were less profitable and deeper in debt.

But that was a week ago, and plenty had changed. More than 136,000 people worldwide had contracted Covid-19 and 5,000 had died. Morge's vacation had ended early after Colorado's governor ordered ski resorts to close. Now, flying over the Great Plains, he knew he had lost his negotiating leverage with his bankers. The lenders were now offering far less money, in the neighborhood of $3 billion. Some of Delta's longtime lenders, including Credit Suisse and PNC, were balking at participating in the loan at all. One banker told a member of Morge's team, "We don't think you need $3 billion. We think you're going to need $10 billion." Their firm, the banker said, was out: They didn't want to lend into a bottomless hole.

The banks that were still agreeing to participate were driving a hard bargain. They were no longer comfortable lending to Delta on faith alone but were instead demanding the liens on some of its airplanes as collateral. Morge was gripped by panic. He honestly didn't know if the banks were going to come through. The airline's lobbying group was about to ask the U.S. government for help, but he didn't know what the appetite would be for industry bailouts. Without a lot of money, and soon, he worried Delta might go bankrupt for the second time in fifteen years.

The final loan would end up being even smaller, just $2.6 billion. The new terms reflected a reality that had gripped America.

CORPORATE AMERICA WAS on its knees. Bill Ackman was in the middle of the biggest trade of his life.

By early March, Pershing Square's traders had put on the trade they hoped would protect the firm if Ackman's doom-and-gloom predictions came true. They had bought more than $1 billion of credit-default swaps on three baskets of corporate bonds: one that included the debt of highly rated companies like General Motors, one of lower-rated ones like Sprint and American Airlines, and one of European companies. All told, they paid $27 million in premiums and commissions. Ackman thought it was the bargain of a lifetime.

Although credit-default swaps are often likened to financial insurance policies, they are different in one key regard: The event they protect against—a borrower defaulting on its debt—doesn't actually have to happen for the policyholder to make money. The swaps themselves are financial investments that gain in value as the event they guard against appears more likely. When the underlying debt—in this case, a pile of corporate bonds—falls in value, the swaps can be sold at a profit. All it would take for Pershing Square's bet to pay off was for the market to get spooked.

It happened fast. As the coronavirus spread across Asia and then into the United States, global investors got scared in a hurry. Corporate bond prices began plummeting as investors worried companies wouldn't have the money to pay them back. From a peak in early March, a benchmark index of corporate bonds maintained by the financial-services firm Bloomberg and the investment bank Barclays fell 15 percent by March 20. On paper, Pershing Square's investment was worth more than $2 billion.

Those huge gains would have made any investor happy. But at the same time his swaps were soaring in value, Ackman's portfolio of stocks, which accounted for the bulk of his firm's investments, had lost more than a quarter of their value. By the first Friday in March, the swaps accounted for 40 percent of Pershing Square's assets— a portfolio so lopsided it looked wildly imprudent. What's more, the Federal Reserve was starting to indicate that it was prepared to step in and calm the bond market, possibly by guaranteeing corporate bonds or buying them itself to stabilize prices and soothe investors' nerves. Either move would cause bond prices to rally, erasing much of the more than $2 billion in paper profits Pershing Square was sitting on. On a single day, March 6, the value of the firm's swaps had fallen $800 million on paper—still hugely profitable, but volatile enough that Ackman had had enough. He called his traders and told them to start selling the position.

It wasn't hard to do. With the markets in full turmoil, investors across the world were now panicking and looking for the same protection that Ackman had bought weeks earlier. Companies deemed safe just a few weeks earlier now appeared in danger of defaulting. The yield on investment-grade corporate debt compared to that of ultrasafe U.S. Treasury bonds, a kind of investor's "fear meter," had tripled since late February, when Ackman had started buying the swaps. It was as if he had bought flood insurance during a drought year for a pittance and sold it during a monsoon.

By the following Monday, his traders were about halfway done. It would take another three days to liquidate the entire position. The trade would ultimately net nearly $2.6 billion in profits on an initial investment of just $27 million—a hundred-thousand-fold return. For comparison's sake, a home run venture capital investment might return a hundred times the money invested over the course of many years. Ackman had done one thousand times better in the span of about three weeks.

It was a sequel of sorts to the 2007 trade that inspired the Hollywood hit *The Big Short,* which followed a handful of hedge fund managers as they bet against the U.S. mortgage market and reaped huge profits when it crashed. Ackman had little in common with that crew, which included a virtually unknown, socially awkward introvert named Michael Burry and a pair of thirty-year-old newbies, Jamie Mai and Charlie Ledley, investing out of their garage. But he had hit on the same sentiment, the one he had named back in February when he spoke to a roomful of bright-eyed wannabe investors in London: The market was wrong. In 2007, investors assumed housing prices would keep going up. In early 2020, they assumed the coronavirus would stay in China.

History might do well to add a fourth criteria to Nassim Taleb's description of black swan events: They're rare, extreme, easily rationalized with the benefit of hindsight—and extraordinarily profitable for those who, by luck or pluck, see them coming.

CHAPTER 8

THE DAY THE WORLD SHUT DOWN

The whistle sounded early, too early. It was seconds from tip-off when referees swarmed midcourt of the Paycom Center in downtown Oklahoma City, where more than ten thousand people had been waiting for the game between the hometown Thunder and the visiting Utah Jazz. The referee had the ball in his hands when the Thunder's head doctor came sprinting out to center court and whispered in his ear. Rudy Gobert, a player for the Utah Jazz, had tested positive for Covid-19. Fifteen awkward minutes later, a voice boomed on the arena's public-address system. The game was canceled.

"Take your time in leaving the arena tonight, and do so in an orderly fashion," it said. "Thank you for coming out tonight. We are all safe."

It was Wednesday, March 11. American sport—and America writ large—had its patient zero.

MARCH 11 WASN'T, by any metric, the worst day of the pandemic. It was not the deadliest or the most infectious, not by a long shot. It wasn't the bottom for financial markets. Unemployment would not peak for another month. But as the crisis stretched on, March 11 would come to serve as a milestone for millions of Americans—

a day that previewed how the virus would ravage the economy, shutter institutions, and strike at the very heart of American culture.

It was the day Covid would be made real for many of us. On March 11, the World Health Organization formally declared a global pandemic. Tom Hanks, that American everyman, announced on Twitter that he and his wife, the actress Rita Wilson, were sick. National Guard troops deployed to New Rochelle, NY, the New York City suburb where one of the first major clusters of community-spread U.S. cases had emerged. The NBA suspended its season following Gobert's diagnosis, followed quickly by other sports leagues and the NCAA, which called off its March Madness tournament just days before tip-off. Disney World shut down its Magic Kingdom. Broadway went dark for the first time since a three-week stagehand strike in 2007. The eleven-year bull market for U.S. stocks officially ended when stock indexes closed the day down 20 percent from recent highs.

From the Oval Office that evening, Trump announced he was suspending air travel to and from continental Europe. The speech, unusually somber and scripted for the perpetually off-message Trump, was arguably the gravest announcement from behind the Resolute desk outside of wartime.

Captured in freeze-frame, the dizzying confluence of events brought reality home for many Westerners who had, until then, viewed the virus as a distant threat. In a matter of a few hours, it hit multiple facets of everyday life: sports, travel, retirement accounts, Hollywood. The coronavirus was no longer an "over there" problem.

For the CEOs of the world's biggest companies, March 11 was a day of unprecedented decisions made on the fly. Their stocks were tanking. Their employees were terrified. For the lucky ones, their business was merely suffering; for others, their business seemed to no longer make sense at all.

—

DAVID SOLOMON HOPPED out of a black town car and approached the guard station outside the White House. The Goldman Sachs CEO had spent the morning of March 11 on Capitol Hill, where he had traded elbow bumps with members of a bipartisan congressional caucus that had been trying to put together a bill to fund coronavirus relief. Wall Street CEOs aren't strangers to the Hill, and on this occasion Solomon had been invited by Josh Gottheimer, a forty-five-year-old New Jersey Democrat who had once been Solomon's camper at a summer camp in upstate New York. The two had stayed close, and the invitation let Solomon occupy a space he was comfortable in: centrist, commonsense, and pragmatically transactional.

But now he had a meeting with the president. The CEOs of the five largest banks had been invited to discuss their response to the spreading virus, which by now had infected 1,267 people in the United States and killed 38. The vast majority of those testing positive for Covid-19 had not traveled overseas and instead had caught the disease from someone in the community.

Not since the last financial crisis, a decade earlier, had the CEOs of the big banks been summoned to Washington like this. Back then, in 2009, a chastened group of executives had slinked to Congress to face the anger of a nation mired in a deep recession that was, to a large degree, the fault of their firms. At least two had taken Amtrak rather than the corporate jet, so deep was the national rancor at Wall Street for having sparked the economic crash.

None of the bankers now assembled in a White House anteroom had been subjected to that congressional tongue-lashing. The 2008 crop of bank bosses had been washed out, some by the scandal and others simply by time. Solomon had taken over just seventeen months earlier. Bank of America's CEO, Brian Moynihan, had been appointed in 2010; Citigroup's Michael Corbat, in 2012. Charlie Scharf had been in charge at Wells Fargo for just five months, hired to clean up after a fake-accounts scandal that had ousted his predecessor. (In fact, Scharf hadn't had to travel far for this meeting. He was already in Washington, having appeared before a congressional committee to answer questions about continued scandals at the bank.) JPMorgan's Jamie Dimon, the only remaining Wall Street CEO to have been in the seat during the 2008 crisis, wasn't there at the White House; he'd been hospitalized after emergency heart surgery to repair a damaged aorta. Filling in was Gordon Smith, JPMorgan's co-president, who joined the CEOs gathered in a waiting area. None wore masks.

The Roosevelt Room's heavy door swung open, and CEOs of the country's biggest hospital systems filed out. They had been there urging the administration to prioritize their patients for coronavirus testing. Doctors and nurses were burning through dwindling stocks of protective masks and gowns, the executives said. Faster test results would rule out some patients and preserve critical gear.

Scharf, the Wells Fargo CEO, noticed Paul Rothman, the CEO of Johns Hopkins Medicine and dean of its medical school. Scharf had graduated from the university and was now a trustee, and the two men had been in touch the week before. Rothman had relayed a concerning message in that phone call; Trump administration officials may have been publicly downplaying the risk of a pandemic, but Johns Hopkins's models were bleak. The two men now exchanged nods as the doctors left their audience with the president and the money men filed in.

The bank CEOs had a friendly audience in the president, who called them "probably the best bankers in the world." And they played the part, eager to show both that their banks were on sound footing and that, unlike in the wake of 2008, when banks had all but stopped lending, they were ready and willing to support the economy. JPMorgan executive Gordon Smith, filling in for Dimon, said the bank had lent out $26 billion in the past forty days to consumers and small businesses. What had been billed as a short event open to the press followed by a more substantive closed-door meeting turned into a public display of confidence from the bosses of the nation's largest banks. "This is not a financial crisis," Corbat said to a row of news cameras.

As the meeting broke up, Trump motioned to the CEOs to follow him, and the group filed into the Oval Office, where they milled around the striped couches. Out of view of the cameras, the CEOs urged the president to put money into testing, which would help direct medical and protective resources to places they were needed most and prevent unnecessary, scattershot lockdowns. "Testing will keep the economy open," Moynihan, the Bank of America CEO, said. Trump nodded, pursing his lips. Then he motioned to the presidential desk, a gift from Queen Victoria built from the wood planks of the HMS *Resolute,* a nineteenth-century Arctic exploration ship.

"You guys want to take a picture?"

BACK IN NEW York, two dozen corporate executives gathered at noon on the forty-first floor of the Hearst Tower on the corner of Fifty-seventh Street and Eighth Avenue in midtown Manhattan. It was their chance to tell Governor Andrew Cuomo what they were seeing and what they needed. The guest list originally included more than a hundred executives, but the night before, the governor's office had called Kathy Wylde, head of the Partnership for New York, a group of city business leaders who had organized the meeting. Cuomo's office was working on a new policy to limit public gatherings—it would be announced the next day, and would cap groups at five hundred—and decided the optics of a large indoor meeting wouldn't be good. So the list had been whittled down to about twenty, including Hearst CEO Steven Swartz; Bill Ford, CEO of the private-investment firm General Atlantic; Pfizer's chief, Albert Bourla; Nasdaq's Adena Friedman; Rob Speyer from real estate giant Tishman Speyer; Dave McInerney from grocery-delivery firm FreshDirect; and Joey Levin from IAC, Barry Diller's conglomerate that owned travel booking site Expedia. Along with the big bank CEOs in Washington, Wall Street, one of New York's largest employers, was represented by a pair of lieutenants, John Waldron from Goldman and his counterpart at Citigroup, Jane Fraser. The governor canceled plans to attend in person and beamed in from Albany along with his health commissioner, Howard Zucker.

All eyes were on Bourla. The day before, Pfizer had announced plans to partner with a German biotechnology firm, BioNTech, to develop a new type of vaccine they hoped would be effective against the coronavirus. Traditional vaccines carried a weakened or dead version of a virus to train the immune system to recognize and attack invading microbes. BioNTech had been experimenting with a different kind of vaccine, one that would instead carry blueprints, written into snippets of genetic code called mRNA, that would turn immune cells into small antibody factories. It had never been successful but had shown promising results in the lab.

"We're going to work as fast as we can, but the virus has a head start," Bourla told the room.

Waldron shared Goldman's plans to split its workforce and tap backup trading floors in New Jersey and Connecticut. Cuomo, known for political blustering and the occasional grandstanding, had few answers. Adena Friedman, the Nasdaq CEO, dialed her head of risk as she walked out onto Fifty-seventh Street. "We've got to shut the offices now. This is going to be a complete disaster. New York isn't ready." Nasdaq's Times Square headquarters closed the next day.

STACEY CUNNINGHAM WALKED the floor of the New York Stock Exchange in the final minutes of the trading day on March 11. When the bell rang at 4 P.M., it was official. The eleven-year bull market, which had enriched investors, cemented America's status as the power center of global finance, and washed away unpleasant memories of the 2008 crash out of which it grew, was over.

A flood of alarming headlines that day had sent stocks lower. Goldman Sachs's economic analysts issued a dire projection that by midsummer, the S&P 500 would be 25 percent lower than it was when the year opened. Boeing drew down a $13.8 billion bank loan, a giant borrowing that suggested severe financial distress at one of America's industrial icons. News reports surfaced that private-equity giant Blackstone had encouraged companies it owned to do the same. The visual of the CEOs of the country's biggest banks summoned to the White House, while intended to reassure markets, had the opposite effect. Why would they be there if it wasn't an emergency?

The Dow Jones Industrial Average, which just a month earlier had been flirting with 30,000, closed that day at 23,553.22. That decline of more than 20 percent officially heralded the arrival of a bear market.

The origins of these terms in financial markets are thought to trace to an old English proverb warning against selling bearskins before catching the bear. That was likely later applied to short sellers, who sell shares of stock they haven't yet bought on the expectation the price will fall, thus tying the "bear" with those betting on a market decline. The provenance of "bull" is less clear, but the terms had become entwined with market sentiment by 1720, when Alexander Pope wrote a poem: "Come fill the South Sea goblet full / The gods shall of our stock take care / Europa pleased accepts the bull / And Jove with joy puts off the bear."

America's bull market had begun on March 9, 2009, in the wake of the near-collapse of the global banking system and still in the midst of the recession it caused. It had charged forward through a European debt crisis; the first-ever downgrade of U.S. government debt; a slowdown of the Chinese economy; rising interest rates (which should theoretically hurt stocks by increasing corporate borrowing costs); and escalating tensions between Washington and Beijing. Now it had been felled by a microscopic virus.

Members of the White House's coronavirus task force crowded into the Oval Office, where they were joined by the president's daughter, Ivanka Trump, son-in-law and senior adviser Jared Kushner, chief economic adviser Larry Kudlow, and a half dozen others. The president sat behind the Resolute desk. The chief medical advisers on the committee, Anthony Fauci and Deborah Birx, pushed to shut down air travel to and from Europe. Birx warned that, if left unchecked, the virus might kill two million people. Faster action, including shutting down international air travel, could keep the death toll at a quarter of a million or less. It was the first time many of the nonscientists in the room had heard potential death tolls laid out so starkly.

Fauci—who had increasingly, to the president's visible annoyance on numerous occasions, given voice to the worsening severity of the virus—warned the group that the outbreak was going to get far worse, and that contact tracing and testing were too slow to contain the outbreak.

Steven Mnuchin stepped out to take a call from Nancy Pelosi. The two had been haggling for days over a congressional spending bill to lessen the impact of the coronavirus. It would end up being about $8 billion when it was announced two days later, but the two had spoken more than twenty times in the preceding day, hammering out what would be included. By the time he returned, a little after 5 P.M., the president had stepped out to attend to another obligation. A smaller group including Mnuchin, Kudlow, Fauci, and National Security Adviser Robert O'Brien soon followed, taking the elevator to the president's private residence on the third floor of the White House, where the discussion continued.

Shutting down air travel would be a huge hit to the global economy and would likely tank the markets, Mnuchin said. Trump had long been obsessed with the stock market's rise during his presidency, and his pleasure had likely contributed to Mnuchin being one of the only Cabinet secretaries to have remained on the job through the first three years of the administration. Eventually the decision was made to shut down flights to and from continental Europe. The job of informing the airline CEOs fell to Mnuchin, who set about finding an empty office in the West Wing—a cramped complex with little office space to begin with that had become an unusually crowded hive of activity in recent days. By luck, the Cabinet Room was open, and he ducked inside.

Doug Parker switched off CNBC. It was all bad news. Covid cases were mounting. Stocks were falling, including his own. American Airlines' stock had lost half its value in four weeks. The company was burning tens of millions of dollars of cash each day. Bookings were a fraction of what they had been. He was now banging around the company's Fort Worth headquarters waiting for the White House to call.

He had gotten a heads-up from his chief of government relations, Nate Gatten, that Trump was going on television later that evening to announce a shutdown of travel to and from continental Europe.

Just a week earlier, the airline CEOs had said—on camera, in the White House, with the president—that they didn't need any money. Parker himself had echoed that sentiment the same day in a private meeting with Mnuchin. But if the federal government was going to stop transatlantic travel, which accounted for anywhere between 10 and 30 percent of the big carriers' business, that was a different story. Parker knew the airlines were going to need money, and if the president asked how much, he wanted to be ready with an answer.

Parker thought back to the lifeline that the government had thrown the airline industry after the 9/11 terrorist attacks: $5 billion in grants and $10 billion in loan guarantees. Parker figured a similarly sized request would be appropriate.

He tapped on the door of a glass-walled conference room where CFO Derek Kerr and his finance team were meeting, printouts and coffee cups scattered on the table. "What do we ask for?" Parker asked.

Kerr chewed his lip for a minute before responding. "Fifty billion dollars."

The number bowled Parker over. But Kerr's math checked out.

American had revenues of about $40 billion and represented roughly 20 percent of the U.S. travel industry. So, with $200 billion in annual revenue, $50 billion was three months' worth. All of a sudden, it didn't seem insane.

The call came at 8:25 P.M. Parker took it from his desk in the open-air suite he shared with his deputies, overlooking the atrium of American's headquarters. President Trump had wanted to call himself, Mnuchin said, but he was getting ready for his Oval Office address, set to go live in half an hour.

"I know what I said last week," Parker began, "but this is now a huge issue for us and we're going to need some relief. We all are." He steeled himself and tried to sound nonchalant. "I think we're going to need something on the order of $50 billion." He had trouble getting the words out of his mouth. It seemed like an enormous ask, and one that was sure to spark backlash from both sides of the political aisle. Free-market Republicans wouldn't like the idea of the government propping up private industry. Progressives would scream "bailout" and chastise the CEOs for not socking enough away while enriching themselves and their shareholders.

But if he expected pushback, he didn't get it. On the other end of the phone in the Cabinet Room at the White House, Mnuchin didn't flinch. He had warned the president in the residence that afternoon that a European travel ban would punch a huge hole in the airline industry. Parker had just put a number on how big a hole. "I understand," he said, and promised to be in touch.

On the drive home from American's campus, a three-hundred-acre spread near the Dallas/Fort Worth Airport, Parker called his wife, Gwen, a former American Airlines flight attendant, who had been at the Dallas Mavericks game against the Denver Nuggets. She had been sitting a few rows behind Mavericks owner Mark Cuban, whose reaction to a message on his phone conveying the news of the NBA's canceled season was caught on camera and broadcast live—an open-mouthed gape that became one of the pandemic's earliest viral moments. "Obviously this is much bigger than basketball," the billionaire owner told ESPN. Officials let the game finish, a Dallas win. It was the last NBA game of the 2020 season.

"YOU CANNOT MODEL a pandemic," Brian Chesky barked at his finance team. The Airbnb CEO was home alone at his house in San Francisco, splayed in bed with his laptop propped up on his knees. He was dialed in to a late-night phone call, where well-intentioned members of his team had spent the day trying to game out the impact of the virus on demand for home rentals.

Tens of thousands of Airbnb travelers were collectively demanding more than $1 billion in refunds on stays they had previously booked but that they were now too afraid to take. Airbnb's policies allowed hosts, the people who actually owned the properties they were renting out, to set their own refund policies, and many chose not to allow them. (Half of Airbnb hosts depend on rentals to pay their mortgage.) The question for Chesky and his lieutenants: Should Airbnb dip into its own pocket to make up the difference? It could cost billions, money that Airbnb—the epitome of a cash-burning, high-flying Silicon Valley startup—could ill afford.

The normally mellow Chesky, who looked younger than his thirty-eight years and tended to give off a "bro-next-door" vibe, was losing patience with his number crunchers. Were they supposed to force customers to choose between eating thousands of dollars or walking into a stranger's home and hoping for the best?

Just a week before, Chesky had been riding high, speaking to a group of executives in a fifth-floor San Francisco meeting space, a former cafeteria now called "Ate, Ate, Ate"—a nod to its prior function and the building's address, 888 Brannan. The facility was originally built by the National Carbon Company as its headquarters and later housed a manufacturing facility for Eveready Batteries in 1916. In 2013 it was converted into Airbnb's global headquarters, complete with the kind of historic industrial touches—original tram tracks still ran through the floor—that had become the hallmark of fast-growing tech companies. It was a high point, literally, with sweeping views of San Francisco Bay and the Golden Gate Bridge beyond. It was there that the CEO had told his staff of his plan to announce the company's IPO at the end of the month.

That was just a week ago. 2020 was supposed to be the year Airbnb left the Silicon Valley nest and took its place among the titans of Wall Street. Now it looked like it might not survive the year.

CHAPTER 9

STRESS TEST

Stephen Scherr trudged into his weekend home in the Hamptons, a moneyed, pastoral spit on Long Island about two hours outside New York City, where many Wall Street executives kept weekend homes. It was a little after 7:30 P.M. on Friday, March 13, and Goldman Sachs's chief financial officer was trying to wrap his brain around the week that had just ended. The stock market had crashed. So had the prices of oil, gold, and corporate debt. Nobody was buying anything. Investors had settled into a defensive crouch, selling much of what they owned for the safety of cold, hard dollars.

Scherr, who oversaw Goldman's $1 trillion balance sheet, had hopped between phone calls with officials in Washington, who sought assurances that the country's fifth-biggest bank was on sound footing. "It's not good out there," he told Justin Muzinich, Mnuchin's top deputy at the Treasury Department, "but we're on top of it."

He was projecting a confidence he only half felt. Wall Street's circulatory system, where securities and cash flow in a smooth loop between buyers and sellers, was clotted by panic. Investors wanted their money and sold anything they could to get it. Billions more were stuck in a sort of Wall Street limbo, as the settling of trades—in normal times, a mundane back-office task—got swamped in paperwork hell. The result was cash pouring out of Goldman at a pace that alarmed Scherr.

On top of it all, he had been stuck in meetings all week about how to transition the firm's thirty-six thousand employees to work remotely, a possibility that seemed unlikely on Monday and inevitable just a few days later. Goldman had plenty of disaster-response plans on the shelf. In 2012, hundreds of sandbags socked away in the basement kept Goldman's power on during Hurricane Sandy while the rest of lower Manhattan went dark. A photo published in *The New York Times* had captured the scene and reinforced among Goldman's leadership the value of planning ahead. Terrorism was always a threat in Manhattan. (The bank had updated its procedures in 2017 after a van plowed through a crowded sidewalk a few blocks away from its downtown headquarters, killing eight people.) But none of the bank's plans anticipated a full-blown pandemic. And that's what Covid-19 now was: The World Health Organization had officially said so two days earlier. Executives across the world—and especially in New York, which had quickly become the epicenter of the outbreak in the United States, with 142 confirmed cases by March 9—had to figure out how to safely empty their offices while keeping their businesses running.

Goldman's smaller workforces across Asia had been split up weeks earlier and sent to backup sites to thin out the crowded trading floors. But Goldman's headquarters, a glass-and-steel skyscraper on the banks of the Hudson River that had cost $2 billion to build a decade earlier, was far more densely populated. Some ten thousand employees poured in daily from communities across New York, New Jersey, and Connecticut, into the company's global nerve center, disembarking from subways and town cars and into tight elevator banks that spilled them out into the eleventh-floor lobby, where they mingled at the firm's in-house Starbucks and packed the leather-cushioned benches that lined the two-story atrium and offered a stunning view of the Statue of Liberty. From there they filtered into office suites, and a tightly packed trading floor that was now a public health hazard.

Scherr, along with Goldman's president, John Waldron, and its chief administrative officer, Laurence Stein, had been tasked with figuring out what to do with all of them. The question had taken on more urgency after the first employee, a contract worker at Goldman's in-house gym, had tested positive for the virus that week. The trio had settled on a split-team approach that was to start the following Monday, March 16. Half of Goldman's New York City employees would report as usual to headquarters. The other half would work from backup sites across the river in New Jersey or their homes. Employees would be assigned to the "blue team" or the "white team," a nod to Goldman's corporate logo colors and an attempt to sow some esprit de corps in a workforce that was growing more rattled by the day.

The plan was simple enough in theory but had been maddeningly complicated to work out, turning three executives of one of the world's most powerful financial institutions into roadies for a hastily arranged concert tour, scrambling for space and equipment. The tedium had worn out the fifty-five-year-old Scherr, who was hoping for a brief respite as he joined his family in the Hamptons. He had barely stepped inside when his cellphone buzzed. It was his neighbor—Goldman's treasurer, Beth Hammack, whom he had dropped off just a few minutes earlier. The two had weekend homes less than a mile apart in Sagaponack and had carpooled from the city together.

Hammack, too, had been hoping for a quiet end to a taxing week. As treasurer, her job was both boring and crucial: making sure the bank had enough cash on hand at all times, in the right places and the right currencies, to cover its financial obligations. Banks like Goldman move billions of dollars around every day buying and selling securities, posting and receiving collateral to underpin open trading positions, funding loans in dozens of countries, and meeting customer deposit withdrawals.

Managing that ledger fell to the forty-eight-year-old Hammack. The daughter of Wall Street legend Howard Morgan, who had helped launch Renaissance Technologies, the hedge fund at the forefront of algorithmic trading, had spent more than half her life at Goldman, much of it as a trader of Treasury bonds. Quick-witted and to the point, she had once responded to a superior's question about why Goldman had a harder time passing regulatory muster than bigger commercial banks like JPMorgan with a poem ("In crisis, JP has inflows," went one line). In 2018 she was named the bank's treasurer, a critical but unglamorous job—invisible in good times and thrown under a glaring spotlight in bad ones—which fairly described the week that had just ended.

She had barely settled in and poured a gin and Fever-Tree tonic, adding a splash of St-Germain elderflower liqueur, when her phone lit up. Cellphone service in the Hamptons is notoriously spotty, after years of wealthy residents objecting to the construction of new towers that might spoil their ocean views, and Hammack had been in a communications blackout during much of the drive home with her boss. As soon as she connected to her home Wi-Fi, emails and voicemails began pouring in from deputies in New York and London, none of them bearing good news. She dialed Scherr.

"Have you had a drink yet?" she asked, looking at hers, untouched and sweating droplets onto the table. He hadn't. "Good, because we have a problem," she said.

Goldman's financial books, tallied that Friday evening, showed that billions of dollars in cash had whooshed out the door during the week and almost none had come in. As Hammack delicately put it to her boss, the market turmoil had resulted in "an inexplicably high amount of liquidity leaving the firm."

Liquidity is the lifeblood system of a modern corporation. It refers to cash and securities like government bonds that can be easily sold in a pinch to fund day-to-day operations and cover outstanding IOUs. Liquidity is important to any company but crucial for banks, which are required by regulators to keep enough cash on hand to ensure that they can make good on their trading obligations, fund their lending commitments, and honor customer withdrawals. Even banks that look rich on paper can find themselves in mortal danger if their liquidity dries up. They can be forced to sell assets to raise cash, which spooks customers into pulling more of their money. The result is an old-fashioned run on the bank, where cash and confidence evaporate in lockstep. It's the equivalent of owning a gold mine but no shovels.

Goldman had plenty of proverbial gold, with more than $1 trillion in assets on its books. And it had, at least for normal times, enough shovels—more than $230 billion in cash and other assets like government bonds, which are generally considered as good as cash, on its year-end books. But the prior week had been anything but normal. Trading clients had retreated from the market chaos and taken their cash with them. Big companies, worried about the spread of the virus, had drawn down on their credit lines, forcing Goldman to fund billions of dollars of loans. Goldman's $230 billion liquidity pool, which looked plenty deep just a few weeks ago, was draining fast.

What's more, much of that pool wasn't actually cash, but rather holdings of government debt. At the end of 2019, Goldman owned more than $100 billion worth of bonds issued by the U.S. Treasury as well as Fannie Mae and Freddie Mac, the quasi-governmental agencies that guaranteed U.S. home mortgages. In normal times, those bonds trade smoothly, and their prices are readily ascertainable through bids from other Wall Street brokers, which meant Goldman could sell them easily enough and know exactly what they would fetch. That's what makes an investment liquid; it's as good as cash.

But during the course of the week, the bond market had seized up. Big gaps had opened between sellers' asking prices and what buyers were willing to pay, in some cases so big that trading dried up entirely. Even U.S. Treasury bonds, normally the most easily tradable financial asset in the world, couldn't be moved in chunks of more than a few million dollars at a time. Without an active buyers' market for these bonds, it was hard to assign them a dollar value, which left Hammack's staff flying blind.

An obscure government rule had added complications. Broker-dealers like Goldman are required to ring-fence cash, meaning that at least once a week, they have to tally up the value of trades that remain open—what they owe clients and what clients owe them—and put the difference aside in protected accounts that can't be touched. With markets now in turmoil, some of those positions were becoming nearly impossible to value. Keeping up with who owed what to whom, and how much cash Goldman needed to set aside in those "lock-box" accounts, was becoming a Sisyphean task.

If the tumult continued much longer, Hammack warned Scherr over the phone that evening, Goldman risked falling below minimum liquidity levels set by the Federal Reserve, which could force the bank to raise cash by quickly selling securities at fire-sale prices. Left unsaid was what would happen next, once word got out. Corporate borrowers, worried about Goldman's solvency, would max out their credit lines. Trading clients would demand extra collateral. Depositors would pull their cash. All of that could force another round of selling, which would result in yet more withdrawals.

Liquidity death spirals had killed investment banks before. In the fall of 2008, Lehman Brothers owned assets worth hundreds of billions of dollars but filed for bankruptcy anyway because it simply ran out of cash. Goldman wasn't anywhere near that scenario, but both Scherr and Hammack had been around long enough to know how this could end.

"Okay," Scherr said after Hammack finished. "Well, I think we should probably go back to the office first thing tomorrow and, you know, figure this out." He said he would come by at 6 A.M. to pick her up. Hammack had been in touch with a deputy in London, Laide Oginni, who was still crunching the numbers at past midnight local time, and now told her to go to bed. "We need you fresh tomorrow," she said.

Hammack picked up her gin and tonic, then thought better of it. She needed to be fresh, too.

By 8:30 A.M. on Saturday, two dozen Goldman executives had

assembled in a spartan conference room on the forty-first floor of the bank's headquarters in lower Manhattan, with views clear to the Statue of Liberty and New York harbor beyond. In addition to Scherr and Hammack, who had carpooled back in Scherr's black Mercedes SUV before dawn, the group included Sheara Fredman, the bank's controller; Brian Lee, its head of risk; Laurence Stein, its chief administrative officer; Phil Armstrong, head of operations, and his deputy in charge of operations for Goldman's trading arm, Ericka Leslie. The ad-hoc group had been assembled to figure out where Goldman's cash had gone, how much more they needed, and how they could get it.

THE FINANCIAL SYSTEM that faced down the turmoil now being spread by the pandemic was not the same one that had crashed in 2008, taking the global economy along with it.

New regulations put in place after that meltdown had reshaped Wall Street, reining in its freewheeling casino culture and shoring up banks' balance sheets. The Dodd-Frank reforms of 2010, the primary legislative response to the meltdown, had satisfied virtually nobody—the law was the result of backroom political compromise and barely squeaked through with a filibuster-proof sixty votes in the U.S. Senate—but they squarely tackled some of the root causes of the mortgage meltdown. Traders at big banks could no longer make giant wagers with house money, which was technically stockholder money but, as the 2008 crisis had shown, was really taxpayer money. Instead, they were recast as mere toll takers, collecting small fees for connecting a client who wanted to buy a stock or bond or barrel of oil with one who wanted to sell. Nor could they pile on huge amounts of borrowed money to juice their returns. Less debt meant banks would be safer and less likely to implode under stress.

Banks now underwent annual "stress tests," simulating how their businesses and vast holdings of securities would fare under a doomsday scenario dreamed up by regulators in Washington. The most recent version, in 2019, had imagined a recession that began in Europe and spilled over into the United States, in which the unemployment rate would hit 10 percent, the stock market would fall by half, and both home prices and interest rates would decline. It was pretty dire stuff to financial executives, and nearly every big bank had passed.

But that was a lab experiment, dreamed up by Washington bureaucrats who, as well-intentioned as they were, couldn't have imagined the living, breathing panic that was playing out in the middle of March 2020. Unlike in 2008, when a crisis in the financial economy spilled over into the real economy, the one where people bought homes and started businesses and traveled, the concern now was the opposite: that what began in the real economy would become a financial crisis. This one, whatever it would become, was not Wall Street's fault. But it was now Wall Street's problem.

The immediate issue was that exploding trading volume had gummed up the plumbing. Trade settlement, the arcane process by which securities are delivered to a buyer and cash is received by a seller, wasn't happening. The value of failed trades on Goldman Sachs's books—pending transactions for stocks, bonds, or other assets—was four times what it should have been by the second weekend in March. There were many reasons, none easy to untangle. Wall Street traders, also now remote, were slower to log trades. The back-office middlemen at custodian banks, which hold securities on behalf of clients, had similarly fallen behind in sending routing instructions.

Clients were also getting cagier about posting collateral. Open trades require both parties to wire cash or other high-quality assets to each other on a regular basis, depending on price changes in the interim. Some are easy enough to figure out: A bet on where Apple's stock price will be in three months can be evaluated with certainty. But more complicated trades are open to interpretation. And the chaotic markets, where asset prices were swinging violently every day, make those calculations even harder. By the second week of

March, the value of disputed trades—essentially, Goldman's ledger of disagreements with its trading partners about who owed whom and how much—was three times its normal level. At the same time, exchanges and clearinghouses were getting more aggressive about demanding collateral from the bank. What in normal times was a bustling two-way street had turned into a dead-end alley. Banks were stuck holding securities they hadn't planned for, without the cash needed to fund them. The result was a drain in liquidity.

Market volatility was being increased by the fact that Wall Street was working from home. Legions of traders now tasked with navigating the choppiest markets of their careers were no longer allowed on the trading floors, where cramped quarters violated the social-distancing guidelines that were now being communicated by public health officials. Goldman's four trading floors in New York, which typically housed three thousand traders, now held fewer than a hundred. Even backup sites in Greenwich and New Jersey were deemed unsafe.

Wall Street trading relies on a heavily digitized, choreographed real estate. Traders use multiple screens to monitor markets and place orders. Massive desktop phone banks provide split-second direct communication to bosses, other brokers, and top clients. Home laptops wouldn't suffice. (Home setups were also problematic from a regulatory perspective. Bank traders are heavily surveilled. Recording software monitors their phone conversations, and certain messaging apps—along with time-wasters like Twitter—are blocked.) Instead, bank executives in Manhattan loaded up Ubers and even their own cars to deliver hardware to keep the firm's vast trading operation, the heart of its money-making machine, humming.

THE SAME WEEKEND, six hundred miles away, a different conclave was under way. The chief executives of General Motors, Ford, and Fiat Chrysler—Detroit's Big Three automakers—dialed in to a conference call at noon on Sunday, March 15, organized by Rory

Gamble, who ran United Auto Workers, one of the country's most powerful unions. UAW represented nearly 400,000 American workers at Ford, GM, Fiat Chrysler, and other companies that produced parts for automotive and aerospace manufacturers.

The three car companies had sent their corporate workforces home starting on March 13, but the union's 150,000 factory workers didn't have that luxury. The health risks posed by a factory setting were obvious. Making cars is a hands-on job, with employees in close proximity handing off parts, congregating in break rooms, and swapping shifts operating heavy machines. A salaried member of the Kokomo, Indiana, local was the first UAW employee to test positive for the virus on March 12, and factory workers had started bringing their own hand sanitizer to plants across the Detroit area. Gamble had assigned his health and safety team to look into best practices for containing the virus. He also tasked the union's lawyers with digging into their contracts with each of the Big Three companies to see what their obligations were in the event of a health emergency.

Gamble had reached out earlier that week, trying to get the three CEOs on the line to discuss closing their U.S. factories as the virus was starting to tear through the country. His goal was to get the Big Three on board, and on record, with a quick and orderly shutdown of their assembly plants, and then use that momentum to do the same with component suppliers and other downstream players whose workers were part of the union.

The phone call was tense. General Motors had just months earlier gone through a strike with its UAW workers that led to a forty-day work stoppage and cost the carmaker, by its own math, up to $4 billion in lost productivity. And a lawsuit that General Motors had filed against Fiat, accusing it of bribing union officials to gain an advantage on its labor costs, festered in the background. (That bribery scandal had ousted the then-head of the union, putting Gamble in the job in November 2019.) Even getting all three CEOs on the line had been a challenge; the companies' lawyers had worried that getting together to discuss labor policy might be a violation of antitrust laws. The irony was obvious. Laws meant to protect workers—by preventing companies from colluding to decrease wages or increase hours—could now put them in harm's way. Gamble had spoken individually with Bill Ford, whom he'd known from his early days as an organizer at a Ford factory union, Local 600, as well as GM chief executive Mary Barra and Fiat Chrysler's chief executive, Mike Manley, and assured them his focus was only on health-and-safety protocols—and that he would avoid any sensitive discussions of production schedules, talk of which might run afoul of federal anti-collusion laws. Still, it had taken phone calls to the executives from Michigan's governor, Gretchen Whitmer, and congresswoman Debbie Dingell, whose district included many auto factories, urging them to do the right thing, to get the executives on the line.

On the call, Gamble pushed the CEOs for an immediate two-week shutdown. Manley pushed back, citing the problem of half-finished vehicles languishing on the assembly line. They would rust, and that was millions of dollars of materials lost. Maybe, Manley suggested, they could wind down the number of workers coming in each day to finish vehicles already in production without starting new ones. But Ford's CEO, Jim Hackett, quickly noted that idea's downside: "The virus doesn't care where the cars are" in the production process, he said. Mindful of their lawyers' instructions not to commit to any changes to their production schedules on the call, the CEOs waffled. They asked for forty-eight hours to come up with a plan.

MORGAN STANLEY HAD two confirmed cases of Covid-19 among its employees, one at its suburban campus in Westchester County, New York, and another in London: a banker who had spent the week before skiing in the northern Italian Alps. And now, on the morning of March 18, CEO James Gorman called them both to see how they were feeling.

Three days earlier he had attended an event at the Australian consulate in New York City, where he had received the country's highest civilian honor, for "distinguished service to the finance and banking sectors." He had wondered whether it was prudent to attend. Events were starting to be canceled across New York, and Governor Andrew Cuomo had banned indoor gatherings of more than five hundred people. This was set to be a far smaller affair, but even so, he had sent a note to the eighteen people attending as his guests, including his college-aged son and a cousin who had flown in from Australia, telling them he would understand if they bowed out. Everyone came anyway and watched the Australian consul general hang a medal around Gorman's neck, a local boy made very good.

Now he was back in his office on the fortieth floor of Morgan Stanley's Times Square headquarters, and he couldn't stop shivering. He had already had maintenance officials in his office once that morning to fix the air conditioning, which seemed to him to be going full blast, but it hadn't worked. He stuck his head out of his office and asked his assistant to get the maintenance guys back. He handed a piece of paper to an aide, joking, "I hope I don't have Covid."

It was early enough in the spread of the virus that jokes like that were still at least a little funny, in a winking sort of way. About 7,300 Americans had been confirmed sick with the disease, now in all fifty states, and 115 deaths had been confirmed from the virus. People were no longer shaking hands, replacing the ritual with showy elbow bumps or fist jabs, and hand sanitizer was the hottest commodity around. But nobody was wearing masks—in fact, government officials were recommending against it—and the idea that daily life would grind to a halt still, even now, seemed unthinkable.

But by early afternoon, Gorman was feeling crummier by the minute. The second run with the maintenance workers hadn't helped, and he had started to feel terrible by early afternoon. The lightbulb went off quickly, as it would for thousands of Covid's early patients, who knew rationally that this disease was out there but didn't believe they could be part of a global pandemic. He walked out of his office, hit the elevator button with his elbow, and wended through the throng in the cavernous lobby to the exit. He didn't want to expose his driver, so he walked the forty minutes to his home downtown and crawled into bed.

By the time he tested positive two days later, he was the firm's thirteenth confirmed case. He holed up in his apartment alone—he and his wife, Penny, had divorced two years earlier—and chugged Pedialyte to stay hydrated. He woke in the morning to sheets soaked through with sweat and a fresh container of chicken soup outside his door, left by his longtime assistant. He forced himself to eat it. He couldn't taste or smell anything. It scared him.

Still, Gorman tried to present an upbeat front. "I'm sick but I'm not ill," he told John Williams, the president of the Federal Reserve Bank of New York, who, as Morgan Stanley's chief regulator, Gorman felt ought to know. Then he told his board of directors. The question was whether to disclose his illness to the public. It was an unusual question for a board of directors, counterbalancing their duty to inform shareholders of material information with medical privacy. They agreed that as long as he stayed out of the hospital, they wouldn't need to. One other thing, he said: They should start thinking about who would take over the company if he died.

On the eighth day, he told his kids. On the phone, his twenty-four-year-old daughter ordered him to hang up and said she would call back on FaceTime. "I just want to see that you're okay," she said. Gorman, a keep-calm-and-carry-on Australian, choked up.

CHAPTER 10

GROUNDED

Doug Parker was driving through the western Tennessee scrubland when his phone buzzed. It was Saturday, March 14, and the American Airlines CEO was on his way home from Nashville, the trunk of his rental car stacked full of the trappings of a college dorm room. He and his wife had moved their daughter out of Vanderbilt, which like other universities across the country had canceled classes and told kids who could to go home. Now Parker was being told he was needed in Washington to lobby the White House for a bailout. Just a week earlier in an off-the-books meeting, he had told Mnuchin that the industry didn't need any money. That had changed dramatically.

Airlines had slashed the number of flights they were running by up to 70 percent. The planes that were in the air were practically empty. The U.S. government had announced a ban on travel to and from continental Europe the previous week, and then just three days later, had extended it to the U.K. and Ireland, which analysts expected would remove the equivalent of another one million aircraft seats from the market. It had been just ten days since Parker and the other airline CEOs had come to kiss the ring in the White House, and they had left with what they'd come for: Trump assured Americans it was safe to fly. Now he had changed his mind, telling reporters earlier that day, "If you don't have to travel, I wouldn't."

To the airline industry, it was a kick when they were already down. Bookings had plummeted—especially worrisome for the summer vacation season, when airlines bring in a large chunk of their revenue. Delta had finagled a less-than-ideal loan and announced plans to retire some of its planes permanently and park others in desert storage temporarily. United, whose top executives agreed to forgo their base salaries through at least the end of June, raised $2 billion from a group of banks and slashed planned capital spending by $2.5 billion. "At the risk of being alarmist," Helane Becker, a well-regarded Wall Street analyst, would write a few days later, "the airline industry is on the brink of collapse."

At an industry conference a few weeks later—held via webcast—Delta CEO Ed Bastian would say that anyone who tried to forecast the impact of the coronavirus on the travel industry through the economic lens of 2008 was misjudging it. It was more like the terrorist attacks of September 11, 2001. Nineteen years ago, passengers worried their seatmate was strapped to a bomb. Now those passengers worried their seatmate was carrying a deadly virus. "This is a fear event," he said.

It was William Douglas Parker, however, not Bastian, who was the only CEO of a major U.S. airline in 2020 who had been a CEO that morning back in 2001. He was thirty-nine years old then, and it was his tenth day on the job running America West, a money-losing regional carrier with a miserable service record and constant union strife. His company didn't lose any planes in the attack, but the drop-off in flying that followed nearly put it out of business. He staved off a bankruptcy filing by convincing the government to give his airline a $380 million loan guarantee in exchange for warrants to buy up to one-third of the company for $3 a share and a promise to cut costs. In the years that followed, he closed unprofitable hubs, started charging for in-flight food, slapped ads on the backs of seatback tray tables, and turned America West into one of the most efficient budget airlines in the country. In 2005, the same year he married a former flight attendant, he merged it with US Airways in a

$1.5 billion deal, the first industry tie-up since the terrorist attacks. America West's name disappeared, and its red, white, and green planes were repainted in US Airways's red and blue, but Parker took the reins of the combined company.

Impish and impulsive, Doug Parker was the mostly lovable rascal of the airline industry, with a moppish head of brown hair and a laugh that tumbled out in a high, raspy chuckle. He had run with the bulls in Pamplona and bungee jumped on his honeymoon. "I take huge pleasure in surprising people," he told an interviewer in 2005. From minor-league beginnings—it doesn't get any humbler than a regional carrier based in Phoenix—he had made it to the industry's majors, but had struggled to mature as a CEO. In 2007, he served a twenty-four-hour jail sentence for drunk driving, his third infraction. He had been pulled over in Scottsdale, Arizona, just hours after Delta had publicly rejected a $9.8 billion hostile takeover bid. He apologized and was swiftly forgiven. He was mischievous but masterful, winning over Washington and then Wall Street.

Six years later, US Airways merged with the far larger American Airlines, which had filed for bankruptcy. The deal created the world's largest airline. It was a gamble even for Parker, a regular at Las Vegas blackjack tables, where he would start out at the twenty-five-dollar-a-hand tables but upgrade to fifty dollars if he was feeling lucky. "As the largest airline in the world, we should be the most profitable," Parker had said the day the merger was completed. "We intend to be." In a sign of his bullishness, he took his pay exclusively in stock, becoming one of just five CEOs in the country at the time who didn't receive any cash as part of their compensation—and forcing him to cut the company personal checks of $10,000 to pay for his health insurance premiums, without a salary for it to be deducted from.

It hadn't worked out that way. The two airlines had different reservations systems, competing routes, and different union contracts. Parker and the scrappy band of executives who had followed him from America West spent years putting out fires. The company's two dozen Boeing 737 MAX planes were grounded in March of

2019 after two fatal crashes. A dispute that same year with union-ized mechanics, whom the company accused of slow-rolling repairs amid a contract dispute, led to thousands of canceled flights. Ameri-can missed its profit projections in 2018 and 2019, and papered over the holes with debt, some $33 billion worth by the start of 2020. It came into the pandemic as the largest but most heavily indebted of the big U.S. carriers.

Still, Parker was the only CEO of a major U.S. airline who had never been through bankruptcy, and he didn't intend to start now. He pulled his car into the garage of his home back in Fort Worth and quickly packed a bag and booked a flight for Washington. He'd done enough driving, and he was the CEO of the largest airline in Amer-ica.

PETER DEFAZIO WAS sitting in his office in the Rayburn building when his secretary buzzed. Nick Calio was on the phone—again. DeFazio was a veteran congressman from western Oregon, an edenic expanse bounded by the Pacific Ocean to the west and the Cascade Mountains to the east, dotted with vineyards in the north and log-ging camps in the southwest. The seventy-two-year-old Democrat was also the chairman of the House transportation committee, which made him just the person Calio, the airline industry's top lob-byist, needed to talk to.

DeFazio's committee was spearheading negotiations over the $50 billion proposed aid package for the industry, whose revenues had plunged in the two weeks or so since the American public had woken up to the health risks posed by the coronavirus. It was one of the largest emergency rescue lines ever dangled in front of American businesses. And while the broad idea had bipartisan support, there was little agreement over what it would look like, how it would be disbursed, and what strings would be attached to the money. Calio had been calling constantly for updates, and the congressman's pa-tience had worn thin. There was only so much he could do until he had assurances from the industry that they could get the necessary approval and concessions from their highly unionized workers.

DeFazio was brusque. "I'm not going to talk to you until you talk to labor," he said.

"You want me to call Rich Trumka?" Calio barked back, referring to the burly, mustachioed chief of the AFL-CIO, the country's largest federation of labor unions, including those that covered tens of thousands of aviation workers. "No," DeFazio said. "You need to call Sara."

Sara Nelson grew up in a small town in Oregon, the daughter of Christian Scientists. Statuesque and poised, she wanted to be a high-school English teacher, but after college, a heavy load of student loans necessitated a more practical route, and in 1996 she joined United Airlines as a flight attendant, based in Boston. She lost several friends on United flight 175, which left Logan Airport on September 11, 2001, and an hour later crashed into the South Tower of the World Trade Center. That tragedy, and United's bankruptcy filing a year later, spurred her to take a bigger role in the flight attendants' labor union, the Association of Flight Attendants, first as its spokesperson and, beginning in 2014, as its president. In five years on the job, she had not only become a fierce advocate for the 85 percent of aviation workers who were unionized but had also embraced a role as a camera-ready attack dog for organized labor, which had seen a decline in membership and negotiating power across the country. In a 2019 speech railing against the federal government shutdown, which had left TSA workers unpaid and not showing up for work, she called for a general strike to reassert the power of organized labor—a cross-industry walkout the likes of which hadn't been seen since the immediate aftermath of World War II.

In early March of 2020, she had sketched out a proposal for $25 billion in federal aid to keep airline workers—flight attendants, pilots, mechanics, gate agents, baggage handlers, dispatchers, and others—on the payroll. The proposal was an honest effort to avoid

At the World Economic Forum in Davos, Switzerland, in late January 2020, CEOs and world leaders gave little attention to the coronavirus, by then gripping China. "There's a city of twelve million people that's on lockdown," Treasury Secretary Steven Mnuchin barked to CEOs during a private dinner. *(Bloomberg Collection via Getty Images)*

Morgan Stanley CEO James Gorman, center, on his last trip abroad before lockdown. He told protocol officers for Saudi Arabia's controversial young prince, Mohammed Bin Salman, that he wouldn't be shaking hands.

Chris Nassetta's career was defined by crises—the savings-and-loan meltdown of the early 1990s, the dot-com crash, the 2008 financial crisis, and the pandemic, which emptied Hilton's hotels.

Bill Ackman and his wife, Neri Oxman, at the opening of Oxman's exhibit at the Museum of Modern Art on February 26, 2020. It was the investor's last night out in New York City. *(Photo by Austin Donohue)*

In January of 2020, Delta CEO Ed Bastian keynoted the Consumer Electronics Show in Las Vegas, where 200,000 people gathered, and boasted of the airline's innovations and bright future. *(Bloomberg Collection via Getty Images)*

Custodial workers cleaning the New York Stock Exchange after the closing bell on March 20, 2020, the day the exchange said it would close its iconic trading floor. *(Spencer Platt via Getty Images)*

"Here comes the cavalry," Goldman Sachs CEO David Solomon said, snapping a photo out his office window of the Navy ship *Comfort* as it steamed into New York harbor on March 30, 2020, to set up a makeshift hospital in the pandemic's epicenter.

The president's visit to a Ford factory to tour the company's production of protective gear in May 2020 was uncomfortable from the start. "I guess I have to wear a mask?" *(Brendan Smialowski/ AFP Collection via Getty Images)*

When the New York Stock Exchange's trading floor partially reopened on May 26, 2020, two months after closing down as a health risk, medical workers screened masked employees. The stock market crashed in the pandemic's early days, only to hit frenzied highs in its later months. *(Johannes Eisele/AFP Collection via Getty Images)*

"Space of One." The final investor meeting before Airbnb's IPO on December 10, 2020. The stock's trading debut the next morning valued the company, once left for dead, at $47 billion—above its pre-pandemic valuation—and made a billionaire of CEO Brian Chesky, bottom left.

the mass layoffs that were almost certain to happen if air travel remained at current levels. But it was also a naked power grab. It called for aviation unions, including the one she ran, to receive seats on airlines' boards to help set strategy and hold management to account. It wanted any airline that received federal aid to have to remain neutral toward union organizing efforts—a clear shot at Delta, where Nelson's union had been eyeing a union drive after several unsuccessful efforts in the past.

It also called for explicit protections for unions if any airline that received government money later filed for bankruptcy. Nelson had been through United's 2002 bankruptcy and seen workers lose pensions, accept steep cuts to pay and benefits, and lose flexibility in setting their schedules. Coming into 2020, the days of chronic airline bankruptcies seemed behind them. Now Nelson felt sufficiently spooked by the pandemic to urge specific protections in case they happened again.

She had sent the proposal to DeFazio on Friday, March 13, typing out an email as she walked through Reagan National Airport on a returning flight from a union convention in Orlando. He responded that Sunday with good news. Nancy Pelosi, the Speaker of the House, had agreed to adopt the proposal as the basis of the Democrats' negotiating position on what by then was shaping up to be the largest economic stimulus package in history.

Nelson was pleased, though by that afternoon she was already starting to feel crummy. She had deplaned in Washington with a clogged ear and spent much of the next few days chugging Lemsip, a British cold and flu drug.

TWO DAYS LATER, on a balmy Sunday afternoon in New York, executives of the country's biggest banks dialed in to a conference call. On the line were the CEOs of Goldman, Morgan Stanley, Bank of America, Wells Fargo, Citigroup, State Street, and Bank of New York, plus Gordon Smith, the co-president at JPMorgan, whose

CEO, Jamie Dimon, was still in the hospital, recovering from emergency heart surgery. It had been almost a week since their Oval Office meeting, which seemed designed mostly to reassure the nation that its banking system was safe. But financial conditions had continued to worsen, and the confidence they had projected in the White House was starting to wane.

Randy Quarles, the head of bank supervision at the Federal Reserve, had called several of them that week to relay that he was getting pressure from European regulators. Christine Lagarde, president of the European Central Bank, the continent's version of the Federal Reserve, had told him that the ECB was likely in the coming days to direct their banks to suspend their buybacks and their dividends. Lagarde had urged Quarles to push U.S. banks to do the same. Otherwise, she warned, European banks would be at a disadvantage to their American rivals. With no dividends, shareholders would sell their stock, which would require banks to pay more to fund their day-to-day operations. Quarles wasn't buying it, and he had said as much to the Wall Street CEOs he had spoken with that week.

His arguments found friendly ears in James Gorman, the Morgan Stanley CEO. Gorman felt strongly that keeping the dividends made sense. For starters, it wasn't that much money. Dividends accounted for about one-third of the biggest banks' capital-return practices; stock buybacks made up the rest. And it would send a dangerous sign to the market. Dividend cuts are seismic events on Wall Street, sending a signal to investors that a company doesn't have enough capital. "It would be creating a capital problem where none existed," he told the executives. They decided not to cut their dividends, at least not until Washington made them.

But they would throw Quarles a bone and agree to suspend their buyback programs. Dividends and buybacks are the two ways that companies return profits back to shareholders, but they aren't the same. Dividends are set, perhaps at 25 cents per share, and are designed to attract investors by promising them steady income. Stock buybacks, meanwhile, which boost the stock price by reducing the number of shares that corporate profits are spread across, are adjusted frequently and opportunistically. If cash is tight, a company might dial back. If the stock price dips and shares look cheap, it might jump in and buy.

They are different in another key respect. While cutting the dividend panics the market, shareholders barely notice when stock buybacks—which are done quietly and only announced at the end of each quarter—are curtailed. Since the 2008 crisis, regulators had pressured banks to keep their total dividend payments to about half the size of their buyback programs for precisely this reason: If the world got scary and cash ran low, the banks could curb their buybacks to preserve capital without having to cut their dividends and raise questions about their health.

It was a contentious decision. The nation's eight largest banks had spent $100 billion buying back their own stock in 2019, which had been central in dragging their share prices out of the 2008 crash. Was now the right time to be alienating stockholders?

Scharf, the Wells Fargo CEO, had a particular problem. He had joined just five months earlier to help clean up a scandal at Wells Fargo, which had been caught opening millions of fake accounts for customers who never asked for them, sometimes charging them fees. As punishment, the Fed had imposed an asset cap on the bank, meaning it couldn't take new deposits or make new loans or buy new assets. If Wells couldn't use its profits to buy back stock, Scharf worried, they would simply accumulate. The bank couldn't put them to more profitable use without testing the limits of the Fed cap, and pissing off regulators wasn't a rosy prospect to a CEO whose two predecessors had been washed out by scandal. Plus, the last thing he wanted to do was give investors any reason not to own his stock, which had badly lagged rivals since the fake-accounts scandal had surfaced back in 2016. He eventually relented, as did Bank of America CEO Brian Moynihan, who had also expressed reservations, and the vote was unanimous in the end.

CHAPTER 11

THE CAVALRY

Jerome Powell took his seat at the head of the polished mahogany-and-granite table in the Federal Reserve's boardroom, under a half-ton brass chandelier that dangled from the twenty-six-foot ceiling. The space, dedicated by Franklin Roosevelt in 1937, had once been a war room, playing host to talks between British and American military leaders during World War II. Now it was the front lines of another battle.

As the airline industry raced to secure a lifeline, another bailout of sorts was being assembled—this one for the financial system itself. Federal Reserve and Treasury officials were hastily putting together a half dozen lending programs that they hoped would calm chaotic trading markets and lessen the risk that what had begun as a health crisis would take down Wall Street and with it, the economy.

The Federal Reserve is the country's chief economic regulator and has a dual mandate of maximizing employment and keeping prices under control. It is tasked with keeping the economy growing at a steady, prudent clip rather than lurching from exuberant boom to painful bust. It has two primary tools at its disposal.

The first is interest rates. The government sets a target rate, known as the "federal funds rate," that serves as a baseline for all kinds of other economic activity, from what banks charge one another to borrow money overnight to what they charge homebuyers to take out a thirty-year loan. When the Fed wants to stimulate a sluggish economy, it lowers the federal funds rate to encourage banks to lend. When it wants to keep a runaway economy from overheating, it raises the rate. If the economy is a furnace, interest-rate policy is the bellows, letting in more or less oxygen to fan a fire on the verge of going out or tamp down one that is burning too hot. The federal funds rate rose as high as 20 percent in the early 1980s as a response to rampant inflation, and dropped to near zero in 2009 to help the economy recover.

The second way the Fed regulates the economy is by controlling the money supply, which it does by engaging in the buying and selling of its own debt. When the Fed buys back Treasury bonds from big banks and broker-dealers, it in effect creates new money, which is paid to the broker and eventually seeps into the economy, increasing the money supply. The reverse happens when it sells those bonds, as the cash it receives is taken out of circulation. These transactions, known as "open-market operations," were last used in size in the years following the 2008 financial crisis. The Fed bought back billions of dollars of its own debt, as well as that of quasi-governmental agencies such as Fannie Mae and Freddie Mac, in an effort to flood an ailing economy with cash that it hoped would be lent out, invested in new businesses, or used to purchase goods and services.

By the middle of March, what had started as a health crisis was quickly becoming a market crisis. Trading in Treasury bonds, considered the safest financial asset in the world and the foundation of the bond market, had become jumbled and frantic as investors sold what they could to raise cash. There were few buyers. Prices swung around wildly. There was even real concern that one of the weekly auctions of new Treasury bills would fail—that the group of two dozen banks and brokers, called primary dealers, who bid on U.S. government debt and move it out into the market, might refuse to buy it at all. That would be a once-unthinkable outcome reflecting cratering investor confidence in Washington and could threaten the dollar's standing as the world's reserve currency. Even in the depths of the 2008 financial crisis, the market hadn't looked like this. Things were even more disjointed in the markets for corporate bonds, municipal bonds, and the wide sea of esoteric instruments that companies and governments across the world depended on to literally keep the lights on.

The Fed had already stepped in once. Two weeks earlier it had cut interest rates and announced it would purchase billions of dollars' worth of Treasury bonds. But it hadn't been enough, and Powell had called an emergency meeting for that Sunday morning. Regional bank presidents dialed in from around the country, as did other participants who had been unable to appear in person, given the meeting's impromptu scheduling and concerns over the virus's spread. Randy Quarles, the banking cop, was stuck back home in Salt Lake City; he usually commuted to Washington on Sunday evenings and back again on Fridays. Lorie Logan, a top markets regulator, dialed in from the fortress-like headquarters of the New York Fed.

She summed up the situation: Markets were in turmoil. The Fed needed to do more—and quickly. All eyes turned to Powell.

Powell was something of an accidental chief of the world's most powerful central bank. A former Wall Street lawyer and investment banker who had worked in George H. W. Bush's Treasury Department before taking up a post at private-equity firm Carlyle, his career little resembled those of his immediate predecessors. Ben Bernanke, the plodding, soft-spoken scholar who had pulled the economy back from the brink in 2008, and Janet Yellen, the even-keeled PhD tapped by President Obama to continue its recovery, had been academics in their prior lives.

And while Bernanke and Yellen had cemented the perception of the Fed as aloof and academic, almost godlike in its remove from Washington's political circus, it was bare-knuckled politics that had put Powell in the job of Fed chair. In 2012, he had been foisted on the Obama administration to fill a vacancy on the Federal Reserve's board of governors after the president's previous two picks for the role had been filibustered by a Republican-controlled Senate. Five years later, with Yellen's term expiring, calls had come from around Washington for President Trump to reappoint her to a second term. In keeping with the perception of the Fed as above party politics, past presidents including Obama, Clinton, and Reagan had all renominated Fed chairs who had originally been chosen by a president of the opposite party.

Mnuchin lobbied for Yellen to be reappointed, but Trump was torn. He was mistrustful of Democratic holdovers. (He also thought Yellen, at just five feet, three inches tall, was too short for the job.) But he liked the tack she had taken at the Fed, in particular a commitment to not raise interest rates too quickly. Trump had built a real estate empire largely by borrowing from—and occasionally stiffing—Wall Street lenders and was enamored of cheap debt. And as president, he often boasted of the booming stock market, a consequence of low interest rates that pushed investors to seek returns in stocks instead of bonds. He didn't want Yellen, but he wanted someone who would continue her policies.

The president landed on Powell, who had by then spent six years as a low-key member of the Fed's board of governors. He had supported the low-interest-rate policy of Yellen's Fed. He had been deputized by Yellen to reach out to Republicans in Congress over the years and was a known entity by many GOP senators. He suited the president's aesthetic leanings, too: With a thick shock of silver-white hair—and brushing up on six feet tall—he was a central banker out of central casting.

And now, halfway into a four-year term, Powell had proven himself to be a more earthly kind of bureaucrat than was typical for the Fed. The oldest of six children born into a well-to-do Catholic family in Washington, D.C., he exuded not exactly warmth but energy and pragmatism. He had worked hard to quietly win over bipartisan support in Congress, stacking his calendar in the early days of his tenure with meetings on Capitol Hill. And he had tried in small but symbolic ways to peel back the curtain of secrecy around the central bank. In 2019, he had invited leaders from business, labor, and the nonprofit sector to the Federal Reserve's inner sanctum, its wood-paneled boardroom, under the slightly clunky auspices of an event dubbed "Fed Listens." As Powell acknowledged the room's specs, including the chandelier that he acknowledged might "lend a certain formality, even stuffiness" to the day's events, he said he hoped the conversation would be "anything but."

Now he sat under that same chandelier, facing the most dire economic situation in more than a decade.

To MANY INSIDE the government, the early days of the coronavirus pandemic bore some resemblance to the 2008 crisis. The S&P 500 index had fallen 20 percent between mid-February and the first week of March. Things were no better in the credit markets. Investors were refusing to lend even to blue-chip companies; on six straight days, no such "investment-grade" bonds, so called because of their high marks from credit-rating agencies such as Moody's and Standard & Poor's, were issued. The price of short-term debt, known as "commercial paper," that corporations rely on to fund their businesses overnight had skyrocketed.

The chaos had spread even into the deepest and most liquid market in the world—U.S. Treasury bonds. These are direct financial obligations of the U.S. government and are seen as the safest investment on the planet because America has never defaulted on its debt. They are the world's piggy bank, considered exchangeable for cash readily and with no impact on the price, and there are enough buyers and sellers that transactions are frictionless. Nearly $600 billion worth of Treasury bonds traded hands every day in 2019.

That had broken down in a matter of days. Brokers accustomed to moving $100 million or more of Treasury bonds in one fell swoop now found few takers for chunks as small as a few million dollars.

"The Treasury market is the foundation, the building blocks for the rest of the market, and the foundation is cracked," Rick Rieder, a senior executive at BlackRock, the giant investment fund, had told *The Wall Street Journal* on March 13.

There appeared to be no single cause, but rather a constellation of factors that threw sand into the market's gears. Wall Street traders were in the middle of a bumpy transition to working from home or remote backup sites, which meant that trades were happening more slowly. Regulations put in place after the 2008 crisis had made banks more resilient but less nimble, less willing to jump into malfunctioning markets to smooth them out. Hedge funds, lulled by years of calm in the markets, had bet big on that calmness continuing by placing wagers against certain measures of volatility. Those trades became unprofitable quickly when volatility soared, and their scramble to get out of them, or to sell other assets to raise cash to offset their losses, had only poured fuel on the fire.

The week before, the Fed had taken some unusual steps to calm the market, including offering nearly unlimited short-term lending to a group of twenty-four big banks, known as primary dealers, that act as the Fed's counterparties in financial markets. When the banks were slow to take the Fed up on those loans, it had pivoted to buying $37 billion in Treasury bonds on Friday.

None of it had been enough. The group gathered in the emergency meeting on Sunday was now tasked with a question: Should they cut rates to zero? Economists are an argumentative bunch by nature, and the group fiercely debated the issue. Loretta Mester, president of the Federal Reserve's regional bank in Cleveland, argued for a smaller rate cut, perhaps to between 0.25 and 0.5 percentage points. Cutting to zero, she argued, would use up all the Fed's firepower, leaving it with an empty gun if the economy continued to tank. (Central banks can take interest rates *below* zero. The idea is to make saving so unattractive—money sitting in bank accounts would dwindle—that people spend instead, spurring economic growth. Negative interest rates had been the reality across much of Europe since the mid-2010s, but the Federal Reserve had been loath to go there.) In the end, Mester was the lone dissent.

At 5 P.M., the Fed announced via a conference call with reporters what amounted to the most dramatic moves by the central bank in more than a decade. It announced an enormous bond-buying program, up to $700 billion—an effort to unclog the market and steady prices that had swung wildly as investors ran for the exits. It also lowered interest rates again, this time effectively to zero, to make it easier for companies and individuals to borrow.

The Fed was pulling both of the key levers it uses to regulate the economy at once. Lowering the interest the Fed paid banks on the money they kept at the central bank, Powell hoped, would encourage them to lend it out and keep afloat businesses that were being hammered by the intensifying lockdowns. And by wading back into the bond market, the Fed was assuming its role as the nation's lender of last resort and moving to un-gum markets that had seized up.

They were the central bank's most dramatic interventions in the financial markets in history and a sign of just how quickly the coronavirus had become an economic menace. And they would not be the last: In the weeks that followed, the Fed and Treasury Department would roll out one emergency program after another—to buy up short-term corporate debt, to keep money flowing to big banks, to rescue money-market funds and cash-strapped municipalities, to lend directly to big companies. Some of these programs had been pulled straight out of the 2008 playbook, wielded more decisively and in larger scale than a decade ago. Others were new and stretched the powers of the central bank. Powell would later admit the Fed had "crossed a lot of red lines that had not been crossed before" in its effort—ultimately successful—to keep the economy on the rails.

AT GOLDMAN'S HEADQUARTERS, Stephen Scherr, the bank's CFO, had tuned in to the Fed's press conference in his office on the forty-first floor. The executive suite, tomb-like even on a workday and normally abandoned on a Sunday night, had been a hive of activity since Saturday morning, when the bank's team of crisis managers had been summoned. Assistants had been called in to wrangle the phones, and someone had ordered food. The executives digested the central bank's announcement, which seemed to them smart and reassuringly fast. Back in 2008, it had taken the central bank months to enact similar policies to prop up ailing credit markets. This time it had acted inside of two weeks. Still, $700 billion was barely a drop in the market for U.S. government debt, barely more than a single day's worth of trading volume. And that cash would take weeks to work its way to struggling businesses and households, if it did at all. "This is good," Beth Hammack, the company's treasurer, said. "But it's not enough."

Powell knew as much, and said so to the reporters who'd dialed in to the Fed's conference. Economic regulation falls into two buckets. The domain of central banks like the Federal Reserve is monetary policy, using its twin levers of interest rates and money supply to keep the economy on an even keel. But fiscal policy—the job of collecting taxes and doling out government spending—is left up to the legislature. The Fed was doing what it could to calm financial markets but could do little to help households and businesses weather what looked increasingly likely to be a sustained recession. The kind of stimulus that would be needed to fight it was Congress's job. "We don't have those tools," Powell told reporters. "Fiscal response is critical, and we're happy to see that those measures are being considered. We hope they are effective."

When asked by Edward Lawrence, a reporter at Fox, whether the Fed would consider buying securities other than Treasuries and mortgage bonds, he said the Fed hadn't discussed it—and indeed, its legal power to do so was murky. "We don't have the legal authority to buy other securities other than the ones we already buy, and we're not seeking authority to do so."

The market wasn't buying the Fed's reassurances. Asian stocks opened lower when they began trading Sunday evening. U.S. stock futures fell 5 percent, dashing hopes across Washington and Wall Street that investors would be reassured by the U.S. central bank's decisive action.

Goldman's CEO, David Solomon, who had wrapped up his call about the buyback suspension and popped into Scherr's office two doors down from his own, keyed on the lead lining to the Fed's announcement. Since 1994, when the central bank had started making its interest-rate actions public, it had never cut them so quickly, not even during the worst of the 2008 meltdown.

"You can't think about it as a one-time trade," Solomon told his finance chief. Darkness had fallen and barge lights blinked on the Hudson River below. "People are seeing the Fed now acknowledging this is going to be a bad crisis and that the economy is going to be shut down for a period of time. It makes sense that equity prices are down."

By unleashing the U.S. government's financial firepower on chaotic markets, Powell had hoped to calm them. But in doing so, he had confirmed investors' worst fears. An economic crisis was coming.

CHAPTER 12

IT MIGHT BE ENOUGH

The airline industry's lobbying arm hadn't picked their Washington offices on Pennsylvania Avenue for the upper-floor views of the flight path in and out of Reagan National Airport, but it was a nice touch. On normal days, the group's chief executive, Nick Calio, could hear the fruits of his labors roaring over the skies of the nation's capital. When its member CEOs gathered for their quarterly meeting in the seventh-floor conference room, they did so to a steady backdrop of takeoffs and landings framed by the south-facing windows.

Now, on March 18, the skies were eerily quiet. The CEOs were still there, hastily convened to try to find the billions of dollars they needed to stave off bankruptcy, but the traffic had slowed to a trickle—a reminder of just how much trouble they were in.

American Airlines CEO Doug Parker had flown into D.C. the day before after spending the weekend driving back to Dallas from Nashville. Robin Hayes, the CEO of JetBlue, had driven down from New York, because schedules had been cut so far back that he couldn't get a flight. Munoz, the United CEO who had, in the March 4 meeting with Trump, called himself the "poster child" of a person at risk of getting seriously ill from the coronavirus, had ignored the advice of his doctors and come anyway.

It had been a week since Parker had nervously told Mnuchin that the industry would need $50 billion to stay afloat. The CEOs had come to Washington to figure out what that aid request should look like and how they would try to steer it through the political divide. In normal times, the executives sitting around the conference table on the third floor of the headquarters of Airlines for America were fierce rivals. Now they were united in begging their government for help. That day, March 18, fewer than six hundred thousand Americans would get on a plane: the fewest yet in the weeks-old crisis, down from more than two million at the end of February.

The document that the top lawyers at American, Delta, and United had previously hammered out had asked for $25 billion in grants. Now the industry's hole was twice that. There was no way, the executives knew, that the government was going to simply hand them $50 billion with no strings attached.

The CEOs turned to Mitch McConnell, the Senate majority leader. In a conference call on March 17, they pushed their case for outright grants. When the virus was eventually quashed, Gary Kelly, the CEO of Southwest, asked McConnell, did Washington want a thriving airline industry or a crippled one? Loans would saddle their balance sheets with debt and make it all but impossible, once the crisis had passed, to go back to hiring employees and investing in new planes and technology. "We want to take care of our people. We'd like to take care of our shareholders as best we can," Kelly said. But failure to get help would put the industry "teetering on the verge of bankruptcy."

McConnell, a shrewd politician known for holding his cards close to the vest, was unusually open. He had just flown home to Kentucky on a virtually empty plane, and told the CEOs he understood their predicament. "We are planning on moving way beyond the House bill," which he thought was too stingy in its corporate aid. "We'll sit here until we do. We have you all on our minds."

It all felt unreal to Parker. A week earlier, he had been in Selma, Alabama, with Nancy Pelosi, the Speaker of the House of Representatives, and John Lewis, the civil-rights hero and congressman, to commemorate the anniversary of Bloody Sunday, when Lewis and other protesters were beaten by Alabama state troopers as they tried to cross the Edmund Pettus Bridge on their way to Montgomery. There were small signs of concern—John Lewis, who had what would turn out to be terminal pancreatic cancer, had traveled on a separate bus to avoid sitting near anyone who might be carrying the virus. But it felt largely normal. The group had crowded into a table for ten for dinner. Now he was socially distancing as well as he could in a conference room, surrounded by fierce rivals—all united in begging their government for help.

"Social distance": an oxymoronic phrase that was an early and lasting addition to the pandemic lexicon. Public health experts recommended that people stay at least six feet apart, which was thought to be far enough for the droplets that are naturally cast aloft in conversation to fall harmlessly to the floor. All across America in the early weeks of the pandemic, the phrase and its awkward geographic implications were seen in physical form. Stickers with footprints appeared in grocery store checkout lanes and industrial assembly lines. Office buildings that were still open blocked off alternating desks and sinks. In New York, police repurposed electronic traffic signs that normally signaled roadwork and programmed them instead to remind amblers in Prospect Park to keep their distance.

The airline executives had decided that what they needed to do—beg the government for a bailout—needed to be done in person. And after all, none could claim they couldn't catch a flight to Washington.

Now, leaning into the speakerphone, Parker put a finer point on the industry's request for aid. "If this continues without assistance," he told McConnell, "there won't be an airline industry."

CONGRESS WAS WORKING on what would eventually become the $2 trillion CARES Act, as daunting a legislative feat as anyone could imagine. There was unanimous agreement that major government action was needed, but disagreements on just about everything else.

Democrats favored protections for workers and aid for beleaguered municipal governments, which were staring down a wall of mounting public health costs and declining tax revenues as businesses shuttered, and wanted tougher restrictions on big companies that received federal aid. Republicans were, as ever, wary of government overreach, more protective of big business, and less inclined to help out big-city mayors in coastal cities. Even the issue of how to aid Americans was controversial, with Democrats largely favoring federal aid to state unemployment offices and Republicans favoring direct payments to households.

The prospect of such a giant pot of money—the relief bill's price tag, which had started in mid-March at around $1 trillion, would more than double—had set off a rush in corporate America to get in line at the fiscal trough. Some industries could rightly argue they would be toast without help: The restaurant industry's lobby sought $325 billion. The travel industry requested $250 billion. Boeing wanted $60 billion. Others saw a chance to secure special breaks in a moment when the spigots seemed open. Adidas canvassed Capitol Hill for support for a provision it had long wanted that would allow people to use pre-tax money to pay for gym memberships and fitness gear, even as gyms across the country were closed. The nation's pig farmers, citing meat shortages, renewed their call for the federal government to expedite visas for foreign workers—despite the fact that international borders were shut. Drone makers wanted the Federal Aviation Administration to lift restrictions, noting that drones could provide touchless delivery of goods and medicine; a spokesman for the industry called it "the right kind of opportunism."

The airline industry, whose executives were still holed up on K Street, was lobbying for its own slice of the pie. Nick Calio had spoken with enough legislators on both sides of the aisle to assure the group that some kind of aid, likely tens of billions of dollars, was guaranteed. But congressional Democrats, who had taken the lead in crafting the legislation, were dead set against grants, which they viewed as a corporate giveaway. Mnuchin was similarly opposed to outright grants, and instead had proposed a low-interest loan that would offer the airlines money at below-market rates while protecting U.S. taxpayers from losses.

The CEOs now debated that idea. Gary Kelly, the Southwest chief, was open to it. "If someone is going to give us one-percent money for ten years, that's kind of like a grant," he said. Expected inflation over that period would more than negate the interest charged. But it was still debt, something few CEOs in the room could easily shoulder on their companies' already creaking balance sheets. Government loans would make it harder for them to borrow new money from private investors; nobody wanted to be behind the U.S. Treasury in line for payback. Plus, emergency loans in the wake of the 9/11 terrorist attacks had weakened airline balance sheets and helped tip several of them into bankruptcy in the years that followed.

They landed on a $50 billion proposal that was half grants that would be used to cover payroll and half loans that could be used for other purposes. They proposed the government set up a rainy-day loan fund that the airlines could tap, similar to the so-called "discount window" available to the nation's biggest banks.

Now the question was: What could they give in return? The group was particularly averse to caps on executive pay. Their view was that unlike the 2008 crisis, which had been caused by banks gambling recklessly, the industry hadn't created this problem. The CEOs were more open to limiting their stock buybacks and dividends. They didn't have the money anyway. The industry would also agree to keep serving the airports they had served before the outbreak.

Parker didn't want to furlough anybody. He'd spent years getting to a place where he could honestly tell employees they could come and expect a stable career, free of the bankruptcies and busts of the past. He had taken to attending the graduation ceremonies for American's flight attendants, where he would tell them, "If you want to have this job for fifty years, we're going to be here for you."

He suggested the companies agree not to furlough anyone,

provided the government aid covered their salaries. It made business sense to keep employees up to date on their training, which would make it easier to bring them back into service when demand picked up again. He also knew it was good politics. House Democrats were leading the effort to craft the bill, and he knew organized labor had their ear.

Parker tried to convince the other CEOs, including Hayes, who hinted at his reluctance. JetBlue was in a better financial position and didn't necessarily need the money, Hayes said, and the more economic and political strings that were attached to it, the less he wanted it. Munoz and Kelly told him they were in. But he was worried about Bastian, who hadn't joined the other CEOs in Washington and had sent Delta's head of government affairs, Heather Wingate, in his place.

Delta had a complicated relationship with the lobbying group. It had pulled out for a few years, figuring it could do more to advance its own interests in Washington with the annual $5 million dues, and had only rejoined in late 2019. There was also the financial reality that Delta, along with Southwest, was in stronger financial shape than rivals like American and United. Even in a moment of industry need, competitive hackles are hard to shake, and Parker worried that Bastian might be reluctant to take government money that would benefit his competitors more than his own company.

Parker buttonholed Wingate. "Is Ed going to be okay with this language?" He didn't want to be negotiating with a subordinate, only to have the boss say no at the last minute. She assured him that Bastian was on board.

Meanwhile, Parker was trying to put out fires closer to home. For more than a week, American had been negotiating with four Wall Street banks for a $1 billion loan, money it sorely needed. The company's chief financial officer, Derek Kerr, had called Parker that afternoon to tell him it wasn't going well. Bank of America had bailed, citing a problem with a ratings agency, which to a seasoned executive like Kerr sounded like the kind of thing bankers say when they don't want to lend the money. And now Goldman Sachs was wavering. That was $500 million, gone. Kerr had been hoping for another $250 million from Deutsche Bank, but they were now balking, too. Parker ducked into a storage closet and dialed John Waldron, Goldman's president and chief operating officer. Parker had his talking points in his head and was ready to make his case. But in a sign of how topsy-turvy the world was, it was Waldron who started in.

"Tell me what's going on there," he said, seeking details about how the aid negotiations were going. Parker wasn't sure whether his answer would color Goldman's decision on the loan—a bank might feel more comfortable lending to a company with government backing, or less comfortable lending to one desperate enough to need it—or if Waldron was just sniffing around for the kind of market intelligence that Wall Street thrived on. The airline negotiations had become a public sticking point in the broader rescue package. Goldman had a $1 trillion balance sheet full of investments whose value was swinging wildly as odds for the bill's passage waxed and waned.

Parker was confident that there was bipartisan support for some kind of package and told Waldron as much. Then he delicately brought up the matter of the loan. Goldman was back on board, Waldron assured him. "We're behind you," the banker said. Bank of America, too, was pulled back into the boat after Parker called Moynihan, the bank's CEO. (Moynihan had, in turn, called a senior investment banker and given him the green light—an unusual move by a CEO to get so directly involved in a single transaction.)

The airline CEOs flitted in and out during the afternoon with cellphones pressed to their ears, lobbying congressional members whose support for aid would be crucial. Kelly disappeared for a call with Senator Maria Cantwell. From his office back in Atlanta, Bastian lobbied Senators John Thune and Shelley Moore Capito—both Republican members of the Senate commerce committee, which has oversight of transportation.

Meanwhile, the TV was tuned to CNBC, which was displaying increasingly dire reports on the financial markets. The news channel's airline reporter, Phil LeBeau, came on. "I just talked to Gary Kelly," he said, sharing an update on negotiations between the industry, labor, and Congress. The executives in the room turned in unison to the Southwest CEO, who sheepishly shrugged his shoulders. He had ducked out a few minutes earlier to take a call from the reporter.

Things were moving fast.

AT ABOUT 7:30 that evening, Nick Calio walked into the conference room, hopping mad. "You're not going to believe this," the lobbying executive told the group. He had just received the proposal for airline aid that congressional Democrats were working on, and it had Nelson's fingerprints all over it.

The broad strokes were similar to what the airlines had put together—so similar, in fact, that some of the CEOs would suspect for weeks that someone had leaked the A4A plan and it had wound up in the union's hands. But it also included several proposals that seemed unrelated to the crisis and were instead pet issues of labor and the political left, including designated board seats for union representatives, a ban on using federal money to fight organizing drives, and strict limits on executive pay. As Calio shared the details, the air went out of the room.

Airline CEOs are no strangers to union strife, but negotiations are usually handled by lawyers and government-affairs staffers. Typically, only a handful of sticking points might make it up to the CEO's desk. Now they were wading through dozens of demands, some of which struck them as brazen power grabs that they would never agree to.

The mood shifted quickly from defeatism to combat. The CEOs would enlist Republicans in Congress to push back, working with allies on the Hill to get what they could. Age-old battle lines were being drawn. Industry and labor were retreating to their corners. Calio, a wine connoisseur, broke out a few bottles of red from his own custom blend, and weary executives and staff washed down the evening with Cantina di Calio, a 2016 Bordeaux.

SARA NELSON WAS still under the weather, working from bed in her Washington, D.C., home with her laptop balanced on her knees, when her phone rang. It was Parker, who had put down his wineglass and stepped out of Nick Calio's office.

"What are you guys *thinking*?" he said, sounding exasperated. "We're over here trying to save this industry and we get this language that has three-quarters of the people in the room saying, 'the hell with it.'" The union's proposal, including demands that seemed to have little to do with addressing the crisis at hand, was a nonstarter for the CEOs, he told her.

She responded with high dudgeon befitting a seasoned labor advocate. "Haven't they ever heard of negotiating?" she shot back.

Parker sighed. "Sara, this is not a time to negotiate," he said. He knew the coalition of airline CEOs, fragile to begin with, was fraying quickly. "This is starting to fall apart. Can you come over?"

Nelson swept her hair into a ponytail, put on a sweatshirt emblazoned with the logo of the March for Our Lives gun-control movement, and pulled on knee-high boots over her jeans. As she settled in behind the wheel of her car, she got a lump in her throat. She hadn't consulted with anyone. No lawyers, no union staffers. Union negotiations are usually heavily scripted affairs, with official memos sent back and forth between a phalanx of lawyers. She was flying solo.

She called Peter DeFazio. The two knew each other well: DeFazio, in Congress since 1987, represented Nelson's hometown district in Oregon, and she got to know him a little bit in the 1990s, when she would bid to crew United flights from Oregon to Washington, D.C., so she could go visit her parents. They became closer after she was named president of the union. (An episode in the early 2000s endeared him to flight attendants everywhere: Congress held hearings to investigate the spraying of pesticides in airplane cabins, and after an industry representative testified that the debugging was safe, DeFazio took out a can of Raid and said he was sure the representative wouldn't mind if he sprayed the pesticide on his seat in the hearing room.) He had been named an honorary member of the union in 2015.

Nelson told him she was on her way to meet the airline CEOs and try to broker a compromise that both industry and labor could get behind. "You're going by yourself?" he asked her, confirming the knot in her stomach, then wished her luck. "Keep me posted. I'll be up."

She drove through deserted Washington streets, arriving at the A4A headquarters, two blocks east of the White House. Security had left for the evening, so Munoz, the United CEO, met her at the door. He had left for the night already but had been called back; owing to Nelson's past work as a United flight attendant, the group thought the presence of the CEO of her onetime employer might be helpful in brokering a peace. She was touched. The science on the coronavirus was still sketchy, but public health officials had warned that people with underlying health conditions were at higher risk.

The warm feelings didn't last long. Circular discussions in the conference room went nowhere for more than an hour. The airline CEOs resisted calls to put representatives of labor unions on their boards of directors and were unwilling to promise not to seek concessions on their union contracts.

Nelson had had enough. During a break, she motioned to Parker and Munoz and ushered them into a small side room. The two airline executives looked like hell, in rumpled suits with deep bags under their eyes.

"The public hates you. You do not have any political goodwill," she said. Any mention of bailouts would turn the public and Congress against the industry, she warned. Nelson held herself out as their best hope. "If we shape this as a workers-first package, we can get it done," she said. Keeping people employed was a universally popular notion, even in a bitterly divided Congress. And with two million aviation workers in the United States, almost everyone in the country knew someone, or knew someone who knew someone, whose livelihoods were at risk. She tapped on her iPhone to pull up a list of the union's proposals, only to realize she had an outdated version, and quickly placed a call.

"You sent me the wrong one," she barked into the handset. "Send me the other one." Parker overheard her end of the conversation and assumed she was chewing out a union underling who had sent the wrong attachment. "All right, Peter, thanks," Nelson said in a clipped tone and hung up. Only then did the CEO realize she was talking to DeFazio, a sitting U.S. congressman and the chairman of the committee they were all hoping would come to their rescue. Nelson, he now understood, had the ear of the congressional Democrats and was calling the shots. Armed with the latest version, she ticked off the demands one by one to the two CEOs. Munoz occasionally put his head in his hands.

A combination of reason and fatigue won out, and a tentative truce was struck near midnight. The airlines, represented by the CEOs and Calio, and labor, represented by Nelson—who assured them she could get other aviation unions on board—agreed to lobby together in Congress for $25 billion in payroll grants. As long as Congress was covering labor costs, nobody would be furloughed. They agreed to disagree on the rest.

It was after 1 A.M. when Parker trudged through the front door and out into tomb-like city streets. He turned to his head of government affairs, Nate Gatten. "It might be enough," he said.

JONNY FINE's PHONE wouldn't stop ringing. A veteran of the corporate bond market, he oversaw Goldman Sachs's investment-grade syndicate desk, managing an army of bankers who helped blue-chip companies sell bonds to investors. It had been a tough sell the past few weeks. With the market in turmoil, it was all but impossible for even highly rated companies to find investors willing to buy newly issued debt. In the week before the Fed's Sunday night announcement, just a handful of new deals had been completed. On one recent day, March 9, just a single investment-grade borrower had been able to complete a bond offering—Johns Hopkins University, which was quickly becoming a household name as a clearinghouse for Covid-19 data.

But now, pacing his patio in suburban New Jersey, Fine saw signs of a thaw. That Tuesday morning, the forty-five-year-old banker was gauging investors' interest in new bond issues from blue-chip companies including Verizon and PepsiCo and getting a warm reception. Not only that, but several investors he spoke with countered with an offer: If Goldman were interested in raising some cash for itself, they would be interested in buying its bonds. To Fine, a fast-talking, shaved-headed Brit, it was a sign that the market was back.

Goldman was very interested. Hammack's team had spent the weekend doing the big-bank equivalent of digging through the couch cushions, chasing down stalled wire transfers and shifting certain trades to subsidiaries where they could be funded more cheaply. They had come up with some liquidity, but it was clear they needed more. Fine relayed the gist of his conversations with investors to Hammack, who immediately saw the opening. "You're my bankers, too," she told Fine and Gaurav Mathur, another senior banker. "Go see what you can do."

Hammack was still worried that the bank's liquidity levels would drop below minimum levels required by regulators. Even if it was a temporary glitch, it would bring a paperwork headache because banks must quickly file plans with the Federal Reserve explaining how they will make up the shortfall. And if it leaked, it would spook clients and investors, who might take their business—and their cash, which was crucial to funding Goldman's day-to-day operations—somewhere else.

But it wasn't just fear that was tilting Hammack toward the idea of raising new money. Goldman had made its biggest killings in times of crisis, when it plunged in as others drew back. The firm's best year on record hadn't come in 2007, the peak of the precrisis boom on Wall Street, but rather in 2009, when rivals had retreated to lick their wounds. The bank had made $20.8 billion in profits that year, nearly all of it from its securities-trading operation.

Goldman's leaders now saw a similar opportunity. This wasn't a time to step back, but rather to lean in—to seize profit opportunities and prove to the market that when things got tough, Goldman Sachs would show up. But to do that, it needed cash. Armed with crucial intelligence gleaned from Fine and its other bankers and traders that investors were tiptoeing back into the market, Goldman decided to float a bond offering.

Companies often put out press releases signaling their intention to sell new bonds, to help pique investor interest and soften up the ground. But if word got out that Goldman was trying to raise cash, it could be interpreted as a sign of weakness. So Mathur and Fine got their orders: Quietly gauge investors' interest. Raise as much as you can get and don't worry too much about what it costs. Scherr, in the middle of updating Goldman's board of directors by phone on the bank's plans, texted Hammack repeatedly, seeking updates from the trading floor.

By the end of the day, Goldman had sold $2.5 billion in thirty-year bonds paying an interest rate of 3 percentage points over the baseline government rate, joining a gold rush of blue-chip companies that had seized on a window of opportunity. The debt was more expensive than Hammack had hoped, but the deal had gone smoothly, and the bonds had traded well in the early going. Take the win, especially in a world with so few. Her ambivalence was shared by weary bond investors and captured in a quote that Tom Murphy of investment manager Columbia Threadneedle gave to *The Wall Street Journal:* "Any day the markets are functioning is a good day."

The sandbags were packed, at least for now, at dozens of America's blue-chip companies—and at their go-to investment bank.

CHAPTER 13

—

FUCKING INTERESTING

Gregg Lemkau looked out over the glittering ocean at the Kukio Golf and Beach Club in Hawaii. Carved into the lava of the main island's Kona coast, the private community was actually a breakaway from the neighboring Hualalai resort, whose homeowners decided they needed a more exclusive enclave. Hualalai had a Four Seasons hotel and was open to day-trippers; at Kukio, members paid $66,000 in annual dues for the privilege of plunking down millions more on property. It had become popular with Silicon Valley's elite, many of whom hopped a private shuttle known as the Kona Express, with twice-weekly flights from Oakland. But it didn't discriminate among billionaires, and counted some of Wall Street's heaviest hitters as members, too. George Roberts, co-founder of private-equity firm KKR, had a home there. So did Warren Buffett's sister. Ken Griffin, the head of hedge fund and trading giant Citadel, once had two.

Lemkau, co-head of Goldman Sachs's investment bank, had bought a home there in 2016, and that morning in late March of 2020, like every morning in the week since he'd left an eerie New York with his wife and kids, he had woken up at 2 A.M. to try to stay connected to his employees. A short distance away, a snorkeling beach that usually teemed with tourists was deserted. He called Egon Durban, a senior executive at private-equity firm Silver Lake, who was just a few hundred yards away, ensconced inside his own home in the island community. In the past, the two would walk the beach and kick around investment ideas—Lemkau the consummate Wall Street banker, full of ideas and energy, and Durban a seasoned investor with an appetite for risk. But now that was out of the question. Lemkau could probably have hurled a baseball and hit Durban's roof, but health experts were warning against in-person contact, so he made his pitch over the phone.

"Have you guys ever looked at Airbnb?" Lemkau asked.

Airbnb had hurtled its way to a $31 billion valuation and made a star of its young chief executive, Brian Chesky. But it was in trouble now. Bookings had evaporated as vacationers canceled trips. And like other tech startups, it was unprofitable, spending heavily on marketing and talent and subsidized services for its customers. It relied on a steady stream of cash that was now at risk of drying up. Lemkau hinted that the company was looking to raise some money and gently prodded to see whether Silver Lake, with its billions of dollars of firepower, would be interested.

In fact, he was being coy. Just a week earlier, Airbnb had hired Goldman and another investment bank, Morgan Stanley, to help it raise money. Chesky had proven himself skilled at managing Wall Street, effectively pitting its two heavyweights against each other in the race to find Airbnb what it badly needed: money. He had tasked Goldman with finding equity investors who would buy private stock in the company, while Morgan Stanley was leading negotiations with a group of banks who held Airbnb's existing $1 billion revolving loan and devising a plan to raise additional debt if needed. The two banks had been Airbnb's go-to advisers for years and had been hired in 2019 to help plan an IPO for mid- or late 2020. But the coronavirus had changed their assignments. Chesky had been monitoring worrisome signs that showed the company's Chinese business cratering, and the trouble had spread to its businesses in Europe and the United States—its largest market by far—mirroring the virus's spread. The IPO he had sketched out over Christmas would have to wait.

Airbnb had about $3 billion in cash in the vault, a massive sum by most standards, but Chesky knew it wouldn't last long. His company had been burning money even before the coronavirus had upended its business, and the refund requests were piling up. So he turned to the same two banks to help pack financial sandbags.

The Goldman team had already reached out to deep-pocketed investors, and three private-equity firms were interested: TPG, Dragoneer, and General Atlantic. All three were existing investors; TPG had led a 2014 fundraising round that valued the company at $10 billion and vaulted it into the elite ranks of the Silicon Valley "unicorn" club. It now seemed interested in doubling down. Dragoneer's chief credential for inclusion was a 2016 investment in Spotify, the music-streaming service, that was similar in structure to what Airbnb was now seeking: a debt investment that would convert into shares of the company at a discounted price when it ultimately went public.

But any good banker knows the key to Wall Street dealmaking is to create a bidding war. And Durban's firm, Silver Lake, was a good bet. The firm had carved out a reputation as a savvy investor in technology companies. It wasn't a traditional venture capital firm that invested in early-stage startups in the hopes of gigantic returns; rather, it favored more mature, proven companies like Dell, the computer giant that it had taken private in a 2013 buyout that had proved to be one of the most successful deals on Wall Street in decades. Silver Lake had also emerged as something of a white knight in the early days of the pandemic. It had invested $1 billion in Twitter just a few weeks before and would, before the month was out, throw a financial lifeline to travel-booking site Expedia. Would they take a look at Airbnb? Lemkau asked his old friend.

"Brian Chesky is the kind of guy you want to back," Lemkau said. He reminded Durban that some of Silver Lake's best investments had been backing visionary founders, ticking off Michael Dell and Jack Dorsey. "He's the real deal."

Durban was politely dismissive. "I just don't know the business well enough to take a view in the middle of all this," he replied. In fact, that very morning, he had warned Silver Lake's top dealmakers in an internal meeting to tread carefully. Good companies desperate for cash could be bought cheaply, but "don't go throwing money at a company like Airbnb," he had said, calling out the home-sharing company by name.

But he trusted Lemkau's opinion. The two were friends in addition to being neighbors in Hawaii. They had done dozens of deals over the years, many of them, like the Dell takeover, which had made Silver Lake billions of dollars. He promised to give it some thought.

LESS THAN A mile away, another iron had been laid on the fire. Alan Waxman, the head of investment firm Sixth Street Partners and another Kukio resident, had also connected with Lemkau at his vacation home on the island. The two knew each other well. Waxman, an energetic forty-four-year-old Texan with a surfer-dude vibe, had spent more than a decade at Goldman before leaving in 2009 to start Sixth Street, with financial backing from TPG, and had since then hired steadily from his old firm—sometimes to Lemkau's chagrin as he saw his own bankers plucked away. But Sixth Street was smart money: In the decade since its founding, the firm had consistently delivered high returns to its investors, mostly by looking at niche investments and constructing complex deals that provided substantial upside but, more importantly, protected the firm from meaningful losses. Its deals tended to be complicated, even for Wall Street, with intricate terms that companies couldn't readily get elsewhere and which churned out reliable returns for Sixth Street.

Waxman had heard through the Silicon Valley whisper net that Airbnb was considering raising money. "Board meeting Wednesday," a venture capitalist had texted him one day in mid-March. "Recent performance is awful. No new bookings, and lots of new refunds. Unclear what the bottom will be, or if we are there yet." Airbnb was looking for a "Spotify-like deal," the tipster said, a reference to a convertible-debt transaction that Dragoneer had done in 2016. That reference was enough to pique Waxman's interest. The Spotify deal had been a home run for investors when the music-streaming service later went public.

"We're very interested," Waxman texted back. Sixth Street wasn't a venture capital firm, and in fact, Waxman had been warning for more than a year that Silicon Valley was a disaster waiting to happen as investors outdid one another slapping sky-high valuations on un- profitable startups. Waxman thought that Airbnb's most recent valu- ation of $31 billion was too high. But he thought there was enough value in what Chesky had built, Silicon Valley hype or not, to be worth backing. Sixth Street could loan Airbnb a substantial amount of money and also receive warrants to buy the stock down the road. He quickly called Jon Winkelried, the co-CEO of TPG, the private- equity firm that Sixth Street was in the midst of a separation from. He knew TPG was an investor in Airbnb, and he wanted to make sure that if Sixth Street made its own bid, he wouldn't be ruffling feathers. "You're good," Winkelried told him.

Waxman's next call was to Durban. He didn't know that Lemkau had pitched the Silver Lake executive just the day before. But Wax- man was thinking about offering Airbnb a $2 billion investment, and that was a lot for a firm of Sixth Street's size, with $34 billion of assets, to take on by itself. Silver Lake, with its deep pockets and sterling reputation among technology companies, could be a good partner. "You know, I just got a call on this," Durban told him. "I said I wasn't interested."

"Well, I think it's fucking interesting," Waxman said. "Let me tell you what we're thinking."

He walked Durban through the deal Sixth Street was consider- ing. The firm would make a $1.5 billion loan that charged about 11 percent a year in interest and would receive warrants to buy about 1.75 percent of Airbnb's stock in the future at a steep dis- count. The price of those warrants ascribed Airbnb a valuation of about $15 billion, less than half of what the company had been valued at in 2017, the last time it had raised money. "The best companies are made coming out of crisis," he said.

Durban was impressed. Lemkau's endorsement of Chesky was still ringing in his head. And the deal Waxman was proposing was conservative enough that Silver Lake was unlikely to lose money. If Airbnb went public at anywhere near its most recent valuation of $31 billion, the warrants would be the equivalent of found gold. Even at a lower figure, Silver Lake and Sixth Street's investment would be senior enough—that is, in line for any cash payouts ahead of venture capital firms and others that owned Airbnb's stock—that they would likely still make money.

Plus, deal envy runs deep on Wall Street. If the deal was good enough to interest Sixth Street, a firm with a reputation as a winner, it was worth looking at. And if Durban could throw an elbow at TPG, a longtime rival, all the better. He hung up and called Lemkau. "Actually, I might be interested in this thing," he said, adding that he'd be happy to team up with Sixth Street. "We know the tech side. They know the structuring side."

On March 27, Sixth Street sent an offer to Airbnb—a $1 billion loan, plus an additional $500 million in debt that would convert to shares of the company.

It was an audacious lifeline to throw. Plenty of smart investors and TV commentators were leaving Airbnb for dead. Who would want to go stay at a stranger's house in the middle of a pandemic? With stay-at-home orders in place in many major American cities, doing so might even be illegal. But for Silver Lake and Sixth Street, the deal epitomized that old Warren Buffett aphorism: It pays to be greedy when others are scared and scared when others are greedy. Most of Wall Street was scared. Durban and Waxman could afford to be greedy.

Airbnb countered the proposal, but only slightly. It didn't flinch at the 11 percent interest rate the loan would charge—it was expensive, but the world was bad and getting worse, and debt in times of crisis was expensive. And the deal looked more attractive than a competing equity investment proposal from TPG, which would have dramatically lowered the value of existing shares in the company held by its early investors, founders, and employees. Airbnb countered with warrants for just 1.5 percent of the company, rather than the 1.75 percent the investors had sought.

Meanwhile, a wrinkle had emerged. Morgan Stanley's bankers had been advising Airbnb on its negotiations with a group of banks to amend the company's existing $1 billion loan, which needed to be extended to allow for a new investment. A March 25 call with those banks hadn't gone well. Banks across Wall Street were being inundated with clients drawing down lines of credit and begging for new loans, and many of them were on edge. One of Airbnb's existing lenders, Bank of America, was refusing to increase and extend the loan without a large increase in the interest rate.

Morgan Stanley's bankers saw an opportunity. "Let's scrap the revolver," Michael Grimes, the firm's top banker in Silicon Valley, suggested, referring to the bank loan. It was an elegant solution that would solve two problems at once. It would sidestep Bank of America's skittishness and would clean up Airbnb's balance sheet to take on new debt as part of the Silver Lake deal. Most companies are limited in how much debt they can carry, either as a practical matter—debt requires cash each year to pay interest—or to avoid unsettling their stockholders, whose money sits behind that of creditors in the line of seniority. An Airbnb executive later called it a "Houdini" move, a seemingly simple escape from a complicated problem.

One problem: Durban had never met Chesky, Airbnb's CEO, and Waxman had met him only a few times, years earlier. Now they were being asked to pony up as much as $2 billion in a matter of days, and they knew as little about the CEO they'd be backing as they did about the internal finances and workings of the company. They did due diligence—Wall Street–speak for sharing internal information with potential investors—over a series of Zoom meetings.

News of this deal hit the tape on April 6. Silver Lake and Sixth

Street were each investing $500 million in Airbnb in a deal that valued the company at $18 billion, a far cry from its last valuation of $31 billion. At the same time, Airbnb said it would ask its hosts to shift toward longer-term stays, hoping to tap into the same urge, especially among city dwellers, that had sent Lemkau, Waxman, and Durban to extended stays in Hawaii in the first place.

Waxman's phone rang almost immediately after the news hit the wire. "What are you thinking?" came the booming voice of Jeff Weiner, the former CEO of LinkedIn and a Silicon Valley veteran.

Waxman sighed. He'd been taking flak from every direction in the few hours since the Airbnb investment had been announced. Investors and experienced executives, many of whom he deeply respected, were flummoxed that anyone would invest in a travel company right now. Nobody was leaving their homes for a carton of milk, much less traveling.

But Waxman was ready to defend his deal. People would eventually go stir-crazy, he told Weiner. And when they did, they would prefer the private setting of an Airbnb rental over the hubbub of a hotel, with crowded elevators and maids coming in and out. Plus, he told the tech veteran, the way the deal was structured, it was almost impossible for Sixth Street and Silver Lake to lose. Their money was at the top of the heap. As long as Airbnb was worth about $2 billion, they were protected. The deal they had just struck valued the company at $18 billion. The only scenario Waxman could imagine for $16 billion being wiped out was another Great Depression.

"Jeff, listen," he said. "If Airbnb isn't worth $2 billion, we've all got bigger problems."

THE SKIES ABOVE Doug Parker's office were quiet. Too quiet, he thought. Once, nearly a thousand daily flights in and out of the DFW Airport had passed over his head. Now there were so few that he knew the sound of the 2:35 P.M. from Charlotte without even checking. Before the pandemic, more than two million Americans boarded a plane each day. When he and his fellow CEOs gathered in Washington, it was six hundred thousand. Now, by the second week of April, it was fewer than one thousand, 5 percent of its peak just a few months earlier.

Never before had demand for air travel dropped so far, so fast, for so long. It was entirely possible that demand for *any* product had never before collapsed with the same speed and totality with which Americans stopped wanting to be on airplanes.

CHAPTER 14

HELL IS COMING

"There's an answer to this problem," Bill Ackman told his wife. It was the morning of March 18 and the two were lounging in bed at their weekend home in Bridgehampton. The number of Americans diagnosed with Covid-19 had tripled in the past three days to 9,200, a trend line that Ackman knew how to read. "It's so simple," he told his wife. "I have an obligation to say something. I should scream it from the rooftops."

The savior complex was classic Ackman. He dug into a company's numbers as deeply as anyone on Wall Street, but in the course of rolling them out, his investment ideas tended to morph from deeply researched financial wagers into holy wars waged on society's behalf. He had spent years campaigning against vitamin supplier Herbalife, which he accused of being a pyramid scheme that preyed on Hispanic immigrants, making them push its protein powders and vitamin shakes on their friends and neighbors and recruit them into the company's sales force. During a three-and-a-half-hour presentation in 2014 meant to convince investors and regulators that he was right, he choked up talking about his grandfather, a tailor's apprentice, who came to America in the nineteenth century. Herbalife's stock, which Ackman had bet $1 billion would collapse, continued to rise. Five years later, Ackman conceded defeat and sold out, ending a fight he had once said he would take "to the ends of the earth."

When he lost a battle for control of Target Corp.'s board in 2009, he had teared up as he quoted John F. Kennedy. "We will pay any price, bear any burden, meet any hardship," he told a roomful of Target shareholders. The episode burnished his reputation for pouring his emotions and ego, not just his money, into his ideas. Critics would say it blinded him to reality and caused him to hold on to losing bets longer than was wise. Supporters said contrarian ideas needed true believers behind them.

By mid-March, the idea that the coronavirus would tank the U.S. economy had sparked that same grandiosity. So Ackman, who had kept a low online profile in recent years amid a string of catastrophically bad investments, took to Twitter for the first time in more than a year. "Mr. President, the only answer is to shut down the country for the next thirty days and close the borders," he tweeted. "We can end this now. The rest of the world will follow your lead."

It wasn't just altruism at work. To Ackman, the solution—a short but swift shutdown of America—was so obvious that it was bound to happen. He fully believed that Trump, confronted with the science, would implement a nationwide lockdown to contain the virus, sparking a recession that would be ugly but fast. Science would prevail. The market rout would reverse. This would all be over in a couple of weeks.

That's why he had told his traders to plow much of the profits from his giant swaps trade back into stocks. Pershing Square added to its holdings of Hilton, Burger King parent Restaurant Brands International, and Lowe's, the home-supply chain, and had bought stakes in Park Hotels and Google. Over the past six days, Pershing Square had bought an additional $2.05 billion in stocks on the theory that the government would—had to—shut down the economy. The virus would pass and markets would rally. It was a classic play for Ackman, an investment thesis wrapped in public-minded nobility.

Soon after he pushed send on his tweet, Ackman's phone rang. It was Scott Wapner, an anchor at the financial news network CNBC. He wanted Ackman on his show around lunchtime to discuss his call to arms.

It was Ackman's first television appearance in more than two years. He could hear the TV muffled from the basement, where his elderly parents were watching, and choked up. Zoom hadn't yet become widespread, so he was calling in rather than appearing on video, and the studio's audio feed was choppy, leaving him unsure at times whether the anchor could hear him. He filled the silences himself, turning in a twenty-nine-minute interview—a veritable monologue in an age of sound bites—that set Wall Street aflame.

"Hell is coming," he told the financial news channel's audience. "We need to shut it down now." America "will end as we know it," he said, "unless we take this option." The second half of his screed— him saying that he was bullish on stocks and was actively adding to his positions—got overshadowed. Even before Ackman had finished speaking live on CNBC, the Dow Jones Industrial Average started to fall sharply. It was already down more than 1,000 points when he went on the air, and it dropped far enough as he spoke that another automatic trading halt was triggered. "Please get Ackman off CNBC before people start jumping off bridges," fellow hedge fund investor Mike Novogratz wrote on Twitter. The Dow would close down 6.3 percent that day, wiping out more than three years' worth of gains.

Over the next few days, Ackman would be blamed for sparking panic. Conspiratorial-minded critics accused him of fanning the flames with apocalyptic positions in an effort to increase the value of his swaps, which would become more valuable as the market fell. In fact, he had already sold that position and was long on U.S. stocks. And his CNBC interview had come against a drumbeat of other worrying news that had spooked investors: Delta Air Lines announced that its monthly revenue was down $2 billion, Detroit's Big Three automakers were shutting down their U.S. factories, and New

York City officials said they were drawing up plans to convert hotels into hospitals.

As he hung up with Wapner, the CNBC anchor, Ackman felt confident he'd sounded the alarm and laid out a clear plan to avert disaster, unaware that he had instead clanged one off the rim. He would soon have to defend his fire-and-brimstone TV appearance against criticism that he was deliberately talking down the market while holding a "short" position that would benefit when it did. In a series of letters to his investors the following week, he explained that he had already sold his bearish position and had in fact been buying stocks.

Ackman's father, a lung cancer survivor, came in from the next room and gave him an air hug.

A WEEK INTO lockdown in New York City, David Solomon had become his own barista. In normal times, the Goldman Sachs CEO would swing by the Starbucks near his bank's downtown Manhattan headquarters on his way to the office. But with much of New York City on lockdown, he was now making his preferred drink at his SoHo townhome. The Wall Street veteran took four shots of decaf espresso and almond milk, over ice, and poured it into a Yeti supercooling mug. He dialed Stephen Scherr, his chief financial officer.

"Do it," he said. Borrow $1 billion from the federal government.

The day before, Solomon and the CEOs of the other eight biggest banks in the country had dialed in to a conference call organized by their trade group, the Financial Services Forum, to discuss borrowing from the Federal Reserve's discount window.

The window is the clearest manifestation of the Fed's role as the economy's lender of last resort. The name is a relic of the days when a bank in trouble—perhaps facing a run on deposits from its customers—would send a representative to a teller window at the Federal Reserve. Today the process is all electronic, but the goal is the same: to prevent bank runs by offering cheap loans to depository institutions, ensuring that they have enough cash to make good on financial obligations such as honoring customer withdrawals. (The worst thing a bank can do is turn away a depositor trying to withdraw their cash. The panic spreads, and customers show up en masse. In fact, this is why many old bank buildings were designed with large lobbies: to avoid even the outside chance that a line might develop at teller windows and spark fear.)

The discount window's last moment in the spotlight was in 2008, when it had kept alive a handful of wounded banks, including Goldman Sachs and Morgan Stanley. The move had calmed investors and pulled both firms back from the brink of bankruptcy. The window had saved the nation's banking system, but in doing so, it had cemented its reputation as the Hail Mary pass of severely wounded financial institutions. As the nation's banking system limped out of the 2008 crisis, the discount window carried a distinct stigma.

Now the country's biggest banks faced a new crisis. The economy was shutting down. Nobody was traveling or eating in a restaurant or buying a home, the everyday commercial activity that keeps banks' coffers full. And they were staring down the barrel of likely huge defaults on corporate loans.

None needed the money at that instant, but they might before this was over. By taking it now and in unison, so the thinking went, they would rid the exercise of stigma. Goldman borrowed $1 billion, and other banks similarly round figures—a large number to a layperson but a rounding error on the ledgers of these trillion-dollar institutions.

THE TRADING FLOOR of the New York Stock Exchange is an icon of American capitalism. It began in 1792, under a buttonwood tree where two dozen brokers gathered to organize their trading in bank stocks and war bonds. They soon built a coffeehouse down on the corner, to provide their new venture indoor comforts. The exchange operated for the next seven decades out of a series of shops and rented office space before moving in 1903, into a newly constructed neoclassical building at the corner of Wall Street and Broad Street whose façade of white Georgia marble and fifty-foot fluted columns came over the next century and a half to symbolize American financial might. An architectural critic at the time said it captured the "very essence of the strenuous energy of this twentieth century."

It was also, as the coronavirus silently spread in early March, a petri dish. Hundreds of brokers and technicians entered 2 Broad Street each morning—down a cramped flight of stairs, then spilling out onto a giant trading floor, where they huddled around screens and shouted orders in a performative nod to an era before trading went largely electronic.

The exchange had sent most of its corporate employees home on March 13, but the hundreds of floor brokers and designated market-makers, the people who crowd onto its trading floor and make markets in stocks, were still coming in. They didn't work for the NYSE, but rather for dozens of niche firms known as specialists. They wanted to be there, and keeping floor folks happy was important.

John Tuttle, the NYSE's vice chairman, had been tasked with reaching out to the state health department to procure tests, and health workers to administer them to workers coming in. Tuttle, whose wife was pregnant, had rented a home in Sag Harbor for two weeks, and on Sunday, March 15, he called his contact at the health department. The state was strapped. The only tests available were not the rapid, self-administered ones that would eventually be more widely used but laboratory-grade tests that needed to be done by a licensed technician, safely stored, and sent away for processing. The department official said they could have staff onsite on Tuesday. "The market opens Monday," Tuttle said. "I need you Monday."

By the next morning, the entrance at 2 Broad Street had been commandeered by a team of nurses sitting behind the security desk, wearing duck-billed KN95 masks and wielding clipboards. As employees entered down the flight of stairs, they were asked a series of questions. Had they been out of the country? Were they feeling ill? Was anyone in their family sick? The first day, thirteen people were tested.

And now, at 11 A.M. on Tuesday, the results had landed in Tuttle's inbox. Two had come back positive: one exchange-floor worker and one corporate NYSE employee.

The next morning, Cunningham, Tuttle, Blaugrund, chief financial officer Scott Hill, and Elizabeth King, the general counsel, dialed in to a call to discuss whether to close the trading floor. Blaugrund joined from a hospital in Westchester, where his son had been admitted, with doctors now trying to figure out what was causing his low oxygen levels and shortness of breath.

Exchange floors had already closed in Philadelphia and Chicago. CME Group, the Chicago exchange giant where traders swap commodities like wheat and hogs as well as financial options, had made the decision to shut down its trading floor the previous week. Its CEO, Terrence Duffy, a lung cancer survivor who was extra sensitive to concerns about the coronavirus, had thrown an elbow to a competitor, telling *The Wall Street Journal,* "I find it kind of amazing that the NYSE trading floor is still open. I thought we were not supposed to have fifty people or more in one location."

It wasn't an easy call for Cunningham. She believed strongly in the value of human brokers, who could, she believed, step in during times of stress and smooth out trading. Whether humans were actually better than supercomputers and software remained a matter of debate among market scholars, but live traders and the cavernous floor they populated were undeniably core to the Big Board's image. Nasdaq had already claimed the high-tech ground; the NYSE's reputation was staked on high-touch nostalgia, and the sight of its trading floor empty would be momentous—and not just for the exchange, Cunningham told her lieutenants, gathered on the line, but for the country. "NYSE is a symbol of American strength and resiliency," she had told a reporter just a few days earlier. "The people on the floor want to be there." Plus, the coming Friday, March 20, was a complicated day of trading for the market. It was a quarterly occurrence known as "quad witching" where stock index futures, stock index options, stock options, and single-stock futures expire on the same day. The result is usually a day of chaotic trading, and Cunningham argued it was important to have brokers on the floor to help smooth out the bumps.

On the other side of the ledger: It wasn't safe. They now had proof. The NYSE had only been testing employees who had failed a temperature check or reported feeling ill. Given what experts had learned about the virus's ability to spread among asymptomatic people, that screening process wouldn't work anymore.

Testing capacity in New York was scarce. The kind of daily, widespread testing that would be required to keep the trading floor open, if it could even be done, would drain resources from hospitals and others. Cunningham made a judgment call, using what in the weeks to come would become a common phrase, one of the many linguistic legacies of the pandemic. The NYSE's trading floor was simply not, at that moment, an essential workplace.

They settled on a strange compromise: The NYSE would announce in the morning that its floor would close, but not until the following Monday, three trading days later. It was an odd position, acknowledging the risks of in-person gatherings while allowing them to continue.

It was just one of countless tough calls that executives were forced to make on the fly in the early weeks of the pandemic. They chose from a range of imperfect options, facing public health guidance that was changing by the day and priorities of personal safety and corporate survival that were in direct competition. Tilting too far toward the former risked creating a financial hole so deep they might never dig out, whenever the virus finally quieted. Tilting too far toward the latter risked lives, to say nothing of a public-relations disaster. Some, like Cunningham, shouldered an extra burden, running companies that were so iconic, so crucial, that a shutdown of their operations would have rattled public confidence in the global economy.

The decisions they made, they hoped, would save their companies and preserve the engine of the U.S. economy for when the virus eventually subsided. But now they were just trying to get through the week.

THE BRIEF MARKET bounce that followed the Federal Reserve's actions, including dropping interest rates to near zero, on March 15, the one that had allowed dozens of blue-chip companies to raise money through debt offerings, had lasted just a single day. On Tuesday, March 17, companies issued $28 billion worth of bonds. Exxon raised $8.5 billion, Pepsi raised $6.5 billion, with both using the money to pay off shorter-term debt, known as commercial paper, that had become wildly expensive. But those deals, it turned out, had slipped through a narrow window. Two days later, it slammed shut.

Investors had been willing to buy newly issued Exxon bonds at 2.25 percentage points above a government rate on Tuesday. But on Wednesday they were demanding 2.39 percentage points over that rate to trade those same bonds in the market. Pepsi's bonds similarly traded down after they were issued. That reset the terms for new bond issuances that followed the next day, which required companies to dangle higher and higher interest rates to find investors willing to buy them. It was a vicious cycle that reflected the perilous state of the financial markets.

Wall Street was one giant self-fulfilling doomsday cycle. Billions of dollars flowed out of mutual funds, which meant those funds had to sell their holdings to meet redemption requests, which drove down prices. "This is really bad," Jonny Fine told his boss, Dan Dees, the co-head of Goldman's investment banking division, on Friday, March 20. "Unless there is some serious policy intervention here soon, the market is going to break."

CHAPTER 15

BAILED OUT

That Saturday, March 21, Doug Parker was back in Dallas, standing in the dining room of his home in the ritzy neighborhood of Park Cities, when Steven Mnuchin called. The American Airlines CEO and the Treasury secretary had been in near-constant contact since the airlines had struck their uneasy late-night truce with the labor unions. In the intervening days, the financial outlook for airlines had only gotten worse. The day before, the number of U.S. airline passengers had dropped below five hundred thousand, just a third of what it had been a week earlier. Carriers were burning millions of dollars each day. The $1 billion that Parker, holed up in a side room at the lobbying headquarters a few days earlier, had cajoled bank executives into ponying up looked laughably insufficient. American needed the kind of money that could only come from Washington.

Mnuchin repeated his opposition to grants, telling Parker that he was in favor only of federal loans that the airlines would have to pay back. The Treasury secretary had powerful allies in Congress, most vocally Pat Toomey, the junior senator from Pennsylvania. Parker, now a de facto spokesman for the industry, tried to come up with other chits the airlines could give, such as extending their commitment to keep less profitable routes that served smaller cities.

"Doug, you've got to understand," Mnuchin said. In the past

week, the economic picture had gone from bad to calamitous. It wasn't just airlines facing a financial abyss. Detroit's auto factories had shut down. Liquidity in the bond market had completely dried up. Trump had invoked a Korean War–era law, the Defense Production Act, to press private manufacturers into service making ventilators and masks. In a supremely unhelpful development, North Korea had test-fired two ballistic missiles. Mnuchin had taken heat even from *The Wall Street Journal*'s ultraconservative editorial page, which that day had published a piece that criticized him for a late and muddled government response and contrasted him with the—in the paper's view—steady leadership of Hank Paulson in 2008. In short, Mnuchin had bigger fish to fry than what exact form the $50 billion the government was going to give the airlines would take. The federal government needed to keep the entire economy from collapsing.

"We're going to get this thing done, and you should know you've done a great job, and you've gotten yourself in," he told Parker. "No other industry is in. But it's $50 billion and it's all loans. There is zero chance there are going to be grants."

Mnuchin's inflexibility wasn't entirely a surprise, but it still felt like a gut punch to Parker. The day before, as signals became clearer that there was no political support for multibillion-dollar grants, he had asked Nate Gatten, American's head of government affairs, if there was anything else they could try. Gatten had come back with a political Hail Mary play. "We need Chuck Schumer to tell McConnell that he's going to withhold Democratic votes unless this provision is in," he said. In other words, Schumer, the leader of the Senate Democrats, needed to publicly say he was willing to tank a $2 trillion piece of legislation that was supposed to save the entire U.S. economy from collapse, just to help the airlines. It was a laughable long shot. Just a few days earlier, Schumer had spoken on the Senate floor, coming out against bailouts for specific industries, arguing instead for more money for state unemployment offices, small businesses, and public hospitals. "Our major focus cannot be based on bailing out airlines, cruises, and other industries," he had said. "Let's remember, corporations are not people. People are people."

Parker saw only one option. Labor was a core constituency for Schumer. Airlines were not. He sighed and picked up the phone and dialed Sara Nelson, the head of the flight attendants' union. "He's not going to do it for us," he told her. "He might do it for you." Nelson promised to try.

As they hung up, Parker looked at his watch and realized he was late. It was his wife's birthday, and the couple was due for dinner at the home of Robert Isom, American's president, a few blocks away from his own twelve-thousand-square-foot home in the upscale Park Cities neighborhood, a few miles north of downtown Dallas and a quick twenty-minute drive to the company's headquarters.

Parker ducked out between the entrée and dessert and called Calio. The two were speaking so often that Calio's teenaged daughter had taken to yelling out, "Uncle Doug is on the phone," when the lobbyist's cellphone would ring in the evenings. Now Calio was putting together an emergency call of the industry CEOs.

Calio confirmed what Parker already knew, thanks to his back-channeling with Mnuchin: The request for grants they had ironed out back in Washington a few days earlier was dead on arrival in Congress. He tried to buck up the group. They weren't getting grants, but there was a record loan package on the table, on financial terms they could all live with. "It's time to take the win, stop fighting, and go run the airlines," he said.

Parker wasn't entirely giving up on a government rescue. Nelson had given him Nancy Pelosi's cellphone number and urged him to reach out. As he picked up his phone, the strangeness of the moment struck him. He'd had little occasion in his career, as pocked with crises as it had been, to lobby members of Congress.

"Madam Speaker, it's Doug Parker from American Airlines," he texted at 10 P.M. that night. "Peter DeFazio suggested I reach out to you to provide you the airline CEO perspective of this bill and the implications of alternative outcomes. I would welcome a conversation with you at your convenience. This is my cellphone." He kept his eye on the phone for the three-dot bubble that would signal a reply being typed out. It didn't come. He climbed into bed, thinking to himself, *We're toast.*

PARTISAN GRIDLOCK CAME to the rescue. That Sunday, March 22, congressional Democrats refused to bring the CARES Act to the floor for a vote, arguing that the bill didn't do enough to expand unemployment insurance and help strapped state and local governments. The vote was a stunning setback after days of back-and-forth negotiations that had produced the biggest government aid package in American history. It was a worrying sign about partisanship—Congress couldn't even come together over an aid package that nearly everyone agreed was necessary—and for seasoned policy types, recalled the initial failure of the Troubled Asset Relief Program on the floor of the House in 2008, a setback that delayed aid to failing financial markets and likely deepened the crisis on Wall Street.

For Parker, though, it was a glimmer of hope. Maybe the airlines were still in the game.

His good mood didn't last. Parker's wife wasn't feeling well. She and their daughter had gotten tested that Sunday afternoon and both came back positive two days later. Parker felt fine but knew he had potentially exposed his fellow CEOs and staffers, dozens of people, over the course of those two days packed into small conference rooms.

He sent them an email at 4:20 P.M. on March 24. "I feel great," he said after sharing the news of his family members' diagnoses. "I was with my daughter for two days before I left home on March 16 and wasn't with either her or my wife until I left all of you on the 19th, so if I do happen to have the virus, hopefully I was not contagious when we all began sharing office space on the 17th (fortunately it cannot spread through conference calls!)."

Parker had informed his top lieutenants, too, but didn't want to alarm the rest of the workforce—or potentially the market, which might react negatively toward the information that he had been exposed and was awaiting test results. "I'd prefer this not become industry news," he wrote, asking his fellow CEOs for their discretion.

He would get it. When his Covid-19 test came back negative five days later, he wrote the group back and thanked them for the fact that the news hadn't leaked. "That's pretty remarkable given that I had to tell every one of our competitors," he wrote. "You all are class acts."

A few days later, on the afternoon of March 25 and late into the evening, he was on the phone every few minutes with Mnuchin, who was hunkered down in an anteroom in the Capitol with a core group of Republican senators. Their votes were crucial to garnering enough support for the coronavirus relief package, which included the billions in airline aid. Majority leader Mitch McConnell was there, along with Senators Pat Toomey, Mike Crapo, and Roger Wicker.

The political fault lines had hardened in the course of the frenzied two-week negotiations, and the five political figures in the majority leader's wood-paneled office late that evening were at loggerheads. Mnuchin kept insisting on loans over grants, for two reasons. First, he had to look out for the American taxpayer, and loans would be paid back with interest. Second, by becoming a creditor to these companies, the government would have more leverage to exact changes, such as limits to executive pay and the attachment of warrants that would deliver the Treasury a profit if their stock prices rebounded. He had a staunch ally in Toomey, the junior senator from Pennsylvania, a small-government Republican opposed to bailouts on ideological grounds. On the other side were a pair of fellow Republicans, lobbying for a higher percentage of the money to be in the form of grants: Wicker, a key vote on the transportation committee, and Crapo, the powerful chair of the Senate banking committee. At one point, Mnuchin and Toomey had called the president, asking him to weigh in. "Work it out yourselves," the president had responded.

Mnuchin kept throwing out ideas, leaning on his background at Goldman Sachs, where he had spent the late 1980s and early 1990s on the trading floor during an era that prized complexity and gave rise to a generation of wholly new financial products. If an investor held stocks but wanted exposure to bonds, or owned variable-rate debt but wanted the certainty of a fixed rate, Wall Street had a product for that. Traders of that era sliced and diced risk, serving clients exactly what they wanted and nothing else—and ensuring a healthy profit for themselves.

That was the position Mnuchin now found himself in. He needed to craft something that felt enough like a grant that the airlines and their Democratic allies in Congress would approve, and enough like loans that he and the anti-bailout camp could accept. And it had to ensure that the Treasury itself, and by extension American taxpayers, were not at risk of serious losses.

One idea he floated to Parker was having the airlines give stock warrants to Treasury alongside a loan. If, when the loan came due, the companies' stock prices had improved enough that the gains on the warrants covered the loan amount, the airlines wouldn't have to pay back the loan. But if they didn't, the airlines would have to make up the difference to the Treasury.

"That's a loan," Parker countered. "You're getting a guaranteed return." And any sane auditor would treat that money as debt on American's balance sheet, which was creaking before the pandemic and by now had billions more in additional loans and bonds piled on.

"If you make this too hard," Parker said, "there are going to be airlines that don't take it. And they're going to end up furloughing people." His company might have been desperate enough to take whatever money it could get, but those in stronger financial shape, notably Delta and Southwest, would almost certainly snub their noses at the terms Mnuchin was offering. And Parker wasn't sure they would be able to ride out a months-long shutdown without it.

"All right, I'll call you back," Mnuchin said. A few minutes later the phone rang again with another complex structure that Mnuchin hoped might thread the needle of compromise. Again, Parker said he couldn't sell it to his fellow CEOs. And on it went, late into the night. Toomey was calling Parker, too, floating some of the same ideas. Parker suspected a game of bad cop/bad cop and worried that the senator from Pennsylvania was prodding the industry's united front to find a weak link—a CEO who might agree and be able to persuade the rest.

As the clock ticked toward midnight, McConnell chimed in. He had largely stayed out of the politicking over the bill, ceding it to Mnuchin and Nancy Pelosi, and had straddled the fence on key sticking points as he tried to corral an unruly caucus. The $50 billion should be evenly divided into grants and loans, he said. Mnuchin stepped into a side chamber and dialed the White House, reaching Trump, who, as often, was up late watching television. Earlier, Trump had made an appearance on Sean Hannity's Fox News television show, telling Hannity that he had pushed back a call with Chinese president Xi Jinping to be able to dial in to the show. Now he was in the residence. Mnuchin briefed Trump on the compromise, telling the president it would pave the way for the broader bill's passage. "Well, whatever you think is best, Steve," he told his Treasury secretary.

Mnuchin returned to the meeting and signed off, with one tweak. He insisted a line be added to the bill that gave him control over the $25 billion in grant money—an authority that he would later use to convert a large portion of the money into repayable loans.

The CARES Act passed the next day, a $2 trillion tsunami of money meant to keep the economy from collapsing. It included billions of dollars in aid for small businesses and overwhelmed hospitals, additional unemployment insurance for those who had lost their jobs, and checks sent directly to millions of Americans. And it included $50 billion for the country's airlines and related business.

Paulson, who had been Treasury secretary during the 2008 crisis, when the department was widely criticized in the public and in Congress for pouring tens of billions of dollars into Wall Street banks, had bristled at the word "bailout." Mnuchin wasn't eager to be tagged with the same label.

WOULD IT BE enough?

The graphic cut like a knife across the front page of *The New York Times*. On Friday, March 27, the paper gave over the page's right column—the most valuable real estate in print journalism—to a chart showing a spike in unemployment claims wrought by the cresting of the coronavirus over the U.S. economy. The previous high for weekly unemployment claims was 695,000, in 1982, and even during the Great Recession, claims peaked at 665,000. The weekly claims were now captured in a graphic that required almost the entire height of the front page: 3.3 million. The headline captured two grim milestones: "Job Losses Soar; U.S. Virus Cases Top World."

American businesses had laid off workers as the coronavirus had cut across the world, sickening millions and bringing lockdowns that hit their sales. By the end of March, ten million Americans had lost their jobs to the virus's economic rampage. Seven thousand were dead, a number that seemed horrifying then but would eventually surpass one million. The Dow Jones Industrial Average, which had broken 30,000 in late February, closed the month at 21,917. Icons of American commerce were powering down, seeking government aid, shedding staff, and wondering whether their businesses even made sense anymore. Millions of small businesses had failed.

It was a breathtaking unraveling of the biggest economy in the world. And even the toll, then unknown, paled in comparison to the loss of life. Around the world, nearly forty thousand were dead and hospitals were full. In New York, still the epicenter of the U.S.

outbreak—and by now the deadliest Covid-19 city on the planet, having overtaken areas in northern Italy—the ambulance sirens were constant. Residents poked their heads out of their windows at 7 P.M. each night, banging spoons on pots to show their appreciation for healthcare workers.

David Solomon, the Goldman CEO, watched on the final day of the month from his office on the forty-first floor as the U.S. Navy hospital ship *Comfort* floated into New York Harbor. The ship was there to provide a floating hospital to the thousands of coronavirus patients that public health officials expected would quickly overrun the city's hospitals, which were quickly filling up.

"Here comes the cavalry," Solomon said to no one, and snapped a photo.

CHAPTER 16

————

MOONSHOTS

On Tuesday, March 17, Jim Hackett, the Ford CEO, picked up the phone in the study of his home in Western Michigan and called the White House. "I want to give you a heads-up," he told Larry Kudlow, Trump's senior economic adviser. "We're going to be shutting the factories down."

The forty-eight hours that Detroit's Big Three automakers had asked for from the UAW during the weekend's call with the union boss, Rory Gamble, had expired. They had wrestled internally about whether to close the factories, weighing the pros and cons. For starters, nobody quite knew how to do it. Industrial companies have contingency plans to shut down an individual plant for maintenance or retrofitting, but shutting off hundreds of plants all at once was another matter entirely. And then there was the matter of starting them back up on the other side of this crisis, which Hackett figured would be a few weeks at most.

But that morning, a piece of news had come in that had convinced him it was the right decision. An hourly worker at a unionized Chrysler plant in Sterling Heights, Michigan, that assembled Dodge Ram pickup trucks tested positive for the virus. The employee hadn't been in the plant in more than a week, but that hardly mattered in the suddenly charged environment of mid-March. The virus was sowing fear across the United States and putting corporate executives on the defensive, as they found themselves accused of prioritizing profit over worker safety. Chrysler had hastily announced a slew of safety measures, including staggering shift breaks to avoid employees crowding into break rooms and providing workers disinfectant, rags, and gloves at the start of each shift so they could sanitize their own stations. But Hackett knew it was only a matter of time before he had to shut down all the company's plants. No sense delaying the inevitable.

Detroit might have been decades past its years as the engine—literally—of the global auto industry, but it was still its symbolic heart. The decision, when it was announced, would likely send shockwaves through the stock market. He worried that Trump might call out the industry on Twitter for—as he told Jim Farley, recently promoted into the role of Hackett's top deputy—"not believing in America." He hoped he might head that off by explaining his thinking directly to the trigger-happy president's top economic counselor.

"I can't speak for Mary," he said, referring to Mary Barra, CEO of General Motors. But Ford, the icon of America's first industrial age, was going dark the next day, he said. Workers would, at least for now, get roughly their full pay, with supplemental pay spelled out in the contract to top off wages covered by state unemployment insurance.

Kudlow gave a heavy sigh. The economy had been on a tear, buoying his boss's prospects for reelection in the fall, and Kudlow told Hackett he had hoped the U.S. economy could muddle through the virus without huge productivity declines. "I know, and we'll get through this," Hackett said. "But we can't have people in there right now." Kudlow said he understood but added, "I'm just afraid I'm not going to be able to get them back to work again, if they're living on the dole."

It was an early inkling of an economic debate that would rage later, after stimulus checks and extra unemployment insurance payments showed many American workers that it was just as profitable to stay home. It would also presage a challenge that would unfold months later, as stores and hotels and restaurants reopened, only to find that many workers they had fired or furloughed were reluctant to come back—some finding it comfortable enough to get by with government aid, others having few childcare options as schools remained shut, and still others wary about catching the virus.

Seeking a bit of a lighter note, Hackett said, "Who knows, maybe we'll make ventilators."

In fact, it was an idea that the CEO had been chewing on for a few days, ever since Boris Johnson, the prime minister of the United Kingdom, which had reported about 1,500 cases and 55 deaths from the coronavirus, had urged industrial manufacturers in Britain to switch their assembly lines over to producing lifesaving medical equipment like masks and ventilators. Hackett had been mulling it over for two days and had now blurted it out almost as a throwaway comment.

"Well, Jim, that would be helpful," Kudlow replied, promising to help clear the way in Washington however he could.

Hackett quickly called Jim Baumbick, Ford's head of enterprise product line management, and told him to get started on a plan. He put Baumbick in touch with Nick LaRusso, chair of medicine at the Mayo Clinic, and John Kennedy, an entrepreneur in the healthcare equipment world. Baumbick had already been thinking about whether Ford could help. A conversation with one of his deputies the week earlier stuck in his mind; the man's sister-in-law was a doctor at Rush Hospital in Chicago, and she had told him that hospital workers were reusing disposable gloves and gowns and using napkins and scarves as improvised masks.

The previous Thursday, March 12, Baumbick had been told to stay home as part of a remote-work pilot. The company had been ironing out a Team A/Team B approach that would de-densify the office, make contact tracing easier if someone did get sick, and allow reinforcements with whom they had not had contact to fill in their spots. "When you go home, take what you need, because you're likely not coming back," he had told his team. Like at Goldman Sachs, the plan was never implemented; by Monday, March 16, the company's entire nonfactory workforce was told to stay home. The factories would close two days later.

Now, from his home in Novi, Michigan, a suburb of Detroit, Baumbick gathered a core team of about a dozen deputies, who between them managed hundreds of engineers. Until recently they had been hard at work on a must-hit secret project underway at Ford: a massive commitment to new electric vehicles, including an all-electric version of its iconic pickup truck, the F-150, which they hoped to roll out in 2021. It was a crucial pivot for Ford, which, like much of the U.S. auto industry, had lost ground to Silicon Valley competitors and foreign carmakers in the race to ditch gasoline-powered automobiles. Now they had a new challenge, one on which, Baumbick told them, the country was counting.

"Ford built bombers; we made iron lungs," Baumbick would later say. "There has to be something we can do." He would soon learn how desperately the help was needed.

DETROIT'S AUTO FACTORIES remained closed. After the first positive coronavirus test, the Chrysler worker on March 17, more came in quickly: a Chrysler worker at a Jeep assembly plant in Warren, Michigan, then one of 2,800 hourly workers at a Ford Bronco assembly plant in Wayne. A Chrysler factory in Detroit churning out Dodge Durangos ground to a halt for ninety minutes after a worker on the assembly line vomited. Maintenance workers refused to clean it up for fear of contracting the virus, hysteria spread, and workers refused to return to the line. Factories that once produced thousands of cars each day lay dormant, hulking symbols of an economy paralyzed by fear.

Instead of walking factory floors or fine-tuning model plans, Baumbick was in his home office, on a call with a junior staffer in the White House's manufacturing office named Christopher Abbott, to talk about what kind of protective medical gear was needed, what the supply chain looked like, and what role Ford might play. Early discussions had centered around ventilators, the complex and expensive machines that keep alive patients whose lungs are too damaged to breathe on their own. As the two were talking, a doctor who was consulting with the White House on the crisis walked into Abbott's office and asked who he was talking to. Abbott put him on speakerphone, and he began describing a medical disaster in the making.

The doctor's biggest concern, he said, was that doctors and intensive-care nursing staff were getting sick. If there was nobody to treat patients, the crisis would escalate. What was more, with hospitals quickly becoming overwhelmed, many were relying on volunteer staff, retired healthcare workers, to come back into service. If they didn't feel safe, they wouldn't come. The immediate need was for face shields and other gear to protect doctors and nursing staff. A Defense Department engineer had been tinkering around with a new design for a device known as a purified-air-powered respirator, or PAPR, that sucks in air, filters it, and feeds it into a hood and face shield, similar to what would top a hazmat suit. These were far simpler than the complex ventilators that kept intubated patients alive and could probably be produced on a mass scale. "If you could fix this, you can save a lot of people," the doctor said.

As he spoke, a light went off in Baumbick's head. He had never heard of a PAPR, but the components sounded a lot like what went into the air-conditioning systems in a car.

He hung up and immediately called his top climate-control engineers. What did Ford have available in high quantity that might work?

That call began one of the biggest public-service corporate moonshots in history, in which Ford revamped factories, now idled by the pandemic, into production facilities for protective gear and medical equipment that was badly needed. Dubbed Project Apollo, named after the movie *Apollo 13,* in which NASA engineers devised the mother of all hacks to keep three oxygen-starved astronauts alive, using a flight manual cover, spacesuit parts, and a sock. This time, the challenge was also a breathing problem. Americans with Covid-19 were suffocating to death, and hospitals didn't have enough of the equipment to save them. And healthcare workers treating an unrelenting flood of Covid patients were breathing in contaminated air without the protective gear they needed.

Baumbick eventually organized his team around three products. One team would work on the PAPR for emergency workers. Within two days, his engineers had come back with a hand-drawn plan for a device that used blower motors from the AC units of F-150 trucks and batteries from the DeWalt power tools that were used on its assembly lines, attached to an air filter and a hood. A Ford plant in Michigan that had churned out Mustang muscle cars for fifty years was converted in a matter of days and was soon churning out bright yellow hoods attached to hoses that would keep clean air flowing. They called them "scrappy PAPRs."

Another team focused on ventilators. Trump was talking about a need for one hundred thousand ventilators, orders of magnitude beyond what was produced each year. Face shields and respirators were relatively simple; ventilators had thousands of parts, each perfectly calibrated to replace the body's ability to breathe on its own. Even if more ventilators could be produced, a grim problem loomed. Public health officials were talking about—and in some cases already at work setting up—military-style field hospitals to handle overflow patients after hospitals had filled up. These facilities would likely not have a surplus of working electric outlets. Baumbick's team found a company in Florida, Airon, that had designed a pneumatic system, which runs on air pressure rather than electric power. If Ford could build a ventilator, it could run without an electrical hookup, powered solely by oxygen tanks.

Baumbick came back to Hackett with his progress. He estimated it would cost about $600 million, money that Ford, with its revenue drying up and a huge debt load and dividend to fund, couldn't easily spare. "Don't stop. Don't look over your shoulder," Hackett told him. "If anyone gives you crap, ask them to call me."

It was an opportune moment for a moonshot. Ford, to its critics, had been stuck in its ways for too long and had ceded ground on the next generation of cars—futuristic, autonomous, electric, cool—to rivals in China and in Silicon Valley, where Tesla was churning out electric cars that were quiet as a whisper but screamed power and sophistication. Hackett had been trying to push the company to move faster, to be more nimble and less siloed. In fact, just then Ford was in the middle innings of designing the electric version of its iconic F-150 truck, named Lightning. The timeline for the project called for a prototype to be ready in less than two years, which would be more than two years faster than the company had ever designed and built a new vehicle. But changing the company's culture had been slow and difficult: Engineers had tended to run Ford, and their natural incrementalism and affinity for tinkering and refining had seeped into the company culture.

But perhaps more than any other American company, Ford had an intentionally and deeply held idea that in times of crisis it should help the country. Its founding family, which still controlled the company through super-voting shares, had long felt it was their duty to step up in times of national crisis. During the 1940s the company made iron lung machines for polio patients. During World War II, it shut down its production of civilian vehicles to dedicate its resources to the war effort, churning out tens of thousands of airplanes, engines, gliders, and generators—despite the fact that Henry Ford, then nearing eighty and still the company's CEO, was an ardent pacifist who had opposed America's entry into the war.

Forty days after Baumbick's original call with the White House, the first shipment of PAPRs left for the New York area, where more than eight thousand people had died. Ford would produce more than forty thousand by the end of July. A 3D printing site in Spain, which once produced quick-turnaround prototypes of new steering wheels and crankshafts, churned out five thousand face shields per day. Ford engineers drove from Michigan headquarters to a 3M facility in South Dakota that was producing crucial N95 masks to make its assembly lines more efficient.

All this while trying, and at times failing, to keep its own workers safe. While office workers across the world retreated into their home offices and kitchen tables, at first somewhat giddily and then more grumpily as the pandemic wore on, millions of American workers—and their counterparts in countries around the world—did not have that luxury. They kept showing up at manufacturing plants and meatpacking facilities, stocking grocery shelves and driving warehouse forklifts, piloting jet planes and city buses, in the presence of a deadly virus.

Companies across the world pivoted, retooling assembly lines, and rerouted supply chains to tackle the crippling shortage of protective equipment needed by healthcare workers. Baseball teams turned their uniform-making factories to producing masks and hospital gowns. Joe Tsai, vice chairman of Chinese e-commerce giant Alibaba, brokered a secret deal to get 2.6 million masks out of China, where they had been held up by government officials offended by President Trump's escalating "Kung Flu" rhetoric. An Alibaba jet delivered them to New York. Coca-Cola donated twenty-nine thousand pounds of plastic to a small bookbinding outfit in Baltimore, which started churning out face shields.

MEANWHILE, ANOTHER AMBITIOUS project was underway in Washington. With millions of Americans out of work and small businesses in danger of failing, Mnuchin was sketching out a rescue plan for them. It would eventually be called the Paycheck Protection Program, or PPP, and it would go from a bumpy start to become a model government program—well-designed and implemented and the kind of technocratic, commonsense effort too often derailed by politics.

Mike Faulkender took his tie off the hook on the back of the door of his office, inside the giant stone building that houses the Treasury Department. He was the assistant secretary for economic policy, overseeing a small group of PhD economists tasked with keeping a finger on the pulse of the U.S. economy, the largest in the world at $21 trillion in annual output. Mnuchin had relaxed the dress code for the skeleton Treasury staff that remained working in the office after mid-March, when most staffers were sent home. Ties were optional except for business in Congress or the White House. Today he was heading to the Senate to fix a problem.

His boss, Mnuchin, had proposed the outlines of a rescue package that would guarantee workers at small businesses eight weeks of pay, with the government covering six of those. Small-business payroll in the United States was an estimated $50 billion a week, so Mnuchin's opening proposal was a $300 billion pot. He ended up being negotiated up to $350 billion.

But then the Senate got ahold of the bill. The small-business committee, chaired by Florida Republican Marco Rubio and Maryland Democrat Ben Cardin, had in a matter of days vastly expanded the bill and its price tag. Their plan called for seventeen weeks of payroll, as well as funds to cover utilities, rent, and mortgage payments. Faulkender's team had crunched the numbers, and the price tag was well over $1 trillion. A trillion dollars. That was more than the 2008 troubled-mortgage purchase program; more than the 2009 stimulus, a combination of tax cuts, an expansion in food assistance and unemployment programs, and infrastructure spending meant to drag the economy out of the crash. Despite the rapidly growing alarm about the economic effects of the coronavirus, a trillion-dollar program just seemed wildly high, even if Rubio and Cardin felt they had enough support in Congress for it. It had fallen to Faulkender to go walk them through the math.

The Capitol, closed to visitors and nonessential personnel, was a ghost town. Faulkender was met by a staffer and escorted to a hearing room, where Rubio and Cardin, along with Jeanne Shaheen, a

Democrat from New Hampshire, and Susan Collins, a Republican from Maine, were fanned out, socially distanced, around the dais.

It just wasn't going to work, Faulkender told them. Cardin called him a "bean-counter." Faulkender would later tell friends it was one of his proudest moments.

THE PAYCHECK PROTECTION Program stumbled out of the gate.

Congress had approved $350 billion in loans for companies with fewer than five hundred employees, which could be forgiven by the government if the recipients used at least 75 percent of the money to keep paying employees. Actually getting that money out the door was the job of Jovita Carranza, who had been appointed to run the Small Business Administration just a few months earlier. But to the bank executives tasked with processing applications and actually making the loans, the program was a mess.

What kind of information did they need to collect from borrowers? Would they be able to sell the loans after they had funded them? Many banks weren't already approved SBA lenders; could they participate? Could the SBA's loan system, which had processed just $6.6 billion in loans in all of 2019, even handle the flood of applications that would be coming in? On the evening of April 2, the night before the PPP was set to open, the Treasury Department still hadn't issued the final versions of many forms that both banks and borrowers would need to apply.

Banks were only allowed to charge 0.5 percent interest on the loans, less than what many smaller banks had to pay their depositors and other creditors. The rate was also too low to entice money managers to buy the loans from the banks. Banks worried their balance sheets would clog up with unprofitable loans. (The evening before the program's opening, Mnuchin said the interest rate would be increased to 1 percent at the request of community banks.) Tony Wilkinson, chief executive of a trade group for lenders that originate SBA loans, told *The Wall Street Journal* that the draft version of the form was "not as simple as we hoped," and that as the lenders learned more about the program, "their likelihood of participation is getting smaller and smaller."

JPMorgan Chase told its small-business customers a day prior that it didn't expect to start accepting loan applications on the broadly advertised April 3 date, and told reporters it was still awaiting guidance from the SBA and Treasury Department before making loans. Bank of America only planned to give PPP loans to small-business clients who'd already established deposit accounts and loans at the bank as of mid-February.

Small banks nationwide faced their own uncertainty. Maine Community Bank in Biddeford, Maine, had already fielded more than three hundred inquiries about the program before its opening day, and had few answers to give. "Until we get that guidance from the SBA," CEO Jeanne Hulit told *The Wall Street Journal* on April 2, "we are on hold."

At the White House, a press conference was arranged to try and quell those concerns. Faulkender had been at the office until 2 A.M. the previous night, at which point he had passed off the guidance to Treasury's lawyers, who were still tweaking the language.

"I believe we just put up the federal register with the new guidelines for lenders," Mnuchin said.

Treasury had not done so. Back at the department's headquarters, lawyers were still haggling over the fine print. Faulkender called a deputy general counsel assigned to the small-business program. "Post the damn thing," he said. By around 4:30 P.M. on the PPP's opening day, 9,779 loans worth about $3.2 billion in total had been approved.

Over the next two months, $525 billion would be handed out to more than five million borrowers—almost exactly what the beancounters at Treasury had modeled out. Most would never be paid back—95 percent, in the final telling. It was an unprecedented lifeline for America's small businesses, and politically, it was a powerful argument against the populist critiques to come: that the government had, for the second time in twelve years, bailed out big business.

The program's effectiveness would be debated as the pandemic ebbed. As with any gusher of money that size, many businesses that weren't in dire straits took advantage. Researchers at Brown University would later determine the program had saved only about a million and a half jobs, at a cost of $377,000 apiece. Faulkender would publicly defend the program, which Treasury credits for saving eighteen million jobs. It certainly saved millions of workers from being tossed into the unemployment system, which was drowning under a flood of claims in the pandemic's early days. Businesses that received loans laid off fewer workers than those that didn't, and were faster to rehire, validating the government's forecasts.

Whether or not it is ultimately viewed as a success, the Paycheck Protection Program was perhaps the clearest sign of the federal government's determination not to let the economy crack. While there is ample history of propping up huge corporations in times of crisis—see the support to airlines in the wake of 9/11 or the auto industry's rescue in 2008—never before had Washington's largesse reached Main Street.

CHAPTER 17

FALLEN ANGELS

"The federal government is trying to save Ford!" Jonny Fine screamed into the phone. It was Thursday, April 9, and he had just seen a news flash that had prompted him to dial his boss, Dan Dees, the co-head of Goldman Sachs's investment bank.

The Federal Reserve was expanding a program it had announced three weeks earlier to prop up the bond market, which had been beset by chaotic trading that had made it all but impossible for companies, even highly rated ones, to raise cash. In late March, the central bank had rolled out a program to buy highly rated corporate bonds, those with at least a triple-B rating that reflected the underlying creditworthiness of the companies themselves. (The exact letter scale varies between the three largest credit-rating agencies but generally extends from triple-A at the high end to C at the low end.)

The ratings cutoff seemed a sensible move three weeks earlier when the program, officially known as the Primary Market Corporate Credit Facility, had been set up. The Fed does not lose money—ever. And even in a deepening crisis, it wasn't keen to start using taxpayer money to buy junk bonds. These bonds were low rated for a reason, reflecting financial stress or ballooning debt burdens at the companies. The central bank hoped that by providing a backstop to the highest-rated bonds, it would calm the market at large.

But it hadn't. The bond market had descended into chaos. And that morning, the Fed had announced a small tweak to the fine-print terms of the credit facility. It would have meant little to the average American, but Fine, pacing on the patio of his home overlooking the Hudson River, spelled it out to his boss. Companies that had been rated investment-grade before the pandemic hit but had since been downgraded to "junk" status—that is, that were deemed too risky for most blue-chip investors to own—were now eligible for the program.

It was a curious change. Only about two dozen companies fit the criteria. But it was a striking recognition from the Fed that even healthy companies—those with prudent management and viable businesses that would likely still be viable after the crisis was over—might not make it that long. Many investment funds simply can't hold junk bonds, no matter how much their managers might believe in the company's prospects. When a company is downgraded, those investors sell their bonds en masse, which depresses their prices and can make it all but impossible to issue new bonds at affordable rates. On Wall Street, these companies are called "fallen angels." The first few weeks of the pandemic had minted a few, among them Delta Air Lines, Royal Caribbean—and Ford. In April 2020, the common thread between most of the members of the club was that nobody wanted what they had to sell. Nobody was buying airplane tickets or new cars.

None was in a more precarious spot than Ford, which carried $114 billion of rated debt, twenty-five times as much as Delta. Some $37 billion of its bonds had just been unceremoniously booted out of the investment-grade club and into junk territory, the Wall Street equivalent of being moved to the kids' table at a family function. The downgrade had come despite a full-court press from CEO Jim Hackett and CFO Tim Stone, lobbying the ratings agencies against it, arguing that the setback was temporary and that Ford's balance sheet would be fine.

The downgrade couldn't come at a worse moment. Ford was bleeding cash. Its showrooms were closed, as were most of its assembly lines. Even if it could get them up and running again, nobody was buying cars. Sales of new vehicles had fallen by more than one-third in the first quarter of 2020. On March 19, the company had suspended its dividend in an effort to hoard its cash, and had withdrawn the guidance it had given to Wall Street investors about how much money it expected to make in 2020. It had borrowed $15 billion from an existing line of credit from banks and, as of early April, had about $30 billion in cash on hand—an impressive war chest in normal times but an uncertain lifeline now that its factories were closed.

The company had quietly started talking to bankers about floating a bond deal to raise cash. After the ratings downgrade from S&P on March 25, investors would charge Ford a much higher interest rate to buy the bonds, if they would even agree to buy them at all.

Hackett, at his home in western Michigan, called Powell, catching him at his office in an otherwise largely empty Federal Reserve headquarters. The Ford CEO had made it a habit when in Washington to reach out to government officials and politicians, and had met the Fed chairman before, but was still a little surprised that he picked up. "I know you're busy," he started. He was under pressure from his board, from investors, from competitors, to raise cash, and there was no doubt that Ford needed it. The last thing Hackett wanted was to cut Ford's dividend, which offered steady income to thousands of the company's retirees, not to mention millions of dollars each year to his benefactors, the Ford family.

The credit markets were in disarray, he said, and paying steep interest rates to borrow there would only put more pressure on the company's dwindling cash position. "I don't want to create a lot of noise around trying to raise money that I'm only going to give back," he told Powell. Almost apologetically, he hinted at some kind of federal aid. Was there any alternative?

Powell was a few days away from announcing a massive government program to backstop the bond market, in what would be the most aggressive government intervention in financial markets since the 2008 meltdown. He was tight-lipped but reassuring, repeating a line he had delivered from the Fed podium a few days earlier, this time without the central-bank jargon. "The U.S. government is going to be here, Jim."

Still rattled, Hackett's next call was to Larry Fink, the CEO of BlackRock. He struck a casual tone, one chief executive to another. "Larry, I don't want to put you in a bad position," he said.

In truth, Fink had been in a pretty uncomfortable spot for weeks. BlackRock, the world's largest money manager, had been hired by the U.S. Treasury to implement its bond-buying program, using its huge securities-trading operation to acquire, on behalf of the government, hundreds of billions of dollars' worth of corporate bonds, mortgage bonds, and Treasury bills. The government had announced earlier in March its plans to buy hundreds of billions of dollars in assets to unclog frozen and dysfunctional credit markets and had hired BlackRock to do it.

The assignment was in many ways a coup, an acknowledgement that BlackRock, which Fink had founded in 1988, was one of the most powerful financial firms in the country. But it was also an unavoidable conflict of interest for the firm, which itself managed hundreds of investment funds that owned the very bonds that the U.S. government had now hired BlackRock to purchase. Which bonds to buy, and at what price, wasn't easily boiled down to market science, and it had created at least the opportunity for self-dealing, which Fink knew all too well. Fink was also a titan in the close-knit community of corporate bigwigs, and many of the companies whose bonds he was being asked to analyze—to potentially buy, thereby propping up their prices and throwing a financial lifeline to their corporate issuers—were run by friends of his. It was all just a mess. Enter Hackett.

"I know you have to be independent," he said. "So I'm just going to give you the argument for why I think Ford meets the bill of what you're trying to do. We're exactly the kind of company that you're trying to make sure doesn't do something stupid," like slash investments or outsource jobs to save money. "I'm keeping people employed. I'm protecting workers," he said. Ford had not laid off any of its workers and had shuttered its factories—at the prodding of the auto workers' union, to be sure, but at great cost to its bottom line.

"You're right," Fink said. "Let me see what I can do."

That message made its way to Mnuchin's office, leading to the announcement that had elated Jonny Fine: The Fed was throwing a lifeline. The investment banker had been consulting with Stone, Ford's CFO, and his deputy, Dave Webb, for a week or so but had warned them that there was little appetite in the market for their existing bonds, let alone new ones the company might issue to raise cash.

Now the U.S. government had said it was willing to buy Ford's bonds, which Fine knew would send a message to the rest of Wall Street's investors that they were safe. And right on cue, the price of Ford's existing bonds shot up on the news. Ford bonds that just a day before had traded hands at a nearly 50 percent discount to face value now fetched almost eighty cents on the dollar. In another sign of confidence from the market, the cost to insure the automaker's debt against default dropped nearly 2 percentage points. A contract that would have protected an investor against a default for five years now cost about $77 per $1,000 of Ford debt it covered, down from nearly $100 the day before.

This newfound optimism from bond-market investors opened the door for Ford to issue new bonds to replenish its dwindling coffers. After hanging up with Dees, Fine soon called Stone at Ford. His message: It's now or never.

Ford was one of Goldman's most important clients. The investment bank had taken the carmaker public in 1956 in what was, at the time, the largest stock offering in U.S. history, and had remained its adviser of choice over the years. Sidney Weinberg, Goldman's managing partner for nearly six decades in the mid-twentieth century, had joined Ford's board, and the relationship remained one of the most important ones for the Wall Street firm, worth tens of millions of dollars a year in fees. Now Ford was in trouble, and if it was going to find a way out of its deepening financial problems, Goldman wanted to pave the road.

Don't worry about those traditional measures of creditworthiness, Fine told Stone and Webb. "The only thing that really matters," he told them, "is how much cash do you have and how long have you got" before it runs out? The $30 billion in cash Ford had in its coffers as of April 9 wouldn't last long if it wasn't making cars.

The following Monday, April 13, Ford made a securities filing in which it pre-released some first-quarter financial results that had been set to be announced a few days later, and said it was considering ways to raise cash. New vehicle sales had fallen 21 percent from a year ago during the three months ending on March 31, and that only included a few weeks of full coronavirus impact in North America, which accounted for nearly half of its annual sales. The announcement was a flashing neon sign to the market: We see what you see. The Fed's action had emboldened the company to dip its toe into the capital markets and hope it didn't drown.

Investors indicated that they weren't interested in bonds issued by Ford itself but were open to buying bonds issued by its financing subsidiary, Ford Motor Credit Company, which lent money to consumers buying new cars. That subsidiary was more creditworthy because investors could theoretically seek repayment from the underlying consumers who had borrowed the money.

But Ford called the market's bluff.

Over the next five days, Ford would pull off the largest junk-bond offering in history. The deal was a clear sign that the Fed's efforts were working and that investors, as scared as they might be, were behaving very differently than they had in 2008. What started as a $3 billion bond offering ended up at $8.5 billion, with investor orders totaling nearly $40 billion.

AMERICAN AIRLINES' UNSECURED bonds were trading at about thirty cents on the dollar, a sign that investors believed the company was in serious financial trouble. Some members of the board of directors suggested buying back some of the bonds. Just as companies can repurchase their stock, and often do so when it appears undervalued by the market, they can buy back bonds, too, wiping out some of their debt on the cheap. Derek Kerr, the company's chief financial officer, knew the credit-ratings agencies would probably downgrade that particular series of bonds, which was a tiny portion of the company's multibillion-dollar debt load. But Kerr thought the trade-off might be worthwhile to retire the debt at a steep discount, and so he let officials at the big three ratings agencies—Moody's, S&P, and Fitch—know that American was considering the move.

S&P came back with a bombshell: They were threatening to downgrade the entire company, not just the single bond at issue. (Companies often have multiple sets of bonds, backed by different kinds of collateral, that carry different ratings. Those backed by hard assets like airplanes tend to be highly rated, regardless of the creditworthiness of the parent company itself. Unsecured bonds, like the ones American was considering repurchasing, carry lower ratings.) Such a downgrade would have been catastrophic. It would have clearly marked American as the weakest of the bunch—which it was, though Kerr wasn't eager to point that out. It would have put blood in the water on Wall Street. The prices on all of American's outstanding debt would have plummeted. Any plans to borrow anew would be off the table. The cost to insure those bonds—credit-default swaps like those that had made Bill Ackman a mint in the early days of the pandemic—would have skyrocketed, which could spark a self-fulfilling narrative that the company was in existential trouble. What started as a clever way to save some money might cost the airline its life.

Kerr backpedaled, telling S&P that American wouldn't repurchase the bonds after all, but the ratings agency wouldn't back down. The fact that American was even *thinking* about the move was grounds for lowering its credit rating. This was above Kerr's pay grade. He called his boss and told him the bad news.

Parker was soon on the phone with a group of S&P analysts. "I am the chairman of the board of American Airlines!" he barked. "I can tell you we are not thinking about it."

Crisis averted, for now.

BRIAN CHESKY AWOKE early. It was still dark when he opened a Google document he had been fiddling with late into the night. Airbnb was laying off a quarter of its staff, and he wanted employees to hear it from him. "We cannot afford to do everything that we used to," he wrote. "Travel in this new world will look different, and we need to evolve Airbnb accordingly."

Fired employees would get fourteen weeks' severance pay, plus one week for each year they'd been at the company. They were allowed to keep their company laptops to stay connected during the shutdown, and Airbnb tasked a group of its internal recruiters to help employees find new jobs, a move that cut against the often ruthless anti-poaching ethos of Silicon Valley. Chesky later told a podcast that "you should cut as deep as you need" to keep employees out of limbo.

CHAPTER 18

BEG, BORROW, STEAL

Scott Hamilton, the general manager of the Hilton McLean hotel in Tysons Corner, Virginia, needed hand sanitizer.

In what amounted to a well-intentioned corporate heist, Hamilton dispatched his head of operations a few hundred yards up the tree-lined street that ran through the nondescript office park where the hotel was located. As it happened, Hilton's corporate headquarters was just up the road. The deputy, Mohamed Khalif, walked out fifteen minutes later with a few cartons of cleaning products and hand wipes, which he brought back to the virtually empty hotel.

A warm, sharply dressed forty-six-year-old with a neatly parted head of blond hair, Hamilton started as manager of the Hilton McLean Tysons Corner on March 2, a few days after the first reported U.S. death from Covid-19. He had been transferred from the company's Hilton Hawaiian Village Waikiki Beach Resort in Hawaii. It was undeniably a lifestyle downgrade, trading the white beaches of Oahu for the soulless office parks of Tysons Corner, but the posting was in some ways a step up: The hotel was down the street from Hilton's corporate headquarters, which meant plenty of face time with the company's CEO, Chris Nassetta, who had a habit of stopping by to make small talk with employees.

But a week into Hamilton's new job, the world had changed, and like corporate executives across the globe, Hamilton was now scrambling to keep his employees and customers safe in a world where nobody knew what that meant. The guidance from the CDC was changing by the day: First the virus could live on surfaces—for up to nine days, according to some early reports—and then it couldn't. Masks were unnecessary, and then crucial. All across the world, executives were seeking personal-protective equipment like masks and gowns that were in deadly short supply. He had nabbed some dust masks from the basement of a Hilton DoubleTree in Crystal City, left over from renovations a few years earlier, with no idea if they were still effective. When Hamilton learned that NBC News was coming to do a story about hotel closures, he called up Cintas, the company that provides the hotel with uniforms and cleaning supplies, and told them that if they could get more hand sanitizer down to the property by the next day, they might get their logo on the evening news.

BUT NOW THAT spotlight had become an uncomfortable glare. The Tysons Corner Hilton, just across the Potomac from the nation's capital, made most of its money hosting corporate events, lobbyists, and industry conferences. They had virtually all been canceled. Tourists, too, had vanished. Hamilton hadn't yet had time to house-hunt in the D.C. area and was living in the hotel with his wife and two small children, who used the service elevator to avoid being exposed to the handful of other guests using the main elevator banks. They raided snacks from the hotel gift shop and ate prepared food that a catering company dropped off three times a week.

He swept the parking lot and cafeteria himself, having suspended the company's contract with outside janitors in an effort to save money. Once a day, he walked the halls, thinking of *The Shining*, the 1980 horror film about a haunted hotel, and knocked on doors to see if the guests were feeling okay. At least once, he escorted a symptomatic guest out a fire exit to a waiting ambulance. Most of the remaining guests were part of a large group of more than a hundred

Saudi Arabian diplomats and businessmen who had been unable to leave, stranded outside their country's sealed borders and now living at the Hilton on the kingdom's dime. (It was a pandemic perversion of a highly publicized incident in which dozens of Saudi royals and ministers were held hostage by the country's crown prince in the Riyadh Ritz-Carlton in a display of the young prince's power.)

After perhaps airlines, the hospitality industry was the hardest hit by the pandemic. Business and leisure travel stopped. But their overhead costs did not. The Hilton at Tysons Corner, wedged in a suburban campus in view of Washington, was popular with visitors to the Defense Department and the CIA, both nearby. Hamilton had run a large food and beverage department at a Las Vegas hotel in the 2008 downturn and had seen what happens when people stop traveling.

He furloughed 80 percent of the hotel's staff. He seriously considered shutting it down entirely, but his finance team told him it would cost $600,000 a month to keep the hotel closed, between taxes, utilities, and other fixed costs. It also costs money to reopen a closed hotel from a dead stop. With the Saudi contingent and some government guests who cycled in and out, it was just barely worth keeping the property open with a skeleton crew.

In late April, Hilton announced a partnership with Reckitt Benckiser, the maker of Lysol, to set up new cleaning protocols for their hotel rooms, sealing the doors of sanitized rooms with a sticker telling guests they were safe. (The partnership, advertised as Hilton CleanStay, began with a cold outreach on LinkedIn from Anu Saxena, Hilton's head of supply management, to the CEO of Reckitt. "I'm sure you are in the throes of these strange times," she had written on April 4, striking the kind of tone that would become common in the months ahead.) To give the protocols a medical seal of approval, Nassetta had roped in the Mayo Clinic, where an octogenarian Conrad Hilton had donated $10 million in 1972 to build a laboratory named after him. Leaning a bit on that connection, Nassetta asked whether the prestigious medical center could come up with some cleaning protocols that Hilton could follow. The idea was to slap a seal on every one of Hilton's hotel doors, reassuring guests that it had been sanitized to the standards of the world's best doctors.

So grim was the state of affairs across Hilton that the contingent of trapped Saudi Arabians, stuck there for more than eight weeks, briefly made Hamilton's hotel the highest grossing in the entire company. An executive at Park Hotel & Resorts, which owns both the McLean and Waikiki hotels and licenses the banner from Hilton, joked to Hamilton that he had now managed two of the highest-grossing properties in the company's portfolio.

In another sign of the grimness that the pandemic would continue to heap, in ways direct and indirect, on the country: The hotel got an influx of unexpected and extremely of-the-times guests in January 2021, when it was booked up by National Guard troops brought in after a mob hoping to prevent the certification of the presidential election overran the U.S. Capitol on January 6.

It was classic Andrew Cuomo: direct to the point of bullying.

"I've gotten wind that Ford is going to make ventilators and I want fifteen thousand," the governor of New York told Ford's CEO, Jim Hackett, over the phone. New York had become the epicenter of the outbreak in the United States and was quickly becoming the epicenter in the world.

"We're hustling like you wouldn't believe, but it's got to work," Hackett told the governor. The machines were complicated. The company needed to work around existing patents and test whatever it came up with. It also needed approvals from the Food and Drug Administration certifying that the ventilators were effective and safe. Hackett told the governor Ford likely wouldn't have a working ventilator until June at the earliest.

"That's too late," Cuomo said, and hung up.

It wasn't just Cuomo. The Ford CEO had heard from governors

of a half dozen states including Michigan, Illinois, and Ohio, all scrambling for protective gear and medical equipment. Hackett had been through crises before and was no stranger to dealing with politicians. He had been on the board of Fifth Third Bank, the giant Midwestern lender, during 2008, and had, over a sandwich in western Michigan, discussed with President George W. Bush the government's efforts to shore up the country's teetering banks. But this was different.

The challenge and scariness of the virus was being amplified by politics. No help was coming from the federal government, and state and local officials were tapping informal connections to try to protect their citizens. One such example was playing out in Cuomo's backyard. Mount Sinai, the New York City hospital, was dramatically low on ventilators. It had struck a deal with Joe Tsai, the executive at Chinese e-commerce company Alibaba and owner of the Brooklyn Nets, one of the city's NBA teams, to donate one thousand ventilators and thousands of badly needed face masks. But there was a problem: Trump had been ramping up his anti-China rhetoric, calling the coronavirus "the China virus" or "Kung Flu," and the Chinese government was refusing to let the plane out. Bill Ford called Kathy Wylde of the Partnership for New York and said former Goldman Sachs executive John Thornton was calling and said Cuomo had to talk to the Chinese ambassador.

"Great news," read the email that landed in Kathy Wylde's inbox. "The ventilators donated by Alibaba have been given the green light by the government of China to head to New York City, just in time." The state had just, on April 3, suffered its deadliest day of the pandemic so far. In the previous twenty-four hours, 562 New Yorkers had died, bringing the death toll to 2,953—by far the most of any state.

It was the culmination of a week of behind-the-scenes geopolitical wrangling that involved John Thornton, Joe Tsai, and a phone call between Cuomo and the Chinese ambassador.

—

IT WASN'T JUST Andrew Cuomo giving Jim Hackett a hard time.

The president's visit on May 21 to the Ford plant in Ypsilanti, which had been taken over by Project Apollo, was uncomfortable from the start.

Ford is strenuously apolitical, and especially so in an election year. It had a policy of not hosting candidates from either party this close to an election. What was more, Michigan was a crucial battleground state, and no matter the stated purpose of the visit—to see Ford's respirators—Hackett knew it was going to turn into a campaign event. And then there was the problem that Trump's public statements and actions had downplayed the danger of the virus. He wouldn't wear a mask in public and had dismissed evidence that said they helped slow infections. He had dismissed a study from Columbia University that found thirty-six American lives could have been saved, had the administration moved just a week earlier to encourage social distancing instead of waiting until March 15, calling the university "very liberal."

Still, this was the kind of patriotic moment that Ford had in its DNA, and it was proud to show off what it had built. Hackett had called Trump economic adviser Larry Kudlow at the White House again to extend the invitation, but added that the president couldn't come if he wouldn't wear a mask. Ford was getting ready to reopen its factories and needed 100 percent compliance on mask-wearing from its employees. If the president came maskless, Hackett knew his job of getting his factory workers to take mask-wearing seriously would be harder.

When the president first arrived at the Rawsonville plant, he had already been asked by a reporter about whether he would wear a mask and had brushed off the question. "We're going to look at it," he said. "A lot of people have been asking me that." Bill Ford and Hackett met Trump in a conference room, both executives in masks. Hackett thanked Trump for his administration's aid in helping Ford secure needed approvals from the Food and Drug Administration for its ventilators.

Then Trump turned to Bill Ford and said, "I guess I have to wear a mask?"

"Yes, sir," the executive responded. Trump ducked out of the room and returned with a navy mask with the presidential seal, showing it off for the executives before putting it on. "I look pretty good, don't I?" he said. He noted he would wear it on the factory tour but would probably take it off when he spoke to the press. "I don't want them to think I'm, you know . . ." he said, trailing off.

He would finish the sentence later in front of news cameras, saying he had been wearing a mask earlier but "didn't want to give the press the pleasure of seeing it." Bill Ford, wearing a mask and eye goggles, was asked moments later by a member of the traveling press corps whether he had told the president it was okay not to wear a mask. He merely threw his arms up in an exasperated shrug.

SITTING IN THE study of his western Michigan home, Hackett picked up a pen and then put it down and rubbed his eyes. In the past few weeks, he and his chairman, Bill Ford, had settled into a grim division of labor. When a Ford employee died of the coronavirus, Bill would call the family and Hackett would write a letter, something they could keep.

By the time a late spring arrived in Michigan in early June, the two executives had done the dance a dozen times. Each letter had been hard for Hackett, but this one was the worst. It was the third death in a single family. The first was a man in his sixties, a veteran of the factory floor. When he died, Hackett had written to his two sons. A few weeks later, one of the sons had died, and the CEO had written to the surviving brother. Now he, too, was dead.

There was nobody left to write.

CAPTAIN JASON AMBROSI looked out the window of his eighth-floor office onto the vast expanse of Atlanta's Hartsfield-Jackson

Airport, the headquarters of Delta Air Lines, his employer for twenty years. In normal times, Hartsfield is the busiest airport in the country, with more than a hundred million passengers passing through in 2019. Today, a crisp, sun-drenched afternoon in June, it was virtually empty. The only noise was a deafening one: a claw descending from a crane, ripping an airplane apart.

It was an MD-88, one of several hundred planes that Delta was retiring as it moved during the pandemic to simplify its fleet. The MD-88 was Ambrosi's plane and had been for most of his twenty-year career at Delta. It was an old model, a gas-guzzler, and known as a workhorse—plenty safe to fly but temperamental in the cockpit, which was not as automated as newer models. "Boeing builds airplanes, McDonnell Douglas builds character," went the old pilot saying.

At the start of the pandemic, Delta had forty-seven of these planes in service and was now retiring them. There weren't nearly enough passengers to fill the newer planes it had, and with fewer pilots trained on the old MD-88s, they were of little value to the company. Most of them were being flown to an airplane boneyard in Blytheville, Arkansas, where they would be stripped for parts. But a few needed maintenance before they would be airworthy. There was no sense in fixing a plane just to rip it up, so the company had hired wreck-it crews to do the job right there on its runways.

CHAPTER 19

SPACE OF ONE

David Solomon was seated at Duryea's Lobster Deck in Montauk. The Goldman boss had been up early that Friday, working in the morning from the den of his rented home in the eastern Long Island beach town, and was now meeting friends visiting from New Jersey for lunch at the seafood restaurant, a former local dive serving walk-up lobster rolls that had since transformed into a sit-down restaurant with bottle service.

Solomon heard his name and turned to find a woman in her early twenties. She introduced herself as a first-year Goldman Sachs employee and motioned behind her to a table of a half dozen other young colleagues who, she told the CEO of her company without a touch of sheepishness, had taken the day off and come to the beach. Solomon thanked her for saying hi. "I'm sure you're doing great work," he said.

He turned back to his guests, privately fuming. He would never have had the nerve as a junior employee to approach the CEO, much less in the middle of a workday, much less in the middle of a stretch of remote work that had been grating on Solomon for weeks. He was sick of it.

During the summer of 2020, the fear that had kept people inside and made ghost towns out of once-vibrant cities had receded, or at least been outweighed by their urge to party. New York had buzzed

back to life, with to-go cocktails and throngs packed into the ubiquitous outdoor sheds that had taken over sidewalks all over the city.
In the course of three months, the vibe had gone from funereal to
celebratory. The clang of pots and pans being banged out of windows each night, a communal outpouring of support for medical
and emergency workers, had long since ceased, replaced by the more
familiar before-times sound of revelers out on the town. Solomon
would take weekend walks through New York's trendy downtown
Soho neighborhood where he lived, past outdoor bars and restaurants packed with young people, only to turn up on Monday morning to Goldman's offices—which had reopened in late June for
employees who wanted to come in—to find a ghost town. It seemed
to him that his employees were comfortable enough to risk catching
the virus for a beer, but not to return to the office. To him, it was
proof that that remote work had run amok.

His dyspepsia on the subject struck many of his underlings as a bit
hypocritical, given that Solomon himself had traveled freely for much
of the pandemic, spending weekends—though rarely workdays—at
vacation spots in the Bahamas and the Hamptons. He would also, a
few days after his run-in with the junior analysts in the Hamptons,
perform at an electronic-music festival in Southampton that would
be gravely criticized by public health experts and by the state's governor, Andrew Cuomo, who cited "egregious social-distancing viola-
tions."

Solomon would later admit to Goldman's board that the concert
had been a mistake. But his annoyance remained as the summer
stretched on. Solomon belonged to an earlier, hard-driving generation of financial executives. He had come to Wall Street in the mid-
1980s and spent his early years in the mercenary world of high-yield
debt, first at Drexel Burnham Lambert, where Michael Milken
invented the junk-bond market before being convicted of insider
trading, and then at Bear Stearns, where he raised money for private-
equity barons. He joined Goldman in 1999, just after it went public,

and had risen through the ranks as a hard-driving boss. He had been named CEO in 2019 and had built a reputation as bold, if dictatorial, with a clear vision for the firm and little time for dissent.

Still, he had bent to a changing culture on Wall Street and the attitudes of a newer generation of workers, implementing policies that ensured Goldman's youngest and most overworked employees would have their weekends protected. He had spoken often about the need to work hard but have a personal life. But the pandemic and the subsequent work-from-home regime had upset that balance. Goldman had been quicker than other Wall Street firms to send its employees home—notably, it had avoided the kind of trading-floor outbreak that had swept through JPMorgan's in May, when that bank was still pressuring employees to come to work—but it was all starting to grate on Solomon. Wall Street, to a degree seen in few other industries, is an apprenticeship industry. College graduates join by the thousands and learn on their feet. (Literally so in Goldman's case, where summer interns used to receive on their first day, in addition to their security pass, a folding stool to carry around with them from desk to desk as they shadowed more senior executives.)

In the summer and fall of 2020, as the pandemic waned in some hotspots like New York, executives struggled to figure out what to do with, and how to speak to, the thousands of employees they had sent home months earlier. Childcare was still scarce, leaving many parents pulling double-duty and on the edge of losing their minds. The virus was still prevalent and early news of vaccines, though promising, still had them months away. More than 150,000 Americans, and more than 650,000 people globally, had died by the end of July and 165,000 had tested positive for the virus in the month's final week. But the long Groundhog Day of a summer seemed to many business leaders, including Solomon, to have bred a sense of entitlement, or self-indulgence. Their workers had fled the city for long-term rentals in the Catskills or hot new cities like Austin and

Miami. Those who remained were becoming fed up with months of quarantine and taking advantage of outdoor congregations.

America's great work-from-home experiment was underway.

IN JUNE OF 1729, a great stone building opened in London. It is thought to be the first modern corporate headquarters, the home of the East India Company, the quasi-governmental outfit that by then had claimed swaths of Asia in the name of the crown and capitalism. It was an imposing, magisterial sight in Georgian London: three stories high with five marble columns, topped by a cornice—architecture a historian would later say was designed "to inspire confidence and impress the shareholders." It even had a boardroom, into whose marble chimneypiece had been etched a scene of dark-skinned natives offering up pearls, porcelain, tea, and other exotic riches to Britannia, the helmeted female warrior that personified England.

In the three centuries since then, offices have gotten taller and grander, but their purpose remains the same: part logistical convenience and part projection of corporate might. In the waning days of the twentieth century, as internet connections became faster and more widespread, many predicted the death of the office. A few big companies, including IBM and Yahoo, had embraced remote work, promising freedom to employees and boasting of being able to recruit the best talent in the world, wherever it was. In 2009, an IBM report said that 40 percent of its roughly 386,000 employees in 173 countries "have no office at all." The company had saved $2 billion by nixing fifty-eight million square feet of office space, and held its work-from-wherever policy out as a model for others to copy.

It hadn't lasted. In 2013, Yahoo's new chief executive, Marissa Mayer, ordered its employees back into the office, saying that the spontaneous interaction and human connections were crucial to the company doing its best work. (Yahoo's best work, as it turned out, was behind it; Mayer left in 2017, and the company was effectively sold for parts over the next few years.) IBM did the same four years later.

At the same time, companies invested billions of dollars in gleaming corporate campuses, replacing the watercooler with "innovation lounges" and kombucha bars to lure workers back and encourage the kind of collaboration that Mayer thought so key to corporate success. Some companies took a harder tack; Bloomberg, the financial news and data company, logged what time employees got to work in the morning, and compensated for the heavy hand with the kind of workplace perks more common in Silicon Valley, from afternoon ice cream bars to roving peanut-butter carts. The office culture of the late 2010s, on the eve of the pandemic, was one firmly rooted in physical proximity.

BRIAN CHESKY, TOO, was lonely. The extroverted CEO of Airbnb had been holed up in his San Francisco home for weeks. In normal times, he delighted in dropping in to visit hosts and often stayed in Airbnbs under assumed names to test the experience that travelers were getting. Now he had been stuck inside for weeks.

The lockdowns might have killed Airbnb, but instead they inspired a pivot. Before the pandemic, the company had a small unit that allowed travelers to book experiences rather than accommodations—like wine tasting in Napa or tree-canopy tours in Belize. With travel grounded, Airbnb had taken that business virtual, allowing people to offer virtual experiences like tours or classes. Chesky's favorite was "The Dogs of Chernobyl," a fifty-dollar, hour-long video tour in which a host donned a GoPro camera and roamed the fallout zone of the nuclear-accident site and fed hundreds of wild dogs, descendants of pets who were abandoned when residents fled. (Chesky recommended it to Michael Grimes, his banker at Morgan Stanley, who did the event with his wife and college-aged kids.)

The pandemic also brought about another unexpected opportunity.

By May, Chesky began noticing an uptick in bookings for longer-term stays. The weekend getaways to far-flung destinations were being replaced by stints of several weeks or more, overwhelmingly within a few hundred miles of guests' hometowns. Urban residents were searching for vacation rentals in neighboring towns and cities, so they didn't have to fly.

On July 8, the company hit a momentous milestone. Guest bookings finally climbed back to their daily level before the pandemic began. The IPO that Chesky had been planning at the start of 2020, which had been knocked off schedule when the pandemic began— and which at times that spring, as Airbnb begged Wall Street for money and laid off one-quarter of its staff, looked laughable—was back on the table.

Airbnb's bankers at Morgan Stanley had drawn up a presentation that week meant to do two things: convince Airbnb that it could go public, and get Morgan Stanley hired to lead the IPO. It was titled "Space of One," and it was a refined Wall Street pitch, engineered to land softly on the ears of a prospective client. On the left-hand side of the PowerPoint slide was a column titled "Usual," ticking off the ways that a normal company, in normal times, would position itself to investors. The column on the right read, "Space of One," showing line by line how Airbnb's listing would be different. Most companies went public when their short-term results were strong. Airbnb would go public "during [the] worst travel downturn in a century." Most companies would have managed the crisis "to preserve value solely for shareholders." Airbnb would "embrace change from crisis and serve all stakeholders." One that particularly delighted Chesky: "Going public with an uncertain short term can only attract long-term investors by definition." In other words, Airbnb's financial results since the pandemic's start were so bad—and the crisis's end was still so hazy—that any investor willing to buy its stock had to be prepared to stick around for a long time. That's music to the ears of any corporate executive, who bemoans shareholders who pile in at the IPO, only to flip the stock for a quick buck.

The bankers were coming to their well-rehearsed final act, the part of any deal pitch where the icing gets laid on thick. Any other company's "success narrative"—the story it tells to big investors ahead of the IPO to gin up demand for the stock—would be based on how richly it had been valued in previous fundraising rounds. Investors would be impressed by steadily climbing valuations that showed institutional investors had increasing confidence in the company. But that wouldn't work for Airbnb. Its valuation, once as high as $31 billion, had been cut to just $18 billion in the April investment from Silver Lake and Sixth Street.

Airbnb would buck that trend, the bankers said. Its narrative wouldn't be tethered to a steadily climbing valuation or eye-popping growth. Instead, it would be "based on doing the impossible"—surviving.

CHAPTER 20

———

GO FLY PLANES

Doug Parker was walking the halls of American's headquarters in early June when he passed a glass-walled conference room where his top deputy, Robert Isom, and his chief revenue officer, Vasu Raja, were poring over documents. Raja noticed the CEO and waved him in to hear a pitch so bold it would have been unimaginable just a few weeks earlier.

The economics of flying had changed. The federal government was now covering the payroll for American's 107,000 employees. The planes were a fixed cost; even if they sat on the ground, airlines were still paying the leases. That basically just left jet fuel and landing fees, and Raja had done the math showing that even a flight that was less than half full could cover that. "Everyone is going the wrong way here," Raja had told Parker, and pitched him on aggressively adding back flights in a bid for market share. "What do you think?" he had asked his boss. "Sounds fantastic," Parker said. "That's what we're supposed to do. Go fly planes."

After getting the federal aid back in March, American had leaned in. It brought back about half of the 410 jets it had parked that spring on runways in Tulsa, Pittsburgh, and the New Mexico desert outside Roswell. While its rivals hung back, it added the equivalent of an entire airline to its schedule—some four million seats, roughly the size of a pre-pandemic JetBlue—and by mid-July, it had more than twice as many seats in the air as United and more than Delta by half. Its home hub of Dallas/Fort Worth was briefly the busiest airport in the world. By the end of the month, nearly seven hundred planes were taking off each day, down from the nine hundred of a year earlier but up from around two hundred on the quietest days of the spring. Its lounges had reopened, and the occasional line formed at the Chick-fil-A in Terminal D.

Competitors tongue-wagged. In an internal memo sent to employees in June, United, which had added just 640,000 seats in the month that American had added 1.2 million, said some nameless competitors were operating an "inflated schedule" that would ultimately prove to be a money-losing mistake. Bastian promised Wall Street analysts that Delta would take "the industry's most conservative approach to capacity."

But Parker's latest gamble seemed to be working. American's domestic flights were close to 70 percent full in June—so full that the CEO, on a late-May trip to his vacation home in the Florida panhandle, couldn't get a seat on an American flight and ended up on Southwest, an airline he once compared to a "cattle car." At one point, Raja got an angry call from a senior official at the Centers for Disease Control, who had seen discounted flights American was selling to Daytona Beach. Parker's go-fly-planes strategy, it seemed, was not popular in the public health community.

IT WASN'T JUST air travel. The U.S. economy roared back in the summer and early fall of 2020. Weary of lockdowns and tempted by warm weather, Americans busted out of the pandemic shackles, switching off Netflix and putting their sourdough starters back in the refrigerator. After shrinking by 31 percent in the second quarter, America's economy grew 38 percent between July and October. The country had gained back three-quarters of the jobs that had been lost since the start of the pandemic, and unemployment was at 5.4 percent. Restaurant sales, too, were back at 80 percent of pre-pandemic levels. It wasn't quite enough to erase the economic damage of the spring of 2020—there was still about $280 billion missing from the nation's total economic activity—but it was close.

That was welcome news for Chris Nassetta. The Hilton CEO had stacked financial sandbags back in March, borrowing $1.5 billion from Wall Street and raising another $1 billion from a credit-card points deal it had in place with American Express. Hilton's revenues had fallen by two-thirds in the second quarter. By late June, the company's stock was still at seventy dollars, nearly 40 percent down from its February highs. The CEO who had spent more than two hundred days on the road in 2019—a schedule so punishing it had sent him to Cabo in search of respite—was restless from being stuck mostly in his Arlington home. He had enjoyed the extra family time—his five older daughters had moved back home, joining his youngest, still in high school—but was itching to return to a more normal world. And he worried that investors and customers were writing Hilton off for good. By August of 2020, Hilton's hotels were 40 percent full on a good day. Business travel showed few signs of picking up, and leisure travelers had ditched weekend hotel stays in cities for longer-term larks in more rural areas.

"They think we're dead," he told his wife, Paige, as he scrubbed a stubborn lasagna pan. "We're not."

FLYING MORE PLANES wasn't enough. Even with its new strategy, American Airlines' finances were in trouble. The company had burned $65 million a day in March, $86 million a day in April, which would prove to be the nadir, another $56 million a day in May, and $30 million a day in June, despite cost cuts including freezing pay and cutting its headquarters staff by a third. The company had hoped the $25 billion government loan program, of which $4.8 billion had been allocated for American, would plug its rapidly deepening financial hole, but negotiations over the details of the loans were dragging out. The Treasury Department's bankers, at boutique Wall Street firm PJT Partners, wanted sufficient collateral to protect taxpayers, and American had relatively little to offer. Most of its planes were leased or otherwise financed, and it had already borrowed against its most profitable routes.

Jim Murray, the lead banker at PJT, suggested American put its gleaming new headquarters up as collateral. The three-hundred-acre campus, finished in 2019, was a point of pride for the company. It boasted a new state-of-the-art operations center, modern art, and a sun-filled commissary flanked by purpose-built nature preserves where bobcats lurked. It had cost nearly $1 billion, including some $350 million for the main building, and Parker didn't want to put it on the block. So American's chief financial officer, Derek Kerr, offered an alternative. An outside firm had valued their frequent-flyer program at $25 billion. A dirty secret of the airline industry was that they made more money from their credit-card partnerships with major banks than they did from selling airplane tickets. Kerr asked Murray: Perhaps the U.S. Treasury would accept that instead?

The government's bankers were skeptical. What would happen if American went bankrupt? If the miles accumulated by its frequent flyers were zeroed out, the program would be worthless, exposing the U.S. taxpayer to huge losses. Kerr reassured PJT that wouldn't happen, and that even in past airline bankruptcies, their loyalty programs had emerged intact. "There's value here," he told them.

The $25 billion in payroll support the airlines had received as part of the CARES Act in March was set to expire on September 30, and Parker had been talking to Sara Nelson for a few weeks about whether the political coalition they had glued together back in March might hold for a second round of aid. Nelson told Parker she thought it would, but Nate Gatten, American's head of government affairs, was less optimistic. He told his boss there was less political will to re-up the aid to the airlines. It had been distasteful enough to most of Congress the first time around, and the political fight over a second round of stimulus heading into the fall was sticky enough as it was. Democrats were seeking bigger checks for individual households and more aid for hospitals and state and local governments, while Republicans pushed for a smaller, more targeted package.

Political resentment had spread, too, with some critics wondering whether continued support for the airlines was akin to corporate welfare. There were no earmarks for hoteliers, or real estate owners whose properties emptied out and whose tenants began looking for ways out of their leases. The hundreds of thousands of restaurants that closed had no special carveout, despite impassioned pleas from celebrity chefs and trade groups hastily assembled to lobby on their behalf.

The airline CEOs again gathered for a call in mid-June, this time over Zoom. The unified front they had held back in March, when their dire needs were more or less equal, had begun to fray. As the crisis had dragged on, their underlying strengths and weaknesses had come into the open: Delta and Southwest, which had come into the crisis with less debt and stronger balance sheets, had begun to pull back in their efforts for a second round of aid, while others, notably Parker at American, which carried more debt than its rivals, were gung-ho. Nick Calio, the lobbying organization's boss, had privately told Parker that while Bastian and Gary Kelly of Southwest weren't doing anything overt to stymie then-nascent talks in Washington, neither were they working as hard for it. He had kept the topic of a second round of aid off the meeting's agenda, which instead focused on health and safety, including an update on a study the airlines had commissioned in the spring from Harvard's T.H. Chan School of Public Health.

As the executives ticked through agenda items, Parker piped up. "I have one more thing," he said, and he laid out an idea for a clean extension of the airlines' payroll support program. The loan program that had been so problematic last time wouldn't be part of this. "It sounds like a long putt," Bastian said, "but of course who wouldn't accept that?" That was a vote of confidence as far as Parker was concerned, and as soon as he hung up, he sent an email to Gatten: "This is now the top priority of American Airlines."

But negotiations were dragging on and by June, the company couldn't hold out any longer. Just then, Goldman Sachs, the Wall Street firm known for creative, even deviously creative, thinking when it came to fundraising, came to Derek Kerr with an idea. What about American's intellectual property—logos, patents, and other squishy but potentially valuable assets? American had its iconic "AA" logo, its AAdvantage credit card, plus rights to aa.com and other assets. The government hadn't been willing to accept it as collateral, but maybe private investors would.

An independent appraiser put the value of the trademarks at more than $7 billion, which was enough for the Goldman bankers to raise $1 billion in senior debt. But in a sign of just how fragile investors believed the company was, the interest rate was 11.75 percent. Back in February, American had sold bonds backed by no collateral at all for 3.75 percent. In other words, investors were so worried that American might not pay them back that they charged three times as much in interest—even though, if that had happened, they would have been the proud new owners of intellectual property valued at billions of dollars and slapped on credit cards across the country.

(This wasn't the first time during the crisis that a company had mortgaged a well-known brand to raise cash. When Morgan Stanley bankers were finalizing a fundraising round for Carnival Cruise Line back in the spring, the company had put up its ships and operating permits as collateral. At the last minute, a banker suggested that Carnival's logo and trademark be added to the pot, telling a colleague, "I don't see a lot of demand for 'Morgan Stanley Cruise Line.'")

Between the IP bonds and another $2.15 billion in stock and convertible bonds that it issued around the same time, American had enough cash to see itself through another few months.

So it went for one blue-chip company after another in the spring and summer of 2020. Unlike in 2008, when the debt markets were all but closed for more than a year, there was money available, though it was expensive.

The company's daily cash loss would not fall to under $10 million until March of 2021, and would not turn positive until April, a full year after the crisis had begun. Over those twelve months, American would raise nearly $23 billion in new cash, about two-thirds of it from the federal government and the rest in a smattering of stock and bond deals in the market.

KERR HAD FINALLY scored a win. The PJT bankers representing Treasury said they were willing to accept the airline's credit-card program as collateral for the $4.8 billion in loans the airline had been allocated out of the CARES Act.

Its bankers at Goldman, ever sensing an opportunity, suggested a bait and switch. Why didn't American take that government stamp of approval to the market instead and see if investors would accept it? Greg Lee, one of the firm's senior investment bankers, pitched Kerr on the idea in midsummer, a few weeks after the bank had sold the IP-backed bonds.

There were two advantages to this for American, the banker said. First, it would leave the company with its more traditional assets—planes, spare parts, and, if it came to that, its headquarters—that it could use to borrow from private investors in the future. Second, it would let American keep certain commercial details to itself. Unlike other airlines that had a single credit-card partner, American had two: Citigroup and Barclays. The company had worked hard to keep the exact details of the two deals secret, to play the banks off each other for better terms when they occasionally renegotiated their contracts. If the Treasury had claim to its credit-card program, that might make those contracts a matter of public record. Any airing of the loyalty program details would inevitably anger either Citigroup or Barclays—and now wasn't a good time to be pissing off banks,

Kerr knew. The company could be more selective in its disclosures to private investors and at least keep the details of its contracts off the U.S. government's website. There was some logic to the deal, he admitted.

But American had just weeks earlier been forced to pay 11.75 percent interest to get bond investors to lend against its intellectual property. Treasury was offering to lend against the credit-card program at 3.75 percentage points above a benchmark rate, and Kerr knew it was a good financial deal. "Forgive me if I'm not basking in the warm glow of Goldman Sachs," he asked Lee, "but what's it going to cost me?" The banker chuckled. "A lot more," he said, noting that investors would probably demand 10 or 11 percent.

Treasury's deal won. (Goldman would soon pitch the same deal to United Airlines, which became the first carrier to sell bonds backed by its loyalty program to the market. Delta would follow in the fall. American would eventually do the same, in March of 2021, once it had repaid Treasury and taken back the rights to its program. The bonds carried an interest rate of about 5 percent, roughly half what Goldman had quoted Kerr ten months earlier.)

It got another $700 million when Southwest, which was in far stronger financial shape, decided not to take the money. There was a date in the fall by which the airlines had to say whether they were actually going to borrow the money, and Delta didn't do it. So American got Delta's money, another $2 billion, bringing its total government borrowings to $7.5 billion. (The American executives were flummoxed; even if Delta didn't need the money, they figured the company would take it just so it didn't go to a rival.)

AIRLINES ARE QUICK to trumpet new routes they are opening. But they close routes quietly. That's what made a press release that American issued on August 20 unusual. It was a list of fifteen small cities that it would cut service to starting in October—places like Sioux City, Iowa, and Kalamazoo, Michigan. This was pure politics, meant to rile up congressional members whose districts were serviced by those airports. "The airline will continue to reassess plans for these and other markets as an extension of [federal aid] remains under deliberation," the company said.

Parker was back in Washington, reprising the role he had played back in March as chief dealmaker for an airline industry that had received billions of dollars in government aid and now needed billions more. He had traded the Willard Hotel, in an eerie and desolate downtown, for the Four Seasons in Georgetown, where at least a few restaurants were open and he could walk down to the water, which he did almost daily in the sweltering D.C. heat, more often than not with his phone pressed to his ear. He became a well-known figure in the largely empty hotel, checking in with the manager about occupancy rates. Most days they were in the single digits. "I feel you, man," Parker said.

On September 10, he dialed in to a call with Nancy Pelosi. The speaker had been hard to get on the phone, a caginess that reflected the political corner she had been backed into. The presidential election was looming large, and the political wisdom was hardening around the idea that if another big aid package was passed, it would buoy Trump's chances of reelection and help Republicans hoping to wrest control of the House, which would cost Pelosi her Speaker's gavel.

What's more, the united front of organized labor that had helped the Democrats muster the votes for the first round of aid back in March was now fraying. The American Federation of Teachers was pushing for money to be set aside to help schools reopen safely, and its president, Randi Weingarten, had made no secret of her displeasure about another carveout for airline employees. That had contributed to Pelosi's caucus holding a firm line on additional aid to state and local governments, which had become a crucial sticking point in the negotiations. (Such aid would also help public hospitals hit hard by the pandemic.)

Also joining the call, at Pelosi's request, was Peter DeFazio, the

House transportation committee chair who had assumed the role during the airline aid negotiations of subject-matter expert. He was in a foul mood—wildfires were raging across western Oregon and he, along with thousands of his constituents, had been evacuated from his house—and quickly hijacked the conversation.

"Nancy, you're fighting the wrong fight," DeFazio said. Democrats' insistence on pushing for more money for state and local governments was well-intentioned but short-sighted. American and United had warned that without an extension of the federal aid, they would furlough more than thirty thousand employees. "Let's go get what we can get. Then we'll use that and we'll win the election and then we'll go back and get more. If we don't win the election, we've got bigger trouble anyway." The congressman carried on in an uncharacteristic rebuke of his party's leader, seeming to forget that Parker was there at all. Parker hit mute and turned to his chief lobbyist, Gatten. "Just let him go," Gatten said. "He's fighting your fight."

DeFazio kept going, urging Pelosi to soften her stance. Come September 30, he said, tens of thousands of airline workers would be out of a job. "Nancy, they're not bluffing. We have to get this done," he said. Then the line went muffled, like someone was holding a hand over the receiver and talking in the background. DeFazio came back on. "I have to go," he said. "I'm being evacuated." *Click.*

CHAPTER 21

THE YOLO ECONOMY

It looked like God had picked up the world, shaken all the people out of it, and put it back down again. James Gorman was walking through an empty Times Square, on his way to the office. It was October 8, 2020. He had spent nearly three months alone in his apartment, a sudden shock for a man who had scarcely spent a week straight in New York City since becoming CEO of Morgan Stanley ten years earlier. He had taken long walks at night to think, strolling past dark restaurants and shops boarded up as racial-justice protests had gripped much of New York City, and the nation, after the May death of a Black man, George Floyd, at the hands of the Minneapolis police.

Gorman was the thirteenth Morgan Stanley employee to come down with Covid-19. More than twenty would die, including a security guard who worked outside the CEO's office on the bank's executive floor. It had taken Gorman ten weeks to feel like himself again. Deep breaths elicited a crackle from his lungs and a tightness in his chest. Every day, he tried to see if his sense of smell had returned by shoving his nose into a jar of Vegemite, a black, savory spread made from brewer's yeast that is beloved in his home country of Australia and unrecognizable as food to the rest of the world. That morning, he had dipped his finger into the jar and licked it. Nothing yet.

He had begun 2020 with a major takeover, the deal for E*Trade. He was about to announce another one.

It had started in June. Morgan Stanley, whose own money-management arm was a minnow on Wall Street, had coveted Eaton Vance for years. It was a major retailer of Eaton Vance's mutual funds and other products through its retail brokerage. Gorman had reached out to Tom Faust, the CEO of Eaton Vance, about acquiring it. The two had chatted over Zoom, Gorman in his Manhattan apartment and Faust in his weekend home in Maine. Gorman's team had given him a lighting setup, but it kept falling over, and he had shoved it in a closet weeks earlier.

The timing, he knew, was bad. A second wave of Covid had roiled markets again over the summer and sparked the kind of lockdowns that could hamper the economy for years. He didn't care. He had ignored naysayers when Morgan Stanley had acquired Smith Barney, the giant retail brokerage, in 2012. At the time, he had felt like the boy in *The Polar Express*, hearing a bell that nobody else could. (In 2017, a deputy gave him a silver sleigh bell that he kept on his desk.) He knew it would be expensive. And he knew he would face blowback. All mergers are hard, but those between financial firms often fall victim to cultural infighting that can be fatal. Bankers are egoistic and fickle. Traders are pugilistic. Portfolio managers are preening and secretive. Tossing together these various camps from different firms can be a recipe for disaster. Morgan Stanley had been through one such disaster once already, a 1997 tie-up with Dean Witter that had set off a decade of sniping and management coups that had plagued the firm for years.

"The world is full of executives sitting around trying to buy great properties, cheaply," Gorman told his lieutenants as they debated the wisdom of doing a massive deal for Eaton Vance. "They sit around and remind each other how clever they are for avoiding paying too much. When a door opens, you have to walk through it."

Now he was walking through Times Square for a 7 A.M. conference call with his top deputies to brief them on the deal, which would be announced just before the market opened. It was his first time back in the office in months. On any given day, only about 5 percent of his workers were at the bank's Times Square headquarters.

WHILE MANHATTAN REMAINED half-empty, the world of online stock trading was soaring.

The U.S. stock market charged back fiercely from its depths. On August 19, the bear market that had set in during mid-March officially ended, with the stocks closed at a new record high. It was the shortest bear market in history. More than a dozen new closing highs would be hit by the end of the year. It was a stunning, almost absurd rebound for a stock market that had, just a few months earlier, suffered its worst losses in decades.

Silicon Valley led the way. In a frenzy reminiscent of the dot-com bubble two decades earlier, technology stocks soared, well beyond what even their seemingly pandemic-proof businesses' profits could support. In 2018, Apple had built a new wing of the tech royalty castle when it became the world's first company to be worth $1 trillion; on August 19, as the stock market hit an all-time high, its first since February, it became a $2 trillion company. Amazon and Microsoft weren't that far behind, if a few hundred billion dollars can be counted as trivial, and in Silicon Valley in the late days of the long pandemic summer, it could.

The rally's riches, of course, were not shared evenly. Only about half the country owned stocks, and nearly 90 percent of shares were in the hands of the richest 10 percent of Americans. To be sure, they had also suffered the losses on the way down, but now, as the market hit one record after another, they more than made up for it. (Creative accountants, too, can wring tax breaks out of selectively harvesting investment losses.)

Companies of all stripes found it almost too easy to raise money as summer turned into fall. And if Wall Street was in a giving mood,

Derek Kerr would be there. The American Airlines CFO had spent most of the previous eight months begging for cash—from banks, from bondholders, from Treasury, from Congress, then from banks again. It had mortgaged its frequent-flyer program, the iconic red-and-blue logo emblazoned on the tails of its 950-odd planes—in short, anything that wasn't nailed down. (It drew the line at one big thing—having to pledge his headquarters as collateral for government loans.)

On November 9, investors got the news they had been waiting for since March: Pfizer announced at 6:45 A.M. that the vaccine it had developed in partnership with BioNTech was 90 percent effective in protecting participants in an early study from the virus. They started buying at the opening bell, and by the end of the day, the S&P 500 had hit its second-highest level ever. Even the day's mix of winners and losers was a testament to investors' confidence that, with effective vaccines on the horizon, the pandemic was coming to an end. Netflix, Clorox, Zoom, and Peloton, all pandemic darlings, lost a combined $55 billion in market value. The day's biggest winners were the pandemic's losers—Kohl's, Carnival Cruise Line, and American Airlines, whose stock rose 15 percent.

Sitting in his Fort Worth office—really just a cubicle in the open-air executive floor at American's headquarters—Derek Kerr knew enough to take the money. He called his contact at Bank of America. The airline wanted to sell $500 million in stock, he said, and as a thank-you present for participating in the $1 billion loan that American had needed back in March, the company wanted to hire Bank of America to broker the sale.

It was what's known on Wall Street as a block trade, where a bank agrees to buy a company's shares outright and take on the risk of selling them to other investors. Because of the risk involved—a bank may misjudge the demand and get saddled with stock it can't offload—banks typically charge fees of 4 or 5 percent. But now, in a sign of just how quickly market appetite had turned positive, Bank of America was so sure it could sell the shares at a quick profit that it charged American just under 2 percent. By 8 A.M., it had flipped the shares to investors, making under $1 million for a day's worth in a market that was running on jet fuel.

IT WAS THE dawn of the YOLO economy. The term, short for "you only live once," had been around since at least the 1990s and was popularized in the early 2010s by the rapper Drake, who later apologized for it. After losing out on the word-of-the-year prize to "GIF" in 2012 and being roundly mocked on *Saturday Night Live*, it seemed to have faded out. But a year into the pandemic, it became the motto of a class of Americans who had decided to chuck it all. They quit their jobs, they moved across the country, they put their life savings into moonshot investments. "YOLO!" they would post on Twitter or Reddit. It was a dissonant banner in a year rocked by so much death.

Regular Americans rushed to the stock market by the millions, propelled by boredom, turbocharged by a steady stream of social media hype, and flush with cash from a year of curbed spending and generous government stimulus, which they lovingly called "stimmies" on the Internet message boards like Reddit, where they swapped ideas and egged each other on. They flocked to startups like Robinhood that offered free trades on apps that presented the market as a game to be beaten.

The thundering herd returned. And the cloud of dust it kicked up lifted corporate names from a bygone era: GameStop, a troubled video-game retailer that was once a fixture of suburban malls, and BlackBerry, the original smartphone maker that was beaten at its own game by Apple and Google. AMC, the movie-theater chain whose business and stock had been hammered by the pandemic and had, in the early months of 2020, warned that it might go out of business.

Their defiance in the face of conventional investing wisdom was a financial mirroring of the populism that had rocked the political landscape over the previous few years. Both were fueled by hurt and rejection, a sense that the ruling classes in Washington and on Wall Street had sold out everyday Americans. For the Republican base that had propelled Trump to power, it was political elites. For the Reddit crowd that pushed the stocks of near-bankrupt companies skyward, it was a cabal of hedge funds and banks crushing retail investors under their boot.

Most of these amateur traders likely couldn't have articulated the economic forces pushing them toward such objectively irrational investments. But the science made sense: In a world of ultralow interest rates, the road to riches was not parking a slice of every paycheck in a conservative portfolio of long-term investments, banking on the math of pennies compounded over time. It was in betting it all on a single spin of the wheel, a low-probability but high-payoff bet—a calculus similar to that of many of the voters who, in 2016, had pulled the lever for Donald Trump.

These retail investors pulled professional money managers along with them. In doing so, they upended a balance of power that had, in the post-2008 decade, seen the retreat of individual stock pickers and the dot-com day traders and the rise of asset-management behemoths, who managed trillions of dollars in funds that simply owned a slice of the entire market, matching its financial returns with no expectation of beating them. These firms, the largest of which was Larry Fink's BlackRock, with nearly $10 trillion under its thumb, offered low-cost, prudential investment products, a "set-it-and-forget-it" approach designed to build wealth over time. The retail Reddit army had a different rallying cry: "To the moon."

Fueling the surge, too, was a newfangled product that was being pushed on Wall Street: the blank-check company, in which a money manager would sell shares to the public and use those funds to go acquire a private company, which then became publicly traded by merging with the shell company. Special-purpose acquisition vehicles, known as SPACs, came almost out of nowhere to raise $83 billion in 2020, and would go on to raise another $100 billion in 2021, which their managers used to acquire companies. SPACs and zombie stocks embodied the YOLO economy, which was predicated on the belief that the market could only go up, just months removed from an object lesson to the contrary.

BRIAN CHESKY WAS speechless. During an appearance on Bloomberg Television on the morning of December 10, the reporter had just told him that Airbnb's stock, which would start trading any minute that morning on the Nasdaq stock exchange, looked like it would open at $139 a share. "That's the first time I've heard that number," Chesky said. Chesky's dark, bushy eyebrows shot up and stayed there as he did the math in his head, blinking rapidly. The emergency financing he had raised back in the spring from private-equity firms, which had kept Airbnb afloat, had valued the company at about $18 billion. Now, any minute, the company would be worth more than $90 billion. "I—I don't know what else to say," stammered Chesky, who was now worth $15 billion on paper but couldn't form a complete sentence to save his life. "I'm humbled by it." Airbnb's stock actually did a bit better, opening at $146 a share, valuing the company at just over $100 billion. The bump didn't change the $3.5 billion Airbnb had pocketed when it doled out its IPO shares to select investors, but it was a staggering valuation, especially for a company written off by all but a few savvy investors back in the spring.

In Silicon Valley, "unicorn" is the term for a startup that manages to reach a private valuation of $1 billion. At some point there were so many that investors and journalists stopped counting. Dan Primack, a columnist at Axios, suggested a higher tier for the $10 billion-plus set: "dragons." Airbnb, left for dead just nine months ago and rescued by two Wall Street firms in the equivalent of a Silicon Valley fire sale, was now worth $100 billion.

The company had not only survived but had thrived. Its IPO was one of the biggest in history and told the story of the surprising ways that consumers—those lucky enough to keep their jobs, at least—

kept spending throughout the lockdowns. City dwellers sprang for mountain getaways, and parents driven mad in their tiny apartments splurged on country estates. Peloton sales spiked. So did food delivery orders. Hilton, too, had started by late summer to see a rebound in bookings, not for international or business travel, but for families looking for a place they could drive to for a weekend, just to get away.

Consumer capitalism, even in a pandemic, finds a way.

———

GAMBLES

Doug Parker didn't want to be the guy who ruined Christmas.

He had made a promise to get the twelve thousand workers who'd been furloughed in October, after the government's aid ran out, a paycheck by Christmas and he badly wanted to keep it. American's workers had been through hell—yanked around by politicians, furloughed by the company they trusted, leaving many of them financially strapped. More than nineteen thousand of the company's employees had dipped into their 401(k) accounts to help get through the crisis, pulling out an average of $30,000 apiece. Eight thousand more had borrowed against their retirement savings. The largest group was members of the company's fleet-service crew: the workers who haul luggage, wave planes into the gate, or clean up after the passengers leave them. Most made less than twenty dollars an hour before they were furloughed. They were dipping into a rainy-day fund they didn't have.

And so American Airlines executives gathered in the company's boardroom in Fort Worth on December 21. Parker had made that promise weeks earlier, when prospects for a second round of government aid had looked more likely. But the $900 billion bill, which included an extension of the $25 billion earmarked to cover airlines' payroll, had stalled heading into the presidential election, and now Washington was pure chaos, with Republicans trying to forestall any momentum a Democratic majority, about to take over the presidency as well, might manage. Parker realized he'd made a multibillion-dollar promise he might not be able to afford.

Gatten, the airline's top in-house lobbyist, had dialed in from Washington to provide a prognosis. The bill had cleared the House and looked like it would easily pass in the Senate, but the big question was whether the president would sign it. The official White House account had tweeted its support of the bill, but the chatter in Washington was that Trump, who had decamped for Mar-a-Lago in the wake of his loss to Joe Biden, wouldn't sign it. Gatten said he thought the president would, and that American could start the wheels turning to get thousands of payroll checks cut.

"Hang on a sec," Parker said. He stepped out of the boardroom and dialed Steven Mnuchin, who picked up on the first ring. "I've got to decide right now if I'm going to press a button on these checks," Parker said. "If you were me, what would you do?"

It was a dicey call. The Treasury secretary was certainly under no obligation to throw American Airlines a bone. And in fact, news of the bill's enshrinement into law would almost certainly move financial markets, which meant that Mnuchin needed to keep his cards close. But the two had developed a frank and productive relationship over the past nine months, and with billions of dollars on the line, it was worth a try.

Parker got nothing from the tight-lipped Mnuchin, which he interpreted as a sign that there was a real chance that the president, stewing in a postelection funk in Florida, might just sit on the bill. That meant American was about to spend billions of dollars that it didn't have. Parker kept his concerns to himself as he stepped back into the boardroom. "Screw it," he said, and told his team to cut the checks. American's workers had sacrificed enough already. The least he could do—after a year of furloughs and early retirements and disease and death—was get them a paycheck by Christmas.

The next day, Parker's phone rang. It was Mnuchin, who opened with a nervous laugh. "Did you see what's going on?" Trump had just released a video saying he wasn't going to sign the bill. "The bill they are now planning to send back to my desk is much different than anticipated. It really is a disgrace," he said into the camera. Among his gripes: stimulus checks for the family members of undocumented immigrants, $86 million in foreign aid to Cambodia, $25 million to combat the invasive species of Asian carp, $1 billion for the Smithsonian museums. He also wanted the $600 checks cut to households, which he called "ridiculously low," to be raised to $2,000 and add more money for small businesses.

Mnuchin told Parker that he hadn't anticipated this, but that a nagging doubt was the reason he had been circumspect the day before. "Hang in there," he told the CEO, who had just spent billions of dollars his company didn't have to spare.

SIX DAYS LATER, Parker was in his car in Telluride, Colorado, waiting for his wife to come out of the grocery store. The couple had gone skiing for the New Year, though Parker had spent much of the trip on the phone with his team continuing to fret about American's finances. When the company had cut thousands of payroll checks to employees who had been furloughed earlier in the fall, he had been expecting Congress to pass another round of Covid relief, and for the president to sign it. That still hadn't happened, which meant there was no government money coming in to replace the millions of dollars of employee wages.

The airline industry was still bleeding. An uptick in holiday travel—one that public health officials had sharply criticized and would soon blame for a surge in Covid-19 cases—had done little to drag carriers out of the financial hole that the pandemic had dug. And President Trump had not signed the $900 billion Covid relief bill, the second huge stimulus bill passed by Congress to combat the economic effects of the coronavirus. Parker had been reaching out to anyone he could think of for reassurances; Mark Meadows, Trump's chief of staff, had assured him that he'd done the right thing sending out the checks and that the president would indeed sign the bill into law, which would send billions of dollars in payroll aid to the airlines to compensate for the checks the company had just cut.

In a flash of frustration, Parker dialed Roy Blunt, a Republican senator from Missouri, on his cellphone to see what was going on. Blunt told Parker that he didn't know what the delay was; President Trump had changed his mind and indicated that he would sign the bill, and Blunt himself had personally escorted the bill out to the Washington airport, where Mnuchin and House Speaker Kevin McCarthy had flown it to Mar-a-Lago for the president's review and signature.

Finally, at 7:10 P.M. on Sunday, December 27, Parker's phone dinged with a text from McCarthy. "I got POTUS to sign it." A follow-up read: "The hardest I've ever worked. Mnuchin and I never gave up." Nine minutes later, *The Wall Street Journal* sent out a breaking-news alert confirming that the $900 billion bill, which had spent months tied up in Congress, was now law. Parker sent a message of gratitude that bordered on pandering: "Tens of millions of Americans are better off as a result."

That was certainly true, though it undersold the pain that many had endured while the nation's leaders politicked throughout the late summer and fall. The game of chicken played by the two parties, each angling for an edge in the November election, had been costly. While the economy had added jobs each month between May and November, those gains had steadily dwindled as employers had lost confidence in government action. Cumulatively, those gains amounted to roughly half of the thirty million jobs lost in the first two months of the pandemic. Just a week later, the December numbers would show that the economy had lost 140,000 jobs in the month. The report, economist Daniel Zhao told CNBC, showed the economy was "not just tapping on the brakes, but actually has been thrown into reverse."

What had once been projected, or at least hoped for, as a quick snapback in the economy was slipping away, if it ever existed at all.

CHAPTER 23

SUPPLY AND DEMAND

The roosters were a surprise.

It was February 2022, two years since the onset of the pandemic, and Brian Chesky had decided a few weeks earlier to launch an experiment in the future of remote work and to start with himself. The trend that had saved Airbnb in its darkest days of the crisis—the shift from short-term rentals to longer-term stays—now appeared to be a permanent revolution in the way people lived and traveled. Could it revolutionize how they worked, too? By the fall of 2021, nearly half the nights booked on Airbnb were part of stays that were at least a week long. In the prior year, more than one hundred thousand travelers had booked stays of three months or longer. When Airbnb itself opened twelve slots for people to live in any of its host properties—for free—for a year, more than three hundred thousand people applied.

So Chesky wanted to find out: Could he do it himself? His first stop was Atlanta, then Nashville, then Charleston, a villa in Miami—"because that just seems like the kind of thing you do in Miami," he later told a reporter—and a cottage in Malibu overlooking the Pacific. He had found the nearly two years spent mostly alone in his house in San Francisco, joined halfway through by a golden retriever named Sophie, lonely and stifling.

That's how he found himself outside of Los Angeles, where he had quickly clicked on a listing for a "Fairytale Dream Cottage," a five-thousand-square-foot property built in the 1920s, with backyard waterfalls and a treehouse that promised the kind of quirky getaway that he'd been hoping to sample. But he hadn't read the description carefully enough, overlooking the bit about the chicken herds and miniature pigs that roamed in a fenced-in pasture. Two roosters crowed loudly each morning at dawn, another fact he'd have noticed if he'd more closely read the listing. The office was under renovations, which was how he found himself taking conference calls from a makeshift office in the backyard treehouse. He checked out of his one-of-a-kind stay convinced of two things: that he should read the fine print going forward, and that this was the way of the future.

In April 2022, Airbnb announced that its six thousand employees could work from almost anywhere in the world. It wasn't insignificant: The move required an investment by the company to help its workers navigate visas, taxes, payroll, and other living adjustments in more than a hundred countries. But what Chesky would later call a "giant paperwork nuisance" was, he believed, more than balanced out by the benefits of being able to tap a global talent pool—one that was increasingly wedded to the freedom that, whatever grief and angst the pandemic had brought, was its clear silver lining. Brazil, the Czech Republic, Barbados, and Iceland were among dozens of countries that had announced new fast-track visas for remote workers, hoping to lure the kind of upwardly mobile consumers who might buoy their economies coming out of the crisis.

All across America, CEOs were grappling with newly empowered white-collar employees who, having spent two years freed from the strictures of five-day-a-week commutes and office drudgery, were loath to return. By February 2022, only one in three U.S. employees had returned to the office, based on swipe-badge data in more than one hundred cities. At the same time, airport security checkpoints were seeing about 80 percent of pre-pandemic passenger volume. The stands at NBA games were 95 percent as full as they were in 2019. Americans had gone back to their lives—they just hadn't gone back to the office.

Some bosses chose to fight it. They warned of a dystopian future, where gridded squares on a screen replaced the kind of spontaneous creativity of humming workplaces—to some employees, a take that overestimated the magic of office life and underestimated the drudgery of meetings for meetings' sake and commutes that had become longer and less pleasant as urban infrastructure decayed.

Executives on Wall Street, an apprenticeship business where the pandemic had made both training and compliance monitoring harder, were especially keen to get employees back in headquarters. In the spring of 2021, Morgan Stanley's James Gorman had told employees to be back at their desks by Labor Day or face a potential pay cut: "If you can go into a restaurant in New York City, you can come in to the office," he told them.

But it didn't work. Impatient CEOs had underestimated resistance among employees. And the arrival late in 2021 of the omicron variant, which swept through the country—by the time it receded, more than half the country was thought to have had coronavirus of one variant or another—gave reluctant employees a good reason to stay away. By December, Morgan Stanley's Times Square headquarters was only half-full on a typical day. "I was wrong on this," Gorman told an interviewer, acknowledging that he had misjudged how little enthusiasm employees had for a return to their pre-pandemic commutes and schedules. Companies across the country backpedaled on timelines they had previously rolled out. Lyft, the ride-hailing app, said it wouldn't require workers back in the office until 2023. At Ford, thirty thousand workers had been expected back at the corporate jobs—factory workers had returned nearly a year and a half earlier—but were now told they could keep working at home until at least March. Google and Uber extended optional work-from-home indefinitely.

For years before it began, techno-evangelists had been predicting the death of physical offices and the attendant drudgery, promising that ever-improving software, from ultrafast internet to virtual reality headsets, would let people work from anywhere seamlessly, reclaiming hours once spent commuting and reshaping professional lives. But it had never happened, and past experiments had utterly failed. When Yahoo recruited Marissa Mayer as its wunderkind CEO in 2013, one of her first moves was to tighten work-from-home policies that had loosened under her predecessor.

IBM had been a pioneer of remote work, in 1979 sending five employees at its Santa Teresa Laboratory in Silicon Valley home with boxy computer terminals in the hopes of easing congestion on its office servers. In a 2009 report, later scrubbed from its website, the company boasted that 40 percent of its 386,000 employees worked remotely. In 2017, IBM gave employees an ultimatum: Come back to the office or find a new job. The reversal reverberated throughout the ranks of corporate management because IBM had been, in its own words, "a business whose business was how other businesses do business." If they couldn't make the futuristic, not to mention low-cost, vision of a decentralized workforce viable, nobody could.

And the venture-capital boom of the 2010s, when companies were churning out exactly the kinds of innovations that might have enabled a truly remote office of the future, had in some ways done the opposite, drawing professional boundaries in a twenty-mile radius arcing south from San Francisco. They may have evangelized chat apps and workflow software and video hookups that could enable a work-from-anywhere approach to the clients they pitched, yet their corporate campuses, equipped with nap pods and massage rooms and free meals, blared a single message: We want you in the office.

But the pandemic had changed that. Technology had made it easier to stay connected—FaceTime, Apple's video-chat app for iPhone and Mac, had been around since 2011, while corporate video-conference software had proliferated from the likes of Microsoft, Google, and later, Zoom—but had never had a real-world test of its technical chops or its emotional resonance. The pandemic provided both.

Airbnb was poised to be both a leader and a beneficiary of that new world, profiting from a future of work that was less tied to physical offices. Remote workers would fill its properties, bringing in millions of dollars in revenue. Airbnb's internal research showed that most people didn't like staying in hotels longer than a week. If America's professional workforce was going to hit the road, they'd need somewhere to stay.

SUPPLY AND DEMAND are the two basic forces at work in an economy. How much things cost, what a day's work earns, the pace of innovation—they all depend on the balance between how much of something there is and how badly people want or need it, a law simple enough for a grade-schooler to grasp. Most economies find that balance naturally, even if not always smoothly. Electricity prices go up in a heatwave. Stock prices settle when the supply from sellers matches the demand from buyers. Consumers want smaller, faster electronics, so the antennaed bricks of the 1990s turned into sleek smartphones in less than a decade.

The pandemic upended that balance twice, and nearly all the economic pain it brought—and will continue to bring for years to come—can be explained by that act of disruption. In the early days of the pandemic, supply outstripped demand for nearly everything—flights, hotel bookings, cars, concert tickets, restaurant tables, even labor. The mass layoffs—twenty-two million American jobs were lost in the United States—can be academically, if heartlessly, explained by an oversupply of workers in a world with no demand for their skills.

On the way out of the pandemic, those forces reversed. People emerged from their homes starved of the experiences they craved and, in most cases, wealthier, thanks to two years of government aid and the savings from their long hibernations. That exploding demand ran headlong into massive supply shortages. Factories that had closed down were slow to return to their pre-pandemic outputs. Rolling lockdowns across the world, particularly in China, had snarled global supply chains, leading to historic shortages of components and raw materials. And many of the millions of people who had left the workforce, either voluntarily or as a result of pandemic layoffs, opted not to return.

The result, as any economist could have predicted—and many did—was soaring prices. The U.S. inflation rate, measured by the cost of a basket of commonly purchased goods, from monthly rent to clementine oranges to a set of new brakes and a mechanic to install them, had spent the decade or so that preceded the pandemic hovering under 2 percent annually, meaning that a gallon of milk that cost $3 in 2013 cost about a nickel more in 2014. The Federal Reserve and most other central banks aim for 2 percent inflation, low enough that people and corporations don't think too much about it when making financial decisions but high enough that central bankers can lower them in the event of an economic slowdown without dipping below zero. Low, stable inflation is the goal because it gives economic actors the confidence to make investments like buying a house or building a factory, which in turn keeps the economy growing and unemployment low—the Fed's two main goals.

That got blown to hell in the fall of 2021. And Bill Ackman was waiting.

ACKMAN HAD MADE $2.6 billion on his early-pandemic bet against the bond market, one of the biggest single-trade hauls in Wall Street's history. And he'd done it over the course of about three weeks, giving him an annualized return—the benchmark money managers are judged by—of 300,000 percent, an almost comical figure in a world where double-digit annual returns are considered top-tier. The alchemy of any investment has three main components: thesis, expression, and timing. And Ackman had hit all three: the risk of the pandemic was, in fact, being dramatically underestimated by financial markets; a short investment in bonds was the right way to express that view; and February of 2020 was the right time to do it.

Almost a year later, the world looked very different to the billionaire. The first vaccines had been given. People were weary of lockdowns and ready to spend the money they had saved during a year stuck inside.

He believed the Federal Reserve was behind the ball. The central bank had kept interest rates near zero since the start of the pandemic to protect the economy and keep credit flowing. But jobs were coming back, businesses were reopening, and consumers were spending again, all signs that the economy was recovering quickly, which would likely call for the Fed to take its hand off the scale. The reopening would unleash a flood of consumer spending, sparking inflation not seen for decades and forcing the Fed to intervene by raising interest rates.

So in late 2020 he began putting on another giant trade, this time laying out $177 million on options tied to Treasury bonds that would pay off if interest rates rose. As with his credit bet a year earlier, the event itself—in this case, the central bank raising its benchmark interest rates—didn't have to happen for Ackman's bet to start paying off on paper. Investors simply had to start believing that would happen. And just as in early 2020, when the market woke up, it did so quickly. By late March, Ackman's investment had more than tripled in value. By the fall, concerns about inflation had gripped Wall Street, and the profits kept rising.

In October, he logged on to a Zoom meeting of the Fed's investor advisory committee. The panel, made up of about a dozen Wall Street investors and executives, was created in the wake of the 2008 financial crisis as a sort of kitchen cabinet for the central bank, providing insight into markets and recommendations for policy tweaks and regulatory interventions, with occasional keynotes by members on a pet issue. Ray Dalio, head of the world's largest hedge fund,

Bridgewater, had held forth on bitcoin, and Scott Minerd of investment firm Guggenheim Partners had lamented the lack of liquidity in bond markets.

Today the microphone was Ackman's. He wasted little time criticizing his hosts, the Federal Reserve Bank of New York. A "wait and see" approach to raising interest rates, he argued, was a mistake. Nearly 80 percent of the jobs lost during the pandemic had come back; there were only five million fewer people employed now than in February 2020, he said, and many of them likely by choice. More than four hundred million shots had gone into arms. Just four days earlier, the governor of the Bank of England—Jerome Powell's counterpart in Britain—had changed his tune on whether higher prices were temporary or more permanent and said the bank would "have to act" by raising interest rates. Why was the Fed dragging its heels? Back at home in his Manhattan penthouse, Ackman made the point publicly and more pointedly on Twitter. "We are continuing to dance while the music is playing," he wrote, "and it is time to turn down the music and settle down." The Fed, he wrote, "should begin raising rates as soon as possible."

That he stood to profit wasn't exactly a secret—Pershing Square had disclosed the wager as early as March, and he had tweeted it along with a link to the presentation he gave to the Fed. "We have put our money where our mouth is," he wrote. It was the same playbook he had used throughout his career—part soapbox advocate for his own portfolio and part self-appointed savior, evangelizing from the mountaintop.

It took three more months, but Ackman got his wish. In late January, facing increasing evidence that inflation wasn't, as Powell had repeatedly said, "transitory" but here to stay and needed to be dealt with, the Fed signaled it would begin raising interest rates at its next meeting in March. "This is going to be a year in which we move steadily away from the very highly accommodative monetary policy that we put in place to deal with the economic effects of the pandemic," he said at a stark news conference that underscored the weight of his message. After more than a decade of pouring cheap money into the economy, first to protect its slow recovery out of the 2008 crash and later to keep it afloat during the worst economic shutdown in modern history, the Fed was turning off the tap. Money would no longer be virtually free.

But Ackman had already made his money. Pershing Square had started selling its position in the preceding days and was already out by the time Powell took the podium in Washington. It had made $1.25 billion on the trade.

Ackman, better known for waging war against out-of-touch boards and misguided CEOs, had called the biggest macroeconomic event in history both coming and going. He had taken two theses— first, that the virus would be an economic cataclysm, and second, that the country's recovery would be faster and bumpier than anyone expected—and turned them into $4 billion in profits. In both trades, Ackman had wagered on something that the market thought was a long shot. In early 2020, investors remained unfazed by the virus's advance across Asia, and so they were willing to cheaply sell what amounted to fire insurance. A year later, with contradictory signs about the strength of the economy, traders figured the Fed would keep interest rates low, so they offered long odds to anyone willing to take the other side of that bet.

His black swan had turned green.

CHAPTER 24

THE GREAT RESIGNATION

The succession plans that Jim Hackett and Bill Ford had hatched in January 2020 at the automaker scion's ranch in Palm Springs had been well-intentioned. They had chosen Ford's next chief—Jim Farley, a car nut who had outlasted rivals and won the loyalty of the blue-collar workforce—and laid out a plan for Hackett to announce his retirement at the end of the year and stay on through Ford's 2021 annual meeting in the spring. The two men intended to put the exact timing of the announcement to the board in a formal vote that summer. "I plan on staying in this job," Hackett had told CNBC the day Farley's promotion was announced.

It was a tidy plan by the standards of modern companies, which had come to treat CEO succession less as a managerial baton-passing and more as a coronation. And it was especially so for Ford, which had churned through three chief executives in seven years and spawned a level of palace intrigue more often seen on Wall Street than in the industrial heartland.

But like almost everything else at Ford, and at companies across the world, the pandemic had upended that plan. For starters, Hackett was tired. He had seen the company through an existential crisis. He had staved off financial ruin, reopened its factories, and by some miracle kept production schedules for new models like the electric F-150 pickup truck mostly on schedule. In truth, much of the credit for the production success rested on Farley, who had proven himself a capable operator since his promotion in February to chief operating officer and heir apparent. He had found some $6 billion in savings throughout the company during the downturn, clawing back advertising spends and supplier payments and streamlining factory workflows. He was a skilled marketer and played as well with screw-turning suppliers as he did with back-slapping auto dealers.

And more broadly, as the virus appeared to quiet in the summer of 2020—a brief respite, as it would turn out, before new variants brought second, third, and fourth waves—Hackett sensed the closing of a chapter. Once the pandemic ended, he knew a good CEO would be expected to make up for two years of limited travel, visiting the company's factories and suppliers and dealers all over the world. He didn't have it in him to spend the next year on a plane.

His sense was confirmed by a conversation with Tony Earley, a veteran CEO of the utility industry and one of Ford's longest-serving board members, in mid-June. "How would you feel about Jim taking over in October instead of May?" Earley asked. Earley thought highly of Hackett and reached for an analogy meant to flatter as much as persuade. Michael Jordan, Tom Brady. The greats keep telling themselves they have one more good year in them, Earley said, and they usually stay one too long.

It was all Hackett needed to hear. On a sweltering Detroit afternoon, he rang Bill Ford. "That timeline we set out," he said, "I think we should reconsider it." Farley was going to own the next chapter of Ford, the one without death and government rescues and nightmarish politics, Hackett said to the last remaining grandson of Henry Ford. "He should start now."

On August 4, Ford announced Hackett's retirement and Farley's ascension, a corporate battlefield promotion. The move took Wall Street by surprise—though it was a pleasant one: Ford's shares rose 3 percent that morning. "Don't take it personally," Bill Ford told his outgoing CEO, who reminded him of the comment Hackett had made three years earlier when he had been hired—that Wall Street wasn't going to like him.

By any fair accounting, Hackett's tenure had been mixed. As promised, he had cut money-losing cars from Ford's lineup and streamlined its operations. He had launched new versions of iconic vehicles like the F-150 pickup truck and the Bronco and invested in technologies like self-driving cars and electric vehicles that he firmly believed would guarantee that the company, founded more than a century earlier, would survive the next. But the scoreboard was bleak: Ford's stock had fallen more than 40 percent on his watch, and his restructuring of Ford's overseas operations, an $11 billion revamp, had tanked profits with little to show so far.

Hackett's surprise retirement was one of countless in what became known as the Great Resignation, a mass exodus of employees that touched virtually every industry. More than twenty-seven million Americans quit their jobs between September of 2020 and the end of 2021. They quit fast-food jobs and teaching jobs, left airport runways and malls. Many quit low-paying jobs or those with unpredictable schedules and long commutes. There was no one cause. The economic uncertainty of the pandemic's early days delayed long-planned retirements—just two million Americans voluntarily left their jobs in April 2020, an eight-year low. The long slog of pandemic work forced many to rethink their priorities—what the Texas A&M professor who coined the phrase called "pandemic epiphanies." Blue-collar workers worried about their personal safety. Teachers threw up their hands after two years of remote schooling that, on the whole, didn't work for them or their students. White-collar workers, unshackled during the pandemic from their offices, preferred the freedom they found in home offices or new cities. A lack of childcare and soaring costs—a trend that was itself exacerbated by the thousands of low-paid caregivers leaving the workforce—scrambled household economics and, in some cases, made it not worth continuing to work.

Whether caused by overly generous government benefits that paid people not to work or by a mass-trauma event that forced people to reconsider what really mattered, the result was a labor shortage unlike any seen in decades and a long-overdue scramble by companies to increase pay and benefits. Companies that in the early days of the pandemic laid off thousands by late 2021 faced the opposite problem: They couldn't hire enough workers. Macy's furloughed most of its 125,000 department-store workers in March of 2020. A year and a half later, it raised its starting hourly wage to $15 and rolled out college tuition assistance to lure applicants to some 76,000 positions left open as more than two million retail workers quit their jobs that summer and early fall. Still desperate on the eve of Black Friday, it drafted workers from its corporate office into the roles of shirt folders and shelf stockers, begging human-resource executives and accountants to participate in a program they called "Experience Elevation Elves."

Like so much about the pandemic's course through the global economy and society, it was an almost unbelievably quick reversal. In April of 2020, the unemployment rate in the United States touched nearly 15 percent. By the end of 2021, it was under 4 percent—near all-time lows—and employers were trying to fill ten million open jobs. That imbalance lent new muscle to a nascent labor movement. U.S. companies were paying their employees almost 5 percent more in March of 2022 than they were a year earlier. Target, Amazon, and Costco were locked in a wage battle that saw hourly pay go from fifteen dollars to sixteen dollars to more than twenty dollars.

Labor looks ascendant in other ways. Workers filed 1,174 requests with the National Labor Relations Board to form a union in their workplaces between October 1, 2021, and March 31, 2022, a 57 percent increase from the same period the year before. They represented hundreds of Starbucks locations and an Amazon warehouse in Staten Island, which won one of the most closely watched and hotly contested organizing drives in modern history. These efforts aren't nearly enough to make a meaningful dent in the erosion of labor's power in the past fifty years, during which membership fell from about more than one-quarter in 1960 to just 10 percent in 2018. But the increase in union activity, combined with the fact that big companies increased wages after years of resisting, suggests that the balance of power between management and their employees may be changing. The coronavirus pandemic might one day be looked at as a reset, the pendulum not just naturally swinging but being whipped back in the other direction.

CONCLUSION

Past pandemics, aside from their human toll, sparked seismic shifts in the economies of their times. The Black Death that visited Europe in the mid-1300s is thought to have killed at least one-third of the continent's population. But it helped midwife the birth of capitalist economies, based on market forces rather than patronage. Before the plague, most European workers were serfs, captive to landlords whose fields they cultivated in exchange for protection and sustenance. Like the Covid-19 pandemic, the bubonic plague hit that underclass the hardest. But those who survived found an economy transformed: There weren't enough of them left to till the land. What resulted, albeit somewhat briefly, was bargaining power. Many ceased to be serfs, instead hawking themselves to the highest bidder—the beginnings of the West's first true wage economy. Between 1348 and 1351, England lost almost half its population, and wages rose by two-thirds. Fifty years after the end of the plague, British peasants were earning twice what they had before it began.

The 1918 flu pandemic similarly upended the economy it encountered. Three years of death and political upheaval (mask mandates, as it turned out, were as divisive then as they would be a century later) combined with the toll of World War I created a generation that was disoriented, reevaluating their lives after years of mass death. They took President Warren Harding's call for "a return to normalcy"—he popularized the word itself by misreading "normality" during a campaign speech in 1920—and ran with it. What followed was the Roaring Twenties, a period of social and economic innovation that burst out of years of torpor and malaise.

In the early days of the coronavirus recovery we can see echoes of both of those prior pandemics. Labor is ascendant, and while today's workers don't have as far to go as medieval peasants, their fight for better wages and conditions have gained more traction than at any time since World War II, the last time that home-front workers were a scarce commodity.

And the headiness of the 1920s is readily visible, too. By the start of 2022, the U.S. stock market was 40 percent higher than its pre-pandemic peak two years earlier, and the mania of meme finance quieted but never entirely disappeared. Whether it will come to the same crashing end as the Roaring Twenties is unclear as of this writing but easily imaginable to those with a basic understanding of markets and a sense of history.

What is clear is that the economy that emerges from the pandemic is not the same one that crashed headlong into it. Soaring inflation has consumers doubting the dollars in their wallets for the first time in four decades. Long-overdue digital advances in telemedicine, professional collaboration, and logistics are here to stay. The labor market will take years to find an equilibrium, and that period will test whether America's debt to essential workers—the nurses, public-works employees, delivery drivers, and others—is repaid financially in the form of better pay and more investment. (One early test suggests not: A proposal from the Biden administration for $400 billion in new spending to raise wages for home health aides, among the lowest-paid and most sorely needed healthcare workers, was dropped from the final bill.)

The swift and severe rise in interest rates signals the end of the era of free money. In the years after the 2008 meltdown, financial markets came to rely on the benevolence of central bankers, whose policies produced cheap and readily available debt and rising stock prices—two backdrops that tend to make every investor look like a genius. Without that government backstop, markets will likely be more treacherous, but risks will be better appreciated.

Corporate leadership, too, was tested and redefined by the pandemic. With faith in government understandably eroded, employees turned to their bosses for guidance and America's CEOs gladly stepped up—mostly out of genuine desire to see their companies through, though certainly aided by ego. They became more communicative and transparent, found their voices on policy issues, and reestablished connections with their workers that they had lost during a benign decade that afforded them the right to be distant.

That recasting of the role brings its own challenges, which are just now starting to play out. Engagement is a slippery slope, and what began as uncomplicated stances during the unifying early days of the crisis became more complicated as the pandemic, and the social unrest it fomented, divided the country. Mask and vaccine mandates split employees and customers along ideological lines. Return-to-work mandates did the same along generational lines. Having stepped into the political fray as they rushed to save their companies and reassure their workers, corporate leaders are finding it harder to step back out. The culture wars that have roiled American politics and media are coming squarely for commerce, as seen in controversies at Disney and Delta Air Lines about their corporate responses to political developments in their home states of Florida and Georgia, respectively. Those battles would likely have erupted eventually, but the pandemic inflamed and accelerated them.

The pandemic's economic consequences could have been far worse, and almost certainly would have been without the swift actions taken by officials in Washington. One can debate whether the stimulus checks were too big or mailed out for too long, whether the airline aid simply bailed executives out of years of poor planning, whether tighter oversight or more-tailored criteria would have directed money only to the neediest businesses or households, whether the $6 trillion that the Fed injected into the U.S. economy is to blame for what so far has been a bumpy recovery. But any government response entails a trade-off between speed and accuracy, and the 2020 playbook from financial regulators and elected officials in Congress staved off an economic collapse and ensured that when the virus finally cooled and Americans were ready to eat out again, get on a plane, and return to work, that those restaurants, airplanes, and offices would still be there.

ACKNOWLEDGMENTS

This book would not exist without the extensive cooperation of people who spoke to me over the course of more than a year even as the fates of the companies they helped run or regulate—and indeed, the entire economy—were in peril. It's easy to look back now and see that the economy did not crash, that a repeat of 2008 was avoided. But none of that was clear when many of these sources began to tell me their stories. Through a second wave and then a third, through vaccines and variants, through the social and political unrest the pandemic kicked up, which put extra demands on their time and attention, they kept picking up the phone. I'm grateful.

Paul Whitlatch at Crown was an uncompromising and supportive editor. He absorbed the neuroses of a first-time author with humor and humanity, elevating my writing and focusing me on the big picture time and again. Thanks, too, to Katie Berry at Crown. My agent, David McCormick, validated the idea of this book from the jump and provided a sounding board and sharp edits throughout. Charlie McGee provided crucial research and Julie Tate was invaluable time and again.

The Wall Street Journal was an incredible journalistic home. Thanks to Matt Murray, who cheered me on and mercifully did not bug me about when I was coming back from book leave; to Marcelo Prince, who shepherded the eight-thousand-word article, published in the early hours of April 4, 2020, that convinced me there was a book to be written here; to Charles Forelle, Jamie Heller, Dana Cimilluca, Elena Cherney, and Karen Pensiero for their support as I learned how to do the job, how to tell stories, on their dime. It was a privilege.

A special thanks to Marie Beaudette, my editor at the *Journal*. Her confidence spurred me to take on this project in the first place and her patience was key to finishing it. In our eight years of working together in various roles, she trusted my instincts, chided my casual relationship with deadlines, and encouraged me to tell stories in the most authoritative way possible—all solid training for writing a book.

One challenge of this undertaking was getting smart about industries I had never covered. I had spent years writing about Wall Street, only to find—often at the moment that I sat down at my computer to turn interviews into readable copy—that I knew almost nothing about airlines or retailers or automakers. My *Journal* colleagues generously gave their time and expertise, among them Alison Sider, Craig Karmin, Andrew Ackerman, and the retired legend Sue Carey.

Rob Copeland offered advice on dealing with cagey sources and comfort on those days when the words didn't come. Bradley Hope was a constant source of inspiration and is at least partly to credit for this entire endeavor: In 2019 he introduced me to Paul, my future editor at Crown, telling me that I should write a book someday and telling Paul that he should publish it. What that book would be about seemed not to matter at all to Bradley, who finds epic stories with enviable ease.

Sarah Krouse dropped surgical masks and champagne on my stoop after I finished the proposal that would become this book, back when New York City was lonely and scary. She later read key sections with a critical eye and a healthy allergy to adverbs. Peter Rudegeair shouldered my workload while I was on leave and was a welcome set of ears throughout. Charles Forelle explained the intricacies of monetary policy on more occasions and in more detail than he or I will ever discuss publicly. I'll be forever grateful for his seemingly infinite knowledge and love of a good yarn. Erich Schwartzel, Maureen Farrell, Tripp Mickle, Eliot Brown, Justin Scheck, Kirsten Grind, and Mary Childs—friends whose books I devoured—shared their wisdom.

A special thanks to Ben Smith for his enthusiasm for this project as I left the protective nest of the *Journal* to join Semafor. Thanks also to the Crown team who made this book happen: David Drake, Gillian Blake, Annsley Rosner, Julie Cepler, Stacey Stein, Sierra Moon, Allison Fox, and Sally Franklin. And to Meredith, Ileana, Liz, and Corey for keeping me sane throughout.

To my family: my brother, Ben, the best writer I know; my sister, Diana, whose grit and emojis, texted daily, kept me going; Ally, our glue and my found sister; and my mom, Sherrie, who was silently forgiving when our vaccination status—and the freedom to visit after a year apart—collided with reporting travels. Thanks also to David and Kara, whose sunny California home was a welcome writer's retreat, and to Mary Ellen and Corwin, for everything.

This book is dedicated to my dad, Bob Hoffman. He was my first editor, precise in the well-meaning manner of a great dad and the slightly annoying manner of a great lawyer. He was both. He died in 2017, and I wrote much of this book—and spent much of the pandemic—in his old gardening sweatpants. I wish he could have read it. He'd have had some notes.

NOTES

This book is informed by interviews with more than one hundred people who had a view, either directly or indirectly, into the events it chronicles. It draws from personal recollections, contemporaneous notes, calendars, meeting agendas, and personal communications including emails and text messages. The dialogue is rendered to the best recollection of people who were there or were briefed on conversations.

Unless otherwise noted, statistics around case counts, deaths, and other medical facts about the pandemic come from Johns Hopkins Coronavirus Resource Center, which became the preeminent clearinghouse of pandemic-related public health data.

Prologue

xix   **"some 350 Americans"** Miriam Jordan and Julie Bosman, "Hundreds of Americans Were Evacuated from the Coronavirus Epicenter. Now Comes the Wait," *The New York Times,* February 12, 2020.

xxi   **"The 1918 flu killed"** "1918 Pandemic (H1N1 Virus)," Centers for Disease Control and Prevention, March 20, 2019.

Chapter 1: Borrowed Time

5   **"An official at the U.S. Department of Health"** Lawrence Wright, "The Plague Year," *The New Yorker,* December 28, 2020.

7   **"Corporate profits hit"** Data from Bureau of Economic Analysis, Table 6.19B, Corporate Profits After Tax by Industry, July 30, 2021.

7   **"Benefits like pensions"** James Manyika, Jan Mischke, Jacques Bughin,

Jonathan Woetzel, Mekala Krishnan, and Samuel Cudre, "A New Look at the Declining Labor Share of Income in the United States," McKinsey Global Institute, May 22, 2019.

8   **"Between the end of 2010"** Nonfinancial Corporate Business; Debt Securities and Loans; Liability, Level, FRED Economic Data.

8   **"The price-to-earnings ratio"** Data from Nasdaq, Shiller PE Ratio per Month, August 6, 2022.

10 **"The biggest U.S. airlines"** Arne Alsin, "Stock Buybacks Made Corporations Vulnerable. Then the Coronavirus Struck," *Forbes*, April 24, 2020.

Chapter 2: Champagne Decade

13 **"The company that Conrad had built"** Hilton Worldwide Holdings Form 10-K, United States Securities and Exchange Commission, December 31, 2019.

16 **"Seven thousand miles away"** "CHP Closely Monitors Cluster of Pneumonia Cases on Mainland," Government of the Hong Kong Special Administrative Region, December 31, 2019.

17 **"It was the biggest deal"** Liz Hoffman, "Morgan Stanley Is Buying E*Trade, Betting on Smaller Customers," *The Wall Street Journal*, February 20, 2020.

20 **"Bill had wintered there"** Bryce G. Hoffman, *American Icon: Alan Mulally and the Fight to Save Ford Motor Company* (New York: Crown, 2012).

22 **"He once answered"** Stephen J. Dubner, "Can an Industrial Giant Become a Tech Darling?," November 7, 2018, in Freaknomics, produced by Greg Rosalsky, podcast, MP3 audio, 56:41.

22 **"When he mandated"** Christina Rogers, "Ford's New CEO Has a Cerebral Style—and to Many, It's Baffling," *The Wall Street Journal*, August 14, 2018.

22 **"When asked by a Morgan Stanley analyst"** Joann Muller, "Ford CEO James Hackett, Under Fire from Wall Street, Shows Forbes the Early Fruits of His Turnaround Plan," *Forbes*, September 6, 2018.

23 **"But he was a car nut"** Stephen Edelstein, "Ford's New CEO Races a 1966 Ford GT40 as His Form of Yoga," Motor Authority, October 16, 2020.

25 **"Ringing in his head"** Clare Foges, "This Has Been the Decade of Disconnection," *The Times*, December 30, 2019.

27 **"Bastian laid out"** Eric J. Savitz, "Delta Is Using CES to Talk About Better Baggage Handling, Shorter Lines, and More Wi-Fi," *Barron's*, January 7, 2020.

29 **"Spending on air travel"** "IATA Annual Review 2019," International Air Transport Association, June 2019.

30 **"The first reported U.S. case"** Mike Baker and Sheri Fink, "Covid-19 Arrived in Seattle. Where It Went from There Stunned the Scientists," *The New York Times*, April 22, 2020.

Chapter 3: The Big One

34 **"one early scientific study"** Shu Yang, Peihua Cao, Peipei Du, Ziting Wu, Zian Zhuang, Lin Yang, Xuan Yu, Qi Zhou, Xixi Feng, Xiaohui Wang, Weiguo Li, Enmei Liu, Ju Chen, Yaolong Chen, and Daihai He, "Early Estimation of the

Case Fatality Rate of COVID-19 in Mainland China: A Data-Driven Analysis," *Annals of Translational Medicine* 8, no. 4 (2020).

35 **"There were widespread reports"** Emily Feng and Amy Cheng, "Critics Say China Has Suppressed and Censored Information in Coronavirus Outbreak," NPR, February 8, 2020.

35 **"Chinese officials suppressing information"** Raymond Zhong, Paul Mozur, Jeff Kao, and Aaron Krolik, "No 'Negative' News: How China Censored the Coronavirus," *The New York Times,* December 19, 2020.

38 **"That outbreak, in 2003"** "Airlines May See $10-Billion Loss as SARS Takes Its Toll," *Los Angeles Times,* May 6, 2003.

39 **"It was the next piece"** Mike Colias, "Ford Increasing Electric Vehicle Investment to $11 Billion by 2022," *The Wall Street Journal,* January 14, 2018.

Chapter 4: Bubbles

45 **"Dialing in from the sitting room"** Claire Moses, "Bill Ackman and Friends Just Dropped $91.5 Million on NYC's Second-Most Expensive Apartment Sale Ever," *Insider,* April 10, 2015.

47 **"My name is Bill Ackman"** "A Young Bill Ackman Asks Warren Buffett and Charlie Munger a Question in 1994," YouTube, May 27, 2020, video, 5:12, available at https://youtu.be/Mp4Je5OCIZ0.

47 **"he had plowed 11 percent"** "Investment Manager's Report," Pershing Square Holdings, July 2019.

49 **"The market for credit-default swaps"** Tim Reason, "Who's Holding the Bag? Everyone Knows Banks Are Shedding More Risk These Days. So Where Does It Go?," *CFO Magazine,* October 27, 2005.

49 **"$61.2 trillion three years later"** Iñaki Aldasoro and Torsten Ehlers, "The Credit Default Swap Market: What a Difference a Decade Makes," *BIS Quarterly Review,* June 5, 2018.

51 **"In 2016, lenders were charging"** Federal Reserve Bank of St. Louis, ICE BofA US High Yield Index Option-Adjusted Spread, available at https://fred.stlouis fed.org/series/BAMLH0A0HYM2.

53 **"The next day, February 26"** "CDC Confirms Possible First Instance of Covid-19 Community Transmission in California," California Department of Public Health, February 26, 2020.

54 **"Of the twenty-six previous market slides"** Yun Li, "It Took Stocks Only Six Days to Fall into Correction, the Fastest Drop in History," CNBC, February 27, 2020.

54 **"It's a brand-new thing"** Julia-Ambra Verlaine and Akane Otani, "Wall Street Prepares for Another Unruly Week," *The Wall Street Journal,* March 1, 2020.

Chapter 5: Do You Guys Need Help?

55 **"Founded in 1972"** Eileen Shanahan, "Antitrust Bill Stopped by a Business Lobby," *The New York Times,* November 16, 1975.

59 **"As the meeting wrapped up"** Sam Mintz, "Trump Seeks to Stamp Out Airline Bailout Talk," Politico, March 4, 2020.

62 **"The $8.3 billion bill sailed"** Lauren Hirsch and Kevin Breuninger, "Trump

Signs $8.3 Billion Emergency Coronavirus Spending Package," CNBC, March 6, 2020.

64 **"On March 6, the University of Washington"** Andy Thomason, "U. of Washington Cancels In-Person Classes, Becoming First Major U.S. Institution to Do So amid Coronavirus Fears," *The Chronicle of Higher Education,* March 6, 2020.

Chapter 6: The Great Unwind

66 **"The Microsoft founder and philanthropist"** Noah Higgins-Dunn, "Bill Gates: Coronavirus May Be 'Once-in-a-Century Pathogen We've Been Worried About,'" CNBC, February 28, 2020.

68 **"In the decades since"** Richard Dewey, "The Crash of '87, from the Wall Street Players Who Lived It," Bloomberg, October 16, 2017.

68 **"The circuit breakers were designed"** Avie Schneider and Scott Horsley, "How Stock Market Circuit Breakers Work," NPR, March 9, 2020.

72 **"Peter Cecchini, a strategist"** Paul Vigna, Avantika Chilkoti, and David Winning, "Stocks Fall More Than 7% in Dow's Worst Day Since 2008," *The Wall Street Journal,* March 9, 2020.

73 **"Publicly traded money-market funds"** S. P. Kothari, Dalia Blass, Alan Cohen, and Sumit Rajpal, "U.S. Credit Markets: Interconnectedness and the Effects of the COVID-19 Economic Shock," U.S. Securities and Exchange Commission Division of Economic and Risk Analysis, October 2020.

73 **"Just 211,000 people"** Lucia Mutikani, "U.S. Weekly Jobless Claims Unexpectedly Fall," Reuters, March 12, 2020.

77 **"Mortgage securities in 2008"** David Goldman, "Your $3 Trillion Bailout," CNN Money, November 5, 2008.

Chapter 7: Dash for Cash

82 **"Stock buybacks by companies"** William Lazonick, Mustafa Erdem Sakinç, and Matt Hopkins, "Why Stock Buybacks Are Dangerous for the Economy," *Harvard Business Review,* January 7, 2020; Mark Jewell, "Stock Buybacks Finally Decline in 4Q," *The Seattle Times,* March 28, 2012.

82 **"A few days later, reporters caught wind of the move"** Gillian Tan, "Hilton Draws Down $1.75 Billion Credit Line to Ease Virus Hit," Bloomberg, March 11, 2020.

Chapter 8: The Day the World Shut Down

99 **"News reports surfaced"** Sridhar Natarajan and Heather Perlberg, "Blackstone, Carlyle Urge Portfolio Companies to Tap Credit," Bloomberg, March 11, 2020.

Chapter 9: Stress Test

109 **"Goldman owned"** "Form 10-K Goldman Sachs Bdc, Inc.," U.S. Securities and Exchange Commission, February 20, 2020.

114 **"a forty-day work stoppage"** Michael Wayland, "UAW Strike Cost GM up to $4 Billion for 2019, Substantially Higher Than Estimated," CNBC, October 29, 2019.

Chapter 10: Grounded

119 **"At the risk of being alarmist"** Jamie Freed and Tracy Rucinski, "Governments Scramble to Prop Up Airlines as Virus Forces More Flight, Job Cuts," Reuters, March 17, 2020.
121 **"American missed its profit projections"** "American Airlines Group Reports Fourth-Quarter and Full-Year 2019 Profit," American Airlines Newsroom, January 23, 2020.
122 **"85 percent of aviation workers"** Data provided to author by Association of Flight Attendants.

Chapter 11: The Cavalry

129 **"He also thought Yellen"** Philip Rucker, Josh Dawsey, and Damian Paletta, "Trump Slams Fed Chair, Questions Climate Change and Threatens to Cancel Putin Meeting in Wide-Ranging Interview with The Post," *The Washington Post,* November 27, 2018.
131 **"The Treasury market is the foundation"** Nick Timiraos and Julia-Ambra Verlaine, "Federal Reserve Accelerates Treasury Purchases to Address Market Strains," *The Wall Street Journal,* March 13, 2020.

Chapter 12: It Might Be Enough

138 **"The prospect of such a giant pot"** Erica Werner, Mike DeBonis, and Paul Kane, "Senate Approves $2.2 Trillion Coronavirus Bill Aimed at Slowing Economic Free Fall," *The Washington Post,* March 25, 2020.
138 **"The restaurant industry's lobby"** Kenneth P. Vogel, Catie Edmondson, and Jesse Drucker, "Coronavirus Stimulus Package Spurs a Lobbying Gold Rush," *The New York Times,* March 20, 2020.
147 **"Her ambivalence was shared"** Sebastian Pellejero and Liz Hoffman, "Bond Market Cracks Open for Blue-Chip Companies—Then Slams Shut," *The Wall Street Journal,* March 18, 2020.

Chapter 14: Hell Is Coming

158 **"When he lost a battle for control"** Joe Nocera, "Investor Exits and Leaves Puzzlement," *The New York Times,* May 29, 2009.
163 **"Exchange floors"** John McCrank, "Nasdaq Keeps Philadelphia Trading Floor Closed Due to Protests," Reuters, June 1, 2020.
163 **"Its CEO, Terrence Duffy"** Justin Baer and Alexander Osipovich, "Some Asset Managers Argue Markets Should Close, NYSE Urged to Close Trading Floor," *The Wall Street Journal,* March 17, 2020.
165 **"On Tuesday, March 17"** Sebastian Pellejero and Liz Hoffman, "Bond Mar-

ket Cracks Open for Blue-Chip Companies—Then Slams Shut," *The Wall Street Journal*, March 18, 2020.

Chapter 15: Bailed Out

166 **"the number of U.S. airline passengers"** "TSA Checkpoint Travel Numbers (Current Year Versus Prior Year(s)/Same Weekday," Transportation Security Administration.

167 **"Trump had invoked"** Maegan Vazquez, "Trump Invokes Defense Production Act for Ventilator Equipment and N95 Masks," CNN, April 2, 2020.

167 **"Mnuchin had taken heat"** Kate Davidson and Bob Davis, "How Mnuchin Became Washington's Indispensable Crisis Manager," *The Wall Street Journal*, March 31, 2020.

167 **"Our major focus"** Sam Mintz, "Democrats Look to Stave Off 'Blank Check' for Airlines," Politico, March 17, 2020.

173 **"The previous high"** Ben Casselman, Patricia Cohen, and Tiffany Hsu, "Job Losses Soar; U.S. Virus Cases Top World," *The New York Times*, March 27, 2020.

Chapter 16: Moonshots

180 **"Trump was talking"** Reuters Staff, "Trump Says U.S. Will Make 100,000 Ventilators in 100 Days," Reuters, March 27, 2020.

181 **"was an ardent pacifist"** David Long, *Henry Ford: Industrialist* (New York: Cavendish Publishing, 2016).

184 **"Tony Wilkinson, chief executive of a trade group"** Ruth Simon, Peter Rudegeair, and Amara Omeokwe, "The Rush for $350 Billion in Small-Business Loans Starts Friday. Banks Have Questions," *The Wall Street Journal*, April 2, 2020.

185 **"Maine Community Bank in Biddeford"** Ruth Simon, Peter Rudegeair, and Amara Omeokwe, "The Rush for $350 Billion in Small-Business Loans Starts Friday. Banks Have Questions," *The Wall Street Journal*, April 2, 2020.

185 **"PPP's opening day"** Bob Davis, Ruth Simon, and Peter Rudegeair, "Small Firms See Hiccups Applying for New Loans," *The Wall Street Journal*, April 4, 2020.

186 **"Researchers at Brown University"** Scott Horsley, "Did Emergency PPP Loans Work? Nearly $800 Billion Later, We Still Don't Know," NPR, April 27, 2021.

186 **"Faulkender would publicly defend"** Michael Faulkender and Stephen Miran, "Time for a Second Round of PPP," *The Wall Street Journal*, December 17, 2020.

Chapter 18: Beg, Borrow, Steal

199 **"It had struck a deal"** Reuters staff, "NBA, Knicks, Nets Help Donate One Million Masks," Reuters, April 4, 2020.

Chapter 20: Go Fly Planes

210 **"While its rivals hung back"** Alison Sider, "Airlines Add Flights as Travel Slowed by the Coronavirus Starts to Pick Up," *The Wall Street Journal,* June 4, 2020.

211 **"After shrinking by 31 percent"** "Gross Domestic Product (Second Estimate), Corporate Profits (Preliminary Estimate), Second Quarter 2022," Bureau of Economic Analysis, August 25, 2022.

214 **"Political resentment had spread"** Andrew Ross Sorkin, "Were the Airline Bailouts Really Needed?," *The New York Times,* March 16, 2021.

Chapter 21: The YOLO Economy

222 **"shortest bear market in history"** Saqib Iqbal Ahmed and Noel Randewich, "Say Goodbye to the Shortest Bear Market in S&P History," Reuters, August 18, 2020.

222 **"Apple had built"** Rob Davies, "Apple Becomes World's First Trillion-Dollar Company," *The Guardian,* August 2, 2018.

222 **"on August 19"** Jessica Bursztynsky, "Apple Becomes First U.S. Company to Reach a $2 Trillion Market Cap," CNBC, August 19, 2020.

222 **"Only about half the country"** "Share of Corporate Equities and Mutual Fund Shares Held by the Top 1%," Federal Reserve Bank of St. Louis, June 29, 2022; "Share of Corporate Equities and Mutual Fund Shares Held by the 90th to 99th Wealth Percentiles," Federal Reserve Bank of St. Louis, June 22, 2022; Lydia Saad and Jeffrey M. Jones, "What Percentage of Americans Owns Stock?," Gallup, May 12, 2022.

223 **"On November 9, investors got the news"** "Pfizer and BioNTech Announce Vaccine Candidate Against COVID-19 Achieved Success in First Interim Analysis from Phase 3 Study," Pfizer, November 9, 2020.

225 **"Special-purpose acquisition vehicles"** Ken Shimokawa, "SPAC and Equity Issuance Finish 2021 with Strong Momentum," *S&P Global Market Intelligence,* February 3, 2022.

Chapter 22: Gambles

231 **"breaking-news alert"** "What's in the $900 Billion Covid-19 Relief Bill," *The Wall Street Journal,* December 27, 2020.

231 **"Just a week later"** Jeff Cox, "Economy Sees Job Loss in December for the First Time in Eight Months as Surging Virus Takes Toll," CNBC, January 8, 2021.

Chapter 23: Supply and Demand

232 **"His first stop was Atlanta"** Brian Chesky (@bchesky), "2. This week I'm in Atlanta. I'll be coming back to San Francisco often, but for now my home will be an Airbnb somewhere," Twitter, January 18, 2022.

233 **"Airbnb announced that its six thousand employees"** Sara Ashley O'Brien, "Airbnb Says Staffers Can Work Remotely Forever, If They Want," CNN Business, April 28, 2022.

233 **"only one in three U.S. employees"** Peter Grant, "People Are Going Out Again, but Not to the Office," *The Wall Street Journal*, February 14, 2022.

234 **"James Gorman had told employees"** Jack Kelly, "Morgan Stanley CEO James Gorman on His Return-to-Work Plan: 'If You Can Go to a Restaurant in New York City, You Can Come into the Office,'" *Forbes*, June 15, 2021.

235 **"When Yahoo recruited"** Jenna Goudreau, "Back to the Stone Age? New Yahoo CEO Marissa Mayer Bans Working from Home," *Forbes*, February 25, 2013.

235 **"IBM had been a pioneer"** Jerry Useem, "When Working from Home Doesn't Work," *The Atlantic*, November 15, 2017.

235 **"The reversal reverberated"** John Harwood, *The Interface: IBM and the Transformation of Corporate Design, 1945–1976* (Minneapolis: Quadrant, 2011).

236 **"The mass layoffs"** Heather Long, "U.S. Now Has 22 Million Unemployed, Wiping Out a Decade of Job Gains," *The Washington Post*, April 16, 2020.

Chapter 24: The Great Resignation

243 **"But the scoreboard was bleak"** Mike Colias, "Ford Swings to a Loss, Misses Analysts' Profit Estimates," *The Wall Street Journal*, January 23, 2019.

243 **"More than twenty-seven million Americans"** "Table 10. Quits Levels and Rates by Industry and Region, Not Seasonally Adjusted," U.S. Bureau of Labor Statistics, August 30, 2022.

243 **"The long slog"** Alex Miller, "A&M Professor Who Predicted 'Great Resignation' Explains Potential Factors of Why Theory Came True," *The Eagle*, January 8, 2022.

244 **"Still desperate"** Abha Bhattarai, "Macy's Offers Corporate Workers a 'Valuable Opportunity': In-Store Shifts," *The Washington Post*, November 17, 2021.

244 **"Workers filed 1,174 requests"** "Union Election Petitions Increase 57% in First Half of Fiscal Year 2022," National Labor Relations Board, April 6, 2022.

Conclusion

247 **"Between 1348 and 1351"** "The Black Death in the Malthusian Economy," The FRED Blog, December 3, 2018.

248 **"They took President Warren Harding's call"** William Deverell, "Warren Harding Tried to Return American to 'Normalcy' After WWI and the 1918 Pandemic. It Failed," *Smithsonian Magazine*, May 19, 2020.

INDEX

ABOUT THE AUTHOR

Liz Hoffman is the business and finance editor at *Semafor*. She spent nine years at *The Wall Street Journal*, leaving in 2022 as a senior reporter covering financial markets, corporate dealmaking, and the machinations of Wall Street. A native of central Pennsylvania, she graduated from Tufts University and the Medill School of Journalism at Northwestern University. She lives in Brooklyn.

ABOUT THE TYPE

This book was set in Sabon, a typeface designed by the well-known German typographer Jan Tschichold (1902–74). Sabon's design is based upon the original letterforms of sixteenth-century French type designer Claude Garamond and was created specifically to be used for three sources: foundry type for hand composition, Linotype, and Monotype. Tschichold named his typeface for the famous Frankfurt typefounder Jacques Sabon (c. 1520–80).